START YOUR OWN

IMPORT/
EXPORT
BUSINESS

Additional titles in **Entrepreneur's Startup Series**

Start Your Own

Entrepreneur
MAGAZINE'S

STARTUP

START YOUR OWN

IMPORT/ EXPORT BUSINESS

Sixth Edition

YOUR STEP-BY-STEP GUIDE TO SUCCESS

The Staff of Entrepreneur Media, Inc. & Jason R. Rich

Entrepreneur Press®

Publisher: Entrepreneur Press
Cover Design: Andrew Welyczko
Production and Composition: Eliot House Productions

© 2021 by Entrepreneur Media, Inc.
All rights reserved.
Reproduction or translation of any part of this work beyond that permitted by Section 107 or 108 of the 1976 United States Copyright Act without permission of the copyright owner is unlawful. Requests for permission or further information should be addressed to Entrepreneur Media Inc. Attn: Legal Department, 18061 Fitch, Irvine, CA 92614.

This publication is designed to provide accurate and authoritative information in regard to the subject matter covered. It is sold with the understanding that the publisher is not engaged in rendering legal, accounting, or other professional services. If legal advice or other expert assistance is required, the services of a competent professional person should be sought.

Entrepreneur Press® is a registered trademark of Entrepreneur Media, Inc.

Library of Congress Cataloging-in-Publication Data
    Names: Rich, Jason, author. | Entrepreneur Press.
    Title: Start your own import/export business : your step-by-step guide to success / the staff of Entrepreneur
        Media, Inc. & Jason R. Rich.
    Description: Sixth edition. | [Irvine, CA] : Entrepreneur Press, [2021] | Series: Entrepreneur
        magazine's startup | Includes index. | Summary: "The staff of Entrepreneur Media, Inc. and Jason Rich provide
        a step-by-step guide to starting your own import/export business. As a successful import/export agent, you
        can net a healthy six-figure income by matching buyers and sellers from around the globe, right from your
        own home. This book is loaded with valuable insights and practical advice for tapping into highly lucrative
        global markets. You'll learn every aspect of the startup process, including: Choosing the most profitable goods
        to buy and sell Setting up and maintaining a trade route Using the internet to simplify your transactions How
        the government can help you find products and customers Essential trade law information to keep your busi-
        ness in compliance How to choose a customs broker The latest government policies Proven methods for find-
        ing contacts in the United States and abroad Plus, you'll gain the tricks of the trade from successful importers/
        exporters and hundreds of valuable resources help you become a player in the lucrative world of international
        exchange"-- Provided by publisher.
    Identifiers: LCCN 2020008244 (print) | LCCN 2020008245 (ebook) | ISBN 978-1-59918-672-6 (trade paperback) |
        ISBN 978-1-61308-429-8 (ebook)
    Subjects: LCSH: Trading companies--United States--Management. | Imports--United States. | Exports--United States
        | New business enterprises--United States--Management. | International trade.
    Classification: LCC HF1416.5 .T87 2020 (print) | LCC HF1416.5 (ebook) | DDC 658.1/1--dc23
    LC record available at https://lccn.loc.gov/2020008244
    LC ebook record available at https://lccn.loc.gov/2020008245

Printed in the United States of America

26 25 24 23 22   10 9 8 7 6 5 4 3 2 1

Contents

Chapter 3
Keeping Tabs on Politics and the Global Economy 27

Chapter 4

Tricks of the Trade for Startups 39

Chapter 5

Daily Operations 57

Chapter 8
Trade Dollars and Sense. 135

Chapter 9
Employees, Insurance, and Business-Related Topics . .153

Chapter 10

Tools of the Trade 165

Chapter 11

Advertising, Marketing, and Distribution 177

Chapter 12
Effectively Controlling Your Finances 209

Preface

Has the topic of international trade piqued your interest? Are you looking into the idea of launching your own import/export business? Well, you've picked up the right book. It contains the information you'll need to get started. However, you should be prepared, because a lot of additional research and education will be required before you're ready to get started.

Starting a business is one of the most exhilarating things you can do for yourself and your family. It's also one of the scariest. Owning your own business means you're the boss, the big cheese, the head honcho. You make the rules and define company policy.

It also means you can't call in sick, especially when you are also the only employee; you can't let somebody else worry about your business earning enough money to cover payroll and expenses; and you can't defer that cranky client or intimidating IRS representative to a higher authority. You're the person in charge!

You've probably picked up this book about starting and running an import/export business for one or more of the following reasons:

- ▶ You have a background in the import/export field, which is ideal.
- ▶ You're already an expert on a specific product category (here in the USA), or you're very familiar with a country or region of the planet.
- ▶ You're an avid fan of the Travel Channel. Your passport is always close at hand, and you think international trade has the potential to be a glamorous and exciting business.
- ▶ You have a background in sales or distribution and feel that sales is sales, no matter where you are in the world.
- ▶ You have no background in any of the above, but believe import/export is a hot opportunity and you are willing to learn more and maybe take a chance.

There is, of course, no wrong answer. Any of these responses is entirely correct as long as you realize they all involve a lot of learning and hard work. This endeavor can also be a lot of fun, as well as provide a high level of personal and professional satisfaction (which is something you probably can't say about a typical 9-to-5 job).

The objective here is to tell you what you need to know to help you decide whether an import/export business is right for you. Assuming it is, this book will help you do the following:

- ▶ Get your business started successfully.
- ▶ Keep your business running successfully.
- ▶ Enhance your networking skills.
- ▶ Discover ways to use technology (a smartphone, tablet, notebook computer, and/ or desktop computer) and the internet to help manage virtually all aspects of your import/export business.

While some aspects of operating an import/export business are highly technical, you'll find that most of the information in this book is user-friendly. Despite that, there is some technical information you will need to learn before moving forward with the successful operation of your business, so expect a learning curve.

To help convey real-world information, throughout this book you'll find quotes from people who are on the front lines of the industry—from all around the world. These people share their knowledge and experience in a way that will help you learn how the import/export business works. In Chapter 14, for example, you'll read in-depth and exclusive interviews with experts from various areas of international trade who share their advice about how to succeed in imports and exports.

This book breaks up a tremendous amount of information into individual, easily digestible chapters, with separate sections that cover just about every aspect related to startup and operations. Think of this book as your general road map. Once you understand what's involved, you'll need to make some decisions, based on the type of import/export business you plan to run, where you plan to operate from, your startup budget, your previous experience, and a variety of other factors. You'll also likely need to pursue some additional (and highly specialized) education.

Throughout this book, you'll find plenty of helpful referrals and resources, including addresses, phone numbers, and websites. Use these resources to help you get up and running faster and more efficiently. For example, be sure to take full advantage of the resource section at the end of the book to help you reduce time spent on doing industry-related research.

For the right type of entrepreneur or small-business operator, running an import/export business can be a fun, rewarding, and potentially profitable experience. But it will take hard work and a significant time commitment. So like any legitimate business opportunity, do not think of this as a get-rich-quick type of business. By reading this book, you'll develop a much better and more realistic understanding of what's involved.

Trading Around the Globe

International trade is one of the hottest industries of the millennium, despite some of the trade restrictions and disruptions in international trade relationships that have occurred in the current political climate. This is not a new type of business opportunity, however. Think Marco Polo. Consider the great caravans of the Biblical Age with their cargoes of silks and spices. You can even go as far back as prehistoric man trading shells and salt with distant tribes. Trade exists because one group or country has a supply of some commodity or merchandise that is in demand by another group or country. This demand creates a need for importers and exporters.

Meanwhile, as the world becomes more and more technologically advanced, and as a society we shift in subtle and not-so-subtle ways toward "one world" modes of thought, international trade becomes potentially more rewarding in terms of demand, profit potential, and personal satisfaction.

This chapter explores the flourishing business of international trade from both the import and export sides. We're about to delve into the steadily rising economic importance of the field and dip into the secrets of the import/export industry, both in the U.S. and throughout the world.

The International Adventurer

The stereotypical importer rides around in his battered Jeep, bargaining for esoteric goods in exotic markets amid a crescendo of foreign tongues. If that's your idea of an international trader, you're right. But you're also dead wrong.

Importing is not just for those lone footloose adventurer types who survive by their wits and the skin of their teeth. It's big business these days.

In 2018, total U.S. trade with foreign countries was $5.6 trillion. This included $2.5 trillion in exports and $3.1 trillion in imports of both goods and services, according to the U.S. Department of Commerce. Goods made up about 67 percent of U.S. exports, although only about 12 percent of those U.S.-exported goods were classified as "consumer goods." One third were classified as "industrial goods," and the rest of the exports fell into the "capital goods" or "services" category.

As for U.S. imports, 80 percent of all U.S. imports were goods (approximately $2.6 trillion in 2018). Capital goods contributed 27 percent of all goods imported (which equated to about $693 billion). Consumer goods, with the top three categories being phone-, TV-, and pharmaceutical-related, represented about $684 billion. Industrial machinery and equipment imports, along with services, also contributed to the $2.6 trillion worth of imported goods.

The hard facts show that as of 2018, the U.S. continued to import ($3.1 trillion) more than it exported ($2.5 trillion), resulting in a total trade deficit of $621 billion. According to the U.S. Census Bureau, "The nation's international trade deficit in goods and services decreased to $52.5 billion in September 2019, from $55.0 billion in August 2019."

As for the country's exporting activities, these involved sending capital goods, industrial goods, consumer goods, and services to more than 200 foreign countries, including everything from beverages and commodes to computer consulting services. A staggering list of other products and services you might never imagine as global merchandise are fair game for the savvy trader. These goods and services are bought, sold, represented, and distributed somewhere in the world daily.

Who's doing all this international wheeling and dealing when it comes to importing and exporting? It's people just like you! The import/export field is not the sole purview of the conglomerate corporate trader. While large companies exported 70 percent of the value of all exports according to the International Trade Association, which is part of the U.S. Department of Commerce, the big guys make up only about 2 percent of all exporters.

This means that the other 98 percent of exporters are small outfits like yours will be—at least when you're starting out. Keep in mind that there is growing competition worldwide. More than 70 percent of the world's purchasing power is located outside the U.S.

Thus, as a savvy importer/exporter, you might eventually do business with emerging markets like China, Colombia, Czech Republic, Indonesia, Korea, Peru, Poland, Sri Lanka, South Korea, and Taiwan.

As of 2018, five countries, including China, Canada, Mexico, Japan, and Germany, supplied more than half of all U.S. imports. These countries alone supplied 58 percent of the $2.4 trillion imported goods. China, for example, benefits from supplying the U.S. with low-cost goods, while countries like Canada, Mexico, and Germany are known for supplying high-quality goods. Meanwhile, Japan's export strategy to the U.S. involves providing specific products to targeted markets and industries (such as fuel-efficient and reliable automobiles, medical equipment, and aircrafts).

The U.S. Loves Importing

Why are imports such big business in the U.S. and around the world? There are lots of reasons, but the three main ones include:

1. *Availability*. There are some things you just can't grow or make in your home country—bananas in Alaska, mahogany lumber in Maine, or Ballpark franks in France.
2. *Cachet*. A lot of things, like caviar and champagne, pack more cachet if they're imported rather than homegrown. Think Scandinavian furniture, German beer,

Russian vodka (and caviar), French perfume, and Egyptian cotton. Even when you can make it at home, it seems classier when it comes from distant shores.

3. *Price.* Some products are cheaper when imported from another country. Korean toys, Taiwanese electronics, and Mexican clothing can often be manufactured or assembled in foreign factories for far less money than if they were made on the domestic front.

Aside from cachet items, countries typically export goods and services that they can produce inexpensively and import those that are produced more efficiently somewhere else. What makes one product less expensive for a nation to manufacture than another? Two factors: resources and technology.

Resources can be in the form of natural products, such as timber and minerals, as well as human resources, such as low-cost labor or highly skilled workers. Technology is the knowledge and tools to process raw resources into finished products. A country with extensive oil resources and the technology of a refinery, for example, will export oil but may need to import clothing.

The U.S. has long been a major import destination for other nations. The top five countries from which the U.S. imports goods are China, Mexico, Canada, Japan, and Germany. We Americans like variety, low prices, and goods with year-round availability. Importing has allowed us to achieve these goals.

Although the U.S. is an experienced exporter of its services (e.g., travel services, and technical, financial, and legal expertise), the exportation of many types of U.S. goods represents a virtually untapped opportunity—one into which few companies have ventured.

Surprisingly, most of those daring exporters are smaller firms. According to a recent report from the U.S. Census Bureau, companies with fewer than 100 employees accounted for about 90 percent of all exporters, while approximately 98 percent of the total exporters were small or medium-size companies (meaning they employ fewer than 500 people). Also surprisingly, most exporters—over 90 percent—shipped goods to fewer than ten countries. The top five export destinations, in order of preference, were Canada, Mexico, China, Japan, and Germany.

According to the U.S. Census Bureau's Department of Commerce, "In 2018, there were 291,802 identified U.S. exporters, accounting for $1.41 trillion in exports of goods of $1.6 trillion total exports of goods." The identified 291,802 U.S. exporters included 72,543 manufacturing-related exporters, 94,267 wholesale-related exporters, and 124,992 miscellaneous or unidentified exporters. Additional information pertaining to U.S. exporting companies in 2017 and 2018 was scheduled for release in April 2020.

Import/Export–The Prequel

What exactly does an international trader do? In the simplest terms, they are salespeople. Instead of peddling domestically manufactured products on their home turf, a trader deals in more exotic merchandise, materials that are foreign to somebody in another country.

The importer/exporter also acts as a sort of international matchmaker, pairing up buyers and sellers of products in different countries. They can operate as a middleman, purchasing merchandise directly from the manufacturer and selling to retailers or wholesalers in another country. Importer/exporters may have their own network of retail distribution representatives selling on commission. As a third permutation, they might hire an outside company to find sales for them. And as a fourth version, they might serve as a consultant for foreign countries that want to export their products but don't know how.

Let's back up a little and take this one step at a time. When you're wearing your import hat, you'll be bringing goods *into* the U.S.

When you've got on your export cap, you'll be shipping things *out of* the country, into foreign markets.

Let's say, for example, that you've decided to import Guatemalan handicrafts. You might have spotted them at an outdoor market while you were traveling through Central America, or maybe you became involved by answering a trade lead—a "want ad" placed by a local artisan group desperately seeking U.S. representation. In either case, you swing into action. You get hold of a price list and some samples, and then, here in America, you ferry the samples around to wholesalers or retailers, generate interest through your top-notch salesmanship, and acquire orders. Once you've made a predetermined number of sales, you purchase the handicrafts from the artisans, ship them to your buyers, and then those buyers pay you.

This may sound complicated, with you busily purchasing merchandise and sending to third parties who haven't yet paid a dime, but there are ways to protect yourself that you'll learn throughout this book. Keep in mind, this is not the only way you'll structure deals. You might, for example, work off a commission as a representative, negotiating payments directly between artisans and buyers so you don't have to put up any money yourself.

Emerging Markets Take Flight

It's no wonder that international trade is a growing industry. Despite the fluctuations in the world economy, the emergence of free market ideas around the globe has created a stimulating environment for international trade opportunities.

As the world faces the always-present challenges of a potential global recession or financial downturn (as has been the case with the COVID-19 pandemic), nations dust themselves off and respond to those challenges. Huge, rapidly expanding markets, like China and India, are expected to become increasingly important due to their large populations and the expansion of their middle classes. On the other side of the International Date Line, Mexico continues to be one of the U.S.'s biggest trading partners.

More and more "emerging markets" around the world continue to become viable trade partners and provide business opportunities for savvy importers and exporters. As of 2019, some of the world's leading emerging markets (listed in alphabetical order) included: Brazil, Chile, China, Colombia, Czech Republic, Egypt, Greece, Hungary, India, Indonesia, Korea, Malaysia, Mexico, Pakistan, Peru, Philippines, Poland, Qatar, Russia, South Africa, Taiwan, Thailand, Turkey, and United Arab Emirates.

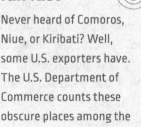

fun fact

Never heard of Comoros, Niue, or Kiribati? Well, some U.S. exporters have. The U.S. Department of Commerce counts these obscure places among the 200-plus countries and territories that import American-made goods.

Earning Potential for International Traders

What can you expect to make as an international trader? That's entirely up to you, depending only on how serious you are and how willing you are to expand. Annual gross revenues for the industry range from $40,000 to $300,000 and beyond, with a median of about $85,000. Some traders work from home, supplementing 9-to-5 incomes with their trading expertise. Others have launched thriving full-time businesses that demand constant attention.

In Maryland, Wahib Wahba heads an export company that, with a staff of five, oversees multimillion-dollar contracts. "There are tons and tons of opportunity for [export] trade," said Wahib. "U.S. manufacturers are behind the clock in exporting." The potential for growth is up to you, if you're willing to put in the time.

"Be prepared to work long hours!" advised Jan Herremans, a trader in Belgium.

"It takes a lot of work," agreed Sam Nelson, a North Carolina export trader.

aha!

You can use Skype, Zoom, WhatsApp, Google Hangouts, or a similar online service to use your internet-connected computer, smartphone, or tablet to make international calls—to landlines or cell phones—often for less than a few cents per minute.

"You have to try with all your energy," said Bruno Carlier, an export manager in France. Wahib echoed this sentiment: "Just keep doing your job. Work on it all the time."

"Do not expect immediate or short-term success," added Lloyd Davidson, a Florida export manager. "Be willing to work around the international clock, if you will; take discourtesies, both foreign and domestic, in stride; maintain the highest standard of personal and business ethics in dealing with your principal and buyer; and learn from your mistakes."

The Startup Costs Associated with International Trade

One of the catch-22s of being in business for yourself is that you need money to make money. In other words, you'll need startup funds. These costs range from less than $5,000 to more than $25,000 for an import/export business. You can start out home-based, which means you won't need to worry about leasing office space. You don't need to purchase a lot of inventory, and you probably won't need employees.

As you'll discover a bit later in this book, your basic necessities will be a computer, printer, scanner/fax machine/copier, smartphone, tablet, and high-speed and reliable internet connection, plus some basic office supplies (including business cards and letterhead). If you already have these items, then you're off to a good start.

Since much of your work will likely require you to make international calls, instead of paying potentially high phone charges, consider setting up an internet-based voice-over-IP calling (VoIP) option.

The Right Stuff

So you've decided running an import/export business is potentially profitable for you. You're willing to invest your money and the time it will take to establish your business. What else should you consider?

Personality. Not everybody is cut out to be an international trader. This is not, for example, a career for

aha!

Check out AllBusiness (www.allbusiness.com), which boasts more than 30,000 members from more than 130 countries. You can get help from and develop business connections with people all over the world. The service offers online resources and tools that will help you start, grow, and manage your business.

LinkedIn (www.linkedin.com) is also a powerful professional networking tool that offers a range of services designed for entrepreneurs and small-business operators.

► **Job Opportunities as a Customs Broker**

If you're interested in pursuing a career as a customs broker, you'll want to understand what people in this line of work do and what their qualifications are, or you need to hire a customs broker to assist you in your import/export business. Be sure to check out this web page on the U.S. Bureau of Labor Statistics website: www.bls.gov/careeroutlook/2016/youre-a-what/customs-broker.htm, and this web page on the U.S. Customs and Border Protection website: www.cbp.gov/trade/programs-administration/customs-brokers/becoming-customs-broker.

the "salesphobic." If you're one of those people who would rather trim your lawn a blade at a time than sell Girl Scout cookies, then you don't want to be in import/export. This is also not a career for the organizationally challenged. If you're one of those let-the-devil-handle-the-details types whose idea of follow-up is waiting to see what happens next, you should think twice about international trading.

Among other vital skills, you'll need to be a good communicator—in-person, over the phone, and in writing. Since you'll be working with people from all over the world, you'll need to learn how to respect other cultures, understand foreign business practices, overcome language barriers, and deal with time zone differences on a daily basis.

Luckily, there are a wide range of technology-based tools and applications to help you communicate with foreign businesspeople. Apps like Grammarly (www.grammarly.com) will help correct your spelling, punctuation, and grammar in outgoing emails and written correspondence, and apps, such as the Office 365 version of Microsoft Word and Outlook, will translate your emails and correspondence into other languages in seconds.

When you need to communicate with people in person who speak another language, a mobile app—like Google Translate on your smartphone—will become a valuable tool.

If, on the other hand, you're an enthusiastic salesperson and a dynamo at tracking things like invoices and shipping receipts, then import/export could be for you. If your idea of heaven is seeing where new ideas and new products will take you, and talking with strangers from different cultures along the way is appealing, then this is a viable career option. Be sure to take the quiz in Figure 1–1 on page 9 to help you quickly determine if you have the personality to succeed as an importer/exporter.

How a Few Experts Got Their Start

Michael Richter, a German trade consultant, let his enchantment with the world be his entry into the industry. "I was simply interested in the worldwide markets and their culture

Traits of the Trade: A Quick Quiz

Do you have a personality that's well-suited for being an ace international trader?

1. My idea of a fun evening is:

    a. Visiting a popular nightclub.

    b. Drinking my favorite coffee while spending hours browsing the Foreign Trade Online website (www.foreign-trade.com/export_trade.htm) and playing with a currency converter app on my smartphone.

    c. Watching movies on Netflix with my friends.

2. When I send Christmas gifts to relatives who live out of state, I usually:

    a. Wait until December 24, stuff the gifts into old grocery bags with the addresses scribbled in crayon, then rush to the post office and stand in a huge line with all the other procrastinators, and hope my gifts arrive on time and intact.

    b. I wrap my gifts carefully in specially selected packaging no later than December 10, call my FedEx or UPS courier (I've already checked to see which is cheaper and faster), then follow up to make sure the gifts arrive on time and intact.

    c. Hope no one notices I forgot to send gifts.

3. I consider myself to be a "people" person because:

    a. Even though I have to force myself, I'm able to interact with people so long as it's not more than once a day.

    b. I love working and interacting with all kinds of folks in person, online, and on the phone.

    c. I enjoy watching other people who interact and communicate well on TV, but I prefer not to do it myself.

4. If I could spend one week a month in a foreign country, I would:

    a. Try to do every activity that is illegal in the U.S.

    b. Try to meet all kinds of people so I could see the world from different perspectives and learn about other cultures.

    c. Be an overbearing American tourist who asks total strangers to take photos of me climbing all over national monuments. I also seek the local McDonald's or KFC in whatever country I am visiting to avoid eating the local cuisine.

Scoring: If you chose "b" for each answer, you passed with flying colors! You're international trader material. You're self-motivated, detail-oriented, and eager to work with people all over the world.

FIGURE 1–1: **Traits of the Trade: A Quick Quiz**

► Gain Real-World International Trade Experience Before Launching Your Own Company

Prior to launching your own import/export business and becoming the company's president and CEO, it certainly helps to have a background in import/export. This might mean "paying your dues" and working for another import/export business to learn the ropes, discover how business works firsthand, and develop the core skillset you'll need.

However, if you don't have previous industry-related experience, should you forget a career in the industry? Certainly not. It's typically possible to start from scratch, if you do your homework and take an organized and well-thought-out approach.

If you're a computer whiz, for example, start out importing or exporting computers or computer-related products or services. If your turf is landscape materials, go green. Launch your import/export business by working with those materials. Go with products or product categories you already understand and have experience working with.

One thing you want to do, however, is determine what knowledge, skills, and experience you're lacking, then take the appropriate steps to compensate. This might mean taking some classes or hiring a business partner with skills or experience that you're lacking.

Don't let the mechanics of international trade, like letters of credit, scare you away. "You have to know what you're doing," advised Wahib Wahba. "Otherwise, you may send a shipment and never get your money just because you spell a name wrong."

But you can get around this: For your first few forays, hire a customs broker or freight forwarder to handle the paperwork for you.

and in developing personal relationships," he explained. "I started being an apprentice—right from the beginning—mostly in investment and construction goods and projects." Now, almost 40 years later, Michael is still in the business—and still enjoying it.

Wahib Wahba, a native of Egypt, started out working overseas as a mechanical engineer for Caterpillar, the world's leading manufacturer of construction and mining equipment. In 1985, he arrived in the U.S., where he promptly started both an MBA degree and a position with a company that sold runway lights and navigational products to airports.

When the company became too heavily involved in domestic sales to handle the international work, Wahib formed a company to take up the slack. The new company also began selling other types of construction projects, from wooden telephone pole installation to railroads, supplying materials, construction services, or both. Soon business was so good that he was able to buy out his former employer.

Wahib stresses that his success developed from his prior experience in the field. "Nobody becomes an exporter overnight," he said. "You have to be coming from somewhere."

Take John Laurino, an international business services provider in São Paulo, Brazil. John learned the ins and outs of import/export as an international purchasing manager for a large company before striking out on his own in 1994.

In Florida, Lloyd Davidson worked in the operations sector of international banking before making the move to his own company. "I decided to expand into export management and export trading," he explained. "I relied on my previous experience in an international environment to support my new endeavors."

Bruno Carlier, who makes his home in Derchigny, France, studied international trade at universities in both France and Spain before completing his schooling in South America by teaching import and export strategy and techniques to others.

"One of my first jobs after my studies was in one of the major French supermarket groups as an import assistant," Bruno said. "I can say that in four months [there], I learned much more than in four years of studies."

But that wasn't enough to get him a job in international trade. Despite a year of teaching in Ecuador and his supermarket job, he lacked hands-on training. Bruno added, "Because I was not considered to have enough experience to work in the [international trade] department of a medium-sized company, I decided to create my own business. Now here I am."

Here, too, are you—on the brink of an exciting new career opportunity, starting your own import/export business. As you can see, there are many paths you can take toward your own niche in the field and many roads that can lead to success. Keep in mind, however, that they all require dedication, hard work, and, especially for those who are newbies in the field, a great deal of learning.

tip

Social media international business discussion groups are full of information for those working in small and medium-sized enterprises (SME). Check out special interest groups on Facebook and LinkedIn, for example. The more you participate in these groups, the more people you'll meet, and the more you'll get out of them in terms of knowledge and networking opportunities.

Future Forecast

Perhaps the import/export business looks like the perfect fit for you—at least, on paper. There is, however, one more thing to take into consideration: the industry prognosis. Will international trading be around for the next 25 to 50 years and beyond?

The odds are good. We may live in challenging times, but they are also interesting times. The world has already experienced world wars, natural disasters, and global financial crises, yet the U.S.—and our trading partners—are still alive and kicking, and, in many cases, thriving.

Do Your Homework!

Before jumping headfirst into the startup operation of an import/export business, do your homework. Decide what area(s) you want to specialize in and what countries or regions you might want to conduct business in. Next, make sure economic forecasts and trends provide a favorable outlook for the type of business you're interested in pursuing.

According to the World Trade Organization (www.wto.org/english/news_e/pres19_e/pr840_e.htm), for example, "Escalating trade tensions and a slowing global economy have led WTO economists to sharply downgrade their forecasts for trade growth in 2019 and 2020. World merchandise trade volumes are now expected to rise by only 1.2 percent in 2019, substantially slower than the 2.6 percent growth forecast in April. The projected increase in 2020 is now 2.7 percent, down from 3.0 percent previously. The economists caution that downside risks remain high and the 2020 projection depends on a return to more normal trade relations."

Meanwhile, an online service called Vault (www.vault.com), which offers in-depth information about the experience of working within a wide range of industries and professions, had this to say about working in the import/export business: "In 2012, more than 304,000 U.S. companies exported goods. Of those, more than 97 percent are identified as small to medium companies employing 500 or fewer workers. The forces that determine the demand for workers in import-export careers are complex. Because so many markets are involved and international trade agreements can change, the outlook for import-export professionals is volatile."

Of course, the WTO and Vault are just two information resources. Scour the internet and seek out up-to-date forecasts and statistics that relate to your business interests, then adjust your business-related goals and business plan accordingly. This book, not to mention Google, offers many reliable resources for performing research that you'll want to take advantage of.

► The Trade War with China Has Had a Global Impact

In early 2018, the Trump administration kicked off a trade dispute with China. The goal was to "fix" trade practices that the administration claimed put U.S. companies at a disadvantage. Meanwhile, China believed that the U.S. government's actions were an attempt to hinder China's growth.

Instead of quickly coming to mutually agreeable trade terms, what began as a dispute escalated into a "trade war" between the U.S. and China, two of the world's largest economies. As of early 2020, an initial trade deal between the U.S. and China has been signed, but *The New York Times*, explained this agreement simply brought "the first chapter of a protracted and economically damaging fight with one of the world's largest economies to a close." In this agreement, China committed to buying an additional $200 billion worth of American goods and services by 2021 and would eliminate or reduce some of the tariffs that it placed on American products.

While initially this seemed like good news for those involved with international trade, new problems began to arise as a result of the Coronavirus global pandemic, which impacted importing and exporting activities between the U.S. and several Asian countries.

Not only has this trade war impacted the ability for U.S.-based import and export companies to do business with China, but the ongoing economic uncertainty has had a negative impact on importing and exporting between a wide range of other nations and on the global economy as a whole. Trade-related restrictions and regulations have constantly been changing, and new fees, taxes, and tariffs have been imposed—some favorable and not so favorable to U.S.-based companies.

As of early 2020, many experienced international trade experts believed that even if the trade war with China were to suddenly and completely be resolved, global trade and economic implications would be impacted for several years to come.

Despite this unsettling and confusing time for those in the import/export business, many continue to successfully navigate and compensate for the changes and have discovered ways to continue earning a profit. In some cases, this has meant avoiding importing and exporting with China and focusing on other countries or regions.

One of your responsibilities as an international trader is to follow and attempt to understand global politics and related economic trends. Be sure to research how a trade dispute or trade war between countries could impact your business, then investigate how to navigate through or around the political turmoil in a way that's favorable for your business interests.

Another excellent place to begin your career-related research is the online Career Center operated by the American Association of Exporters and Importers, also known as the AAEI (https://careers.aaei.org). This is a premier trade organization that represents U.S. companies engaged in global trade. One of the fee-based services offered by this organization is one-on-one career coaching (https://careers.aaei.org/jobseekers/resources/store/monthly_coaching.cfm).

Import/ Export 101

Some international traders do very well importing or exporting services, which can mean a variety of things. As a contractor, you export services and sometimes equipment when your company builds bridges, airports, or telecommunications facilities in a foreign country. As a consultant, you're exporting a service when you

supply your knowledge to a foreign firm. You're importing a service when you purchase the licensing to open
your franchise of a pub that started in England.

In this book, we're talking mainly about importing
and exporting products. If you are trading in services,
some of our information should still be useful to you
(especially Chapter 3). You may also want to consult
Entrepreneur's Start Your Own Consulting Business.

Global trade of any kind involves nations. Where
there are nations, there is government. Anything related
to commerce and government means red tape—miles of
it! Right from the start, you need to find and work with
people who are experienced experts cutting through that
red tape in the fastest, most cost-effective way possible.

Most international traders use freight forwarders
or customs brokers to handle all the details of shipping
and documentation. A freight forwarder is an agent who
acts on behalf of importers and exporters, like you will

tip

Consider exporting your
services. Although the
U.S. has a large trade
deficit, it is a top exporter
of services. Some of
the top service-related
exports in 2019 included:
maintenance and repair,
travel services, insurance-
related services, financial
services, charges/
licensing fees for the use
of intellectual properties,
and telecommunications
services.

soon be. They also work with companies to organize the safe, efficient, and cost-effective
transportation of goods.

Customs brokers are private individuals, partnerships, associations, or corporations
licensed, regulated, and empowered by the U.S. Customs and Border Protection (CBP).
They also help importers and exporters when it comes to meeting the federal requirements
that govern imports and exports. These people earn their living by sorting out government
rules, regulations, forms, and assorted red tape—both foreign and domestic—but they're
also excellent sources of advice on freight costs, port charges, consular fees, and insurance.

Even if you use their services and leave the form filling to them, you should have a
working knowledge of what goes on behind the scenes. This chapter, therefore, takes you
on a whirlwind tour of the import/export world.

The Key Players

Let's look at some of the players involved in the import/export and international trade
industries:

▶ *Export Management Companies (EMCs).* An EMC handles export operations for
  a domestic company that wants to sell its product overseas but doesn't know how

(and perhaps doesn't want to know how). The EMC does it all—hiring dealers, distributors, and representatives; handling advertising, marketing, and promotions; overseeing marking and packaging; arranging shipping; and sometimes arranging financing. In some cases, the EMC even takes title to (purchases) the goods, in essence becoming its own distributor. EMCs usually specialize by product, foreign market, or both, and—unless they've taken title—are paid by commission, salary, or retainer plus commission.

▶ *Export Trading Companies (ETCs).* While an EMC has merchandise to sell and is using its energies to seek out buyers, an ETC attacks the other side of the trading coin. It identifies what foreign buyers want to spend their money on, then hunts down domestic sources willing to export, thus becoming a pseudo-EMC. An ETC sometimes takes title to the goods and works on a commission basis.

▶ *Import/Export Merchants.* This international entrepreneur is a sort of free agent. They have no specific client base, and they do not specialize in any one industry or line of products. Instead, they purchase goods directly from a domestic or foreign manufacturer, then pack, ship, and resell the goods on their own. This means, of course, that unlike their compatriot (the EMC), they assume all the risks (as well as all the profits).

The Supporting Players

Let's say you're an exporter with a hot product to sell. Who do you look for? A buyer, otherwise known as an importer. Here's the rundown on the various types of importers:

▶ *Commission Agents.* These are intermediaries commissioned by foreign firms searching for domestic products to purchase.

▶ *Commission Representatives.* Similar to independent sales reps in the U.S., these folks usually work on a commission basis, and because they don't purchase (take title to) the product, they don't assume any risk or responsibility.

▶ *Country-Controlled Buying Agents.* These foreign government agencies or quasi-governmental firms are charged with the responsibility of locating and purchasing desired products.

▶ *Foreign Distributors.* Similar to wholesale distributors in the U.S., these merchants buy for their own account, taking title to and responsibility for the merchandise.

▶ *State-Controlled Trading Companies.* Some countries have government-sanctioned and controlled trading entities. These agencies often deal in raw materials, agricultural machinery, manufacturing equipment, and technical instruments.

More Major Players

There are, of course, more players than just the importers, exporters, and their cast of distributors and representatives. You'll also be dealing with another major player in the game—government entities.

CBP and ICE

Two important goals of the U.S. Customs Facilitation and Trade Enforcement Reauthorization Act of 2009 were enhancement of supply chain security and trade facilitation. Toward those goals, the U.S. government created the U.S. Customs and Border Protection Agency (CBP) and the U.S. Immigration and Customs Enforcement Agency (ICE).

You may already know customs officers as those people who fixate on you and your luggage with beady eyes as you trudge through the airport on your way home from a foreign vacation. But together these two agencies take on many more tasks than just checking for contraband souvenirs.

According to their websites (www.cbp.gov and www.ice.gov, respectively), these organizations also:

► Assess and collect customs duties, excise taxes, fees, and penalties due on imported merchandise.
► Intercept and seize contraband, including narcotics and other illegal drugs.
► Process people, baggage, cargo, and mail.
► Administer certain navigation laws.
► Protect American business, labor, and intellectual property rights by enforcing U.S. laws designed to prevent illegal trade practices, including provisions related to quotas and the marking of imported goods.
► Enforce the Anti-Dumping Act.
► Provide customs records for copyrights, patents, and trademarks.
► Enforce import and export restrictions and prohibitions, including the export of technology used to make weapons of mass destruction.
► Protect against money laundering.
► Collect import/export data to translate into international trade statistics.

fun fact

The "dump" in the Anti-Dumping Act refers to the practice of flooding a market with an imported product that's far cheaper than a comparable domestic one.

▶ Secure the national borders.

▶ Enforce immigration laws.

▶ Strive to guard against terrorism.

BIS

The Bureau of Industry and Security, also known as BIS (www.bis.doc.gov), is another entity that governs the exportation of sensitive materials (e.g., defense systems, plutonium, and encrypted software). Headed by the Department of Commerce, BIS administers export controls, coordinates Department of Commerce security activities, and oversees defense trade. The BIS manages the export of most merchandise through the Export Administration Regulations, also known as EAR.

Product Category Regulatory Agencies

Beyond CBP, ICE, and BIS, various agencies regulate the importation of sundry products. If you're planning on importing, for example, Cleopatra's magic milk bath, lucky Chinese crickets, cereals, fur coats, or parrots, you'd better check with the agency in charge. Here is a sampling of what you can expect:

▶ *Cheese, Milk, and Other Dairy Products.* Cheese and cheese products are subject to the vagaries of the FDA and the Department of Agriculture. You must have an import license to bring in most cheeses, which are usually subject to quotas administered by the Department of Agriculture's Foreign Agricultural Service. Milk and cream fall under the aegis of the Food, Drug, and Cosmetic Act and the Federal Import Milk Act, and cannot be imported unless you have a permit from the Department of Agriculture, the FDA's Office of Food Labeling, and other agencies.

▶ *Fruits, Vegetables, and Nuts.* Some fresh produce items (including fresh tomatoes, avocados, mangoes, limes, oranges, grapefruit, green peppers, Irish potatoes, cucumbers, eggplants, dry onions, walnuts, filberts, processed dates, prunes, raisins, and olives in tins) must meet import requirements relating to size, quality, and maturity. All these tidbits must have an inspection certificate indicating importation compliance issued by the Agricultural Marketing Service of the Department of Agriculture. For questions, contact the Agricultural Marketing Service. You may also have to deal with additional restrictions imposed by the department's Animal and Plant Health Inspection Service, otherwise known as APHIS, or by the FDA's Division of Import Operations and Policy.

► *Plant and Plant Products.* If you've got a green thumb and want to import garden goodies, be sure you check with the Department of Agriculture first. The agency regulates plants and plant products (including nursery stock, bulbs, roots, and seeds), certain materials (including cotton and lumber), and soil.

► *Radio Frequency Devices.* Also called intentional radiators, these are devices that broadcast radio energy to perform their functions. Cellular phones, smartphones, tablets, "smart" appliances/devices, any devices with wireless connections, Bluetooth connections, wifi, radios, stereos, digital recorders, televisions, walkietalkies, wireless key-access systems, and other radio frequency devices are subject to the radio emission standards of the FCC. If you import these items, you'll need to make sure they comply with FCC standards.

► *Foods and Cosmetics.* Before you import that European miracle fat-melting pill, you'd best check with the FDA to make sure you're not unintentionally bringing in articles that can be considered "misbranded," that is, making false or misleading claims.

Additional Government Agencies Are Involved with Importing Specific Products

Other products that fall under the purview of a government agency, such as the Animal and Plant Health Inspection Service (APHIS), include:

► *Insects*: APHIS

► *Livestock and Animals*: APHIS

► *Meat and Meat Products*: APHIS

► *Poultry and Poultry Products*: APHIS

► *Arms, Ammunition, Explosives, and Implements of War*: Bureau of Alcohol, Tobacco, and Firearms (which falls under the Department of Justice)

► *Radioactive Materials and Nuclear Reactors*: Nuclear Regulatory Commission

► *Household Appliances*: Department of Energy, Office of Codes and Standards, and/or the Federal Trade Commission (FTC)'s Division of Enforcement

► *Flammable Fabrics*: Consumer Product Safety Commission

► *Radiation-Producing Products*: FDA's Center for Devices and Radiological Health

► *Seafood*: FDA and the National Marine Fisheries Service

► *Biological Drugs*: FDA

► *Biological Materials and Vectors*: FDA's Center for Biologics Evaluation and Research and the Centers for Disease Control

► *Narcotic Drugs and Derivatives:* The Drug Enforcement Administration, which falls under the Department of Justice

▶ *Gold and Silver*: U.S. Customs and the FBI

▶ *Caustic or Corrosive Substances for Household Use*: Office of Hazardous Materials Transportation, which falls under the Department of Transportation

▶ *Furs*: FTC

▶ *Textiles*: FTC

▶ *Wildlife and Pets*: U.S. Fish and Wildlife Service and Assistant Regional Director for Law Enforcement for the state in which you're located. For birds, cats, dogs, monkeys, and turtles, check with the Centers for Disease Control in Atlanta, as well as APHIS.

▶ *Petroleum and Petroleum Products*: Department of Energy

▶ *Alcoholic Beverages:* Bureau of Alcohol, Tobacco, and Firearms, as well as the Treasury Department

Don't let this list keep you from treading into international trade waters. Chances are you're not going to be dealing in most of this merchandise, but if any of these goods are where your interests lie, you should know which agency to call for more detailed information. Remember, as the Customs Service people like to say, "Know before you go." If you have any questions at all, ask!

Discover How a Customs Broker or Freight Forwarder Can Assist You

Depending on whether you're importing or exporting, you can also get answers to your procedure questions from a *customs broker* or a *freight forwarder*.

The customs broker (sometimes called a *customhouse broker*) is an important asset to importers. It's their job to know the ins and outs of importing in intimate detail and to handle all the paperwork and details on your behalf. Some brokers are small outfits consisting of a single owner-operator at a single port of entry; others are corporate types with lots of employees and offices in many ports. The U.S. Customs and Border Protection (CBP) licenses them all.

When you hire a customs broker, they act as your agent during the entry process. They prepare and file the entry documents, acquire any necessary bonds, deposit any required duties, get the merchandise released into their custody (or yours), arrange delivery to the site you've chosen, and obtain any drawback refunds.

A customs broker is not a legal necessity, but a good one will make your life as an international trader considerably easier. While the customs broker can become an importer's best friend, a freight forwarder is who an exporter goes to for assistance.

Acting as the exporter's agent, the international freight forwarder uses their expertise with foreign import rules and regulations as well as domestic export laws to move cargo to overseas destinations.

Freight forwarders can assist with an order from the get-go by advising you of freight costs, port charges, consular fees, special documentation charges, and insurance costs. They can recommend the proper type of packing to protect your merchandise in transit, arrange to have the goods packed at the port or containerized, quote shipping rates, then book your merchandise onto a plane, train, truck, or cargo ship. Like a concierge in a upscale hotel, they can get anything you've got anywhere you want it to go.

"There's nothing we say 'no' to," said Ray Tobia, president/CEO of Air Sea International Forwarding. "We try to offer everybody everything, provided it's legal."

Like customs brokers, freight forwarders are licensed, but in this case, by the International Air Transport Association (IATA) and Federal Maritime Commission (for ocean freight). You don't have to use the freight forwarder's services to transport your goods, and not all exporters rely on such services, but they're a definite plus.

Understand the Flow of Products Being Imported or Exported

Now that you're familiar with the players, you'll need to deal with how the merchandise travels from manufacturer to consumers. A manufacturer who uses a middleman who resells to the consumer is paddling around in a three-level channel of distribution. The middleman can be a merchant who purchases the goods and then resells them, or they can be an agent who acts as a broker but doesn't take title to the merchandise.

Who your fellow swimmers are will depend on how you configure your trade channel. We'll discuss this more in Chapter 11, but for now, let's just get acquainted with the group:

- ► *Manufacturer's Representative.* This is a salesperson who specializes in a type of product or line of complementary products; for example, home electronics: televisions, smart home appliances, and smart speakers. They often provide additional product assistance, such as warehousing and technical service.
- ► *Distributor or Wholesale Distributor.* A company that buys the product you have imported and sells it to a retailer or other agent for further distribution until it gets to the end user.
- ► *Representative.* A savvy salesperson who pitches your product to wholesale or retail buyers, then passes the sale on to you; differs from the manufacturer's rep in that they don't necessarily specialize in a product or group of products.
- ► *Retailer.* This is the tail end of the trade channel where the merchandise smacks into the consumer. Yet another variation on a theme, if the end user is not a traditional consumer but an original equipment manufacturer (OEM), you don't need to worry about the retailer because the OEM becomes your end of the line. (Think

Dell purchasing a software program to pass along to its personal computer buyers as part of a bundled package.)

The Rules

Now that you know many of the players and their channels, let's look at some of the rules of the import/export game. As you already know, countries typically export goods and services that they can produce inexpensively and import those that are produced more

► A Caribbean Import/Export Focus

Under the Caribbean Basin Initiative (CBI), designated beneficiary countries in the Caribbean receive duty-free entry of certain merchandise into the U.S., typically most goods produced in the Caribbean Basin region. Although the countries on the list change from time to time, you can generally count on the following being included:

- ► Antigua and Barbuda
- ► Aruba
- ► Barbados
- ► Belize
- ► British Virgin Islands
- ► Curacao
- ► Dominica
- ► Grenada
- ► Guyana
- ► Haiti
- ► Jamaica
- ► Montserrat
- ► Saint Kitts and Nevis
- ► Saint Lucia
- ► Saint Vincent and the Grenadines
- ► The Bahamas
- ► Trinidad and Tobago

efficiently somewhere else. But, as usual, when governments are involved, it's not quite that simple. Countries also tend to block and counter-block sundry items of each other's products in a sort of giant, industrial-sized game of Risk.

Understand Potential Trade Barriers

Trade barriers are set up by national governments to protect certain domestic industries from hefty foreign competition. If the shoe industry in the Land of Oz, for example, makes ruby slippers for $2 a pair, and the Land of Nod manufactures them for only $1 a pair, then Oz might put a tariff trade barrier on any ruby slippers brought in-country from Nod, charging, say, $1.50 per pair in import tax, or duty. Because this extra charge will have to be passed on to the consumer for the Nod people to make a profit, the Oz government figures it can keep its native slippers competitive in the marketplace.

Most trade barriers take the form of tariffs, but they can be camouflaged as quotas on foreign goods or as maximum-frustration builders, like excessive marking and labeling requirements, excessive pollution control regulations, and unfair classification of imports for customs duties. These nontax barriers can be just as costly as tariffs; the cost of getting products qualified for all these special requirements still has to be passed along to the consumer.

warning

Before you decide whether you can trade profitably with a country, you need to know what tariffs or other barriers might stand in your way. For imports, check with the U.S. Customs Service. For exports, ask for help at your local Department of Commerce office, or the commerce department in the country you're interested in. Another viable option is to speak with a knowledgeable freight forwarder.

In recent years, world economists have been pushing the idea that in the long run, trade barriers only hurt our global economy. Some governments have listened, thus the recent trend toward free marketplace initiatives. Other government leaders, however, have taken the opposite approach.

Know Your Quotas!

An import quota is a limit on the quantity of a product that can be brought into the country over a specified period. The Land of Oz, for example, might put a limit on the number of ruby slippers that can be brought into the country each year, say, 10,000 pairs between January 1 and December 31. If a few zealous slipper salespeople fill that quota by February

► **Free Duty-Free Info**

If you are trying to find out if the goods you are importing are considered duty free, start by checking the special program indicator (SPI) for the international trade agreement (i.e., the SPI for GSP) or free trade agreement in the Harmonized Tariff Schedule (HTS), which can be found on the U.S. International Trade Commission's website (www.usitc.gov/tata/hts/index.htm).

You must determine the ten-digit HTS code for the goods. Once you have the HTS code, reference the duty rate in the "Special Rates" sub-column. If the SPI for your trade preference program or free trade agreement is listed, your goods are eligible for the rate indicated.

You could also check with an import specialist at the port of entry through which your goods will enter the U.S.

15, then it's tough luck for anybody else who might be importing ruby slippers for the rest of the year.

The U.S. divides its import quotas into two types: *tariff rate* and *absolute*. Under the tariff rate banner, quota goods can be imported at a sort of "sale" price; you pay a reduced tariff or duty during a given period. There's no quantity limit, so you can bring in as much as you want, but when the special period ends, you pay a higher duty.

Absolute quotas are the quantitative ones. Once the limit's been reached on the product, no more are let into the country until the next time period. Some absolute quotas apply to every country in the world, while others are aimed at certain nations.

Some absolute quotas become filled within moments of the period's official opening time, which is usually at noon on the designated effective date. To deal with this port rush, customs releases everybody's merchandise in prorated portions, based on a ratio between the quota limit and the total amount offered for entry. In this way, each importer gets an equitable chunk of the quota.

Some Countries Play Favorites

A country with "normal trade relations" with the U.S. is one that enjoys trade with Americans *without* additional barriers or duties. France, for example, is an American trading partner, and therefore its imports get the standard rate on most products.

Some countries even get duty-free entry for most types of merchandise. Under a variety of programs, some developing nations receive the freebie treatment as a means of contributing to their economic growth.

To qualify for duty-free trade preferences, your merchandise must meet several conditions, including the following:

► Merchandise must be imported directly from the beneficiary country into U.S. Customs territory (no side trips or detours).

► Merchandise must have been produced in the beneficiary country, meaning that it's entirely the growth, product, or manufacture of that country, or it's been substantially transformed into a new and different product in that country.

► At least 35 percent of the appraised value of the article must consist of the cost or value of materials produced in the beneficiary country and/or the direct costs of processing operations that were carried out in that country.

Because the rules may vary slightly from one trade initiative or pact to another, be sure to check with your customs broker or the director of the port of entry or district where your merchandise will make landfall in the U.S.

Many Countries Offer Viable Import/Export Opportunities

Countries that have trading treaties with the U.S. make good candidates for import/export partners, as do countries with high populations and emerging economies.

► Doing Business with Israel

The United States-Israel Free Trade Area (FTA) agreement provides duty-free entry for certain Israeli products. According to the Jewish Virtual Library, a division of the American/Israeli Cooperative Enterprise, kibitzes are responsible for 5.9 percent of Israel's industrial sales and 8.2 percent of Israeli exports. Plastic and rubber products, metals, and food are all popular Israeli exports. Learn more by visiting: https://ustr.gov/trade-agreements/free-trade-agreements/israel-fta.

Keeping Tabs on Politics and the Global Economy

We're beginning to realize that our planet belongs to all of us. The powers that be— and the importers and exporters in the field—are moving toward a world economy. How are they accomplishing this? International traders contribute by working with (and, in many cases, making lifelong friends with) people all over the globe.

Governments contribute by writing policies that make importing and exporting easier and more profitable for everyone involved. The state of the world's economy also greatly affects international trade, and vice versa. The global financial crisis of 2007 to 2010 had a large impact (as has the COVID-19 pandemic) but governments took numerous measures to assist in the global recovery.

In this chapter we'll discuss trade agreements between nations, the global recession's effect on international trade, the world community's responses to the challenges of recessions, and the current forecast for international trade.

The World Trade Organization Has Clout

The grandfather of modern trade policy is the General Agreement on Tariffs and Trade (GATT), which is an international agreement designed to reduce trade barriers between countries. First instituted in 1947 when World War II was still a fresh wound in millions of minds, it remains the primary international trade instrument used around the globe. It is now under the auspices of the World Trade Organization (WTO).

The WTO was formed in 1995. It has more than 160 members accounting for more than 90 percent of all world trade.

Based in Geneva, the WTO has a Secretariat, a Ministerial General, and a General Council that acts as a dispute settler, a Goods Council, a Services Council, and an Intellectual Property Council, as well as a host of committees.

The WTO's prime directive is to ease trade barriers around the world, help developing nations pull themselves up into the mainstream, and give smaller businesses in all nations more opportunities to join the world marketplace. The precepts it upholds are the following:

- ▶ Trade should be conducted without discrimination.
- ▶ Domestic industry should be protected only through tariffs and not through restrictive policies.
- ▶ All parties should reduce tariffs through negotiations.
- ▶ Members should work together to overcome trade problems.

warning

As is the case with any industry, the import/export business has its share of scam artists and charlatans. Be wary of unsolicited interest, especially if it is accompanied by requests for payment, samples, or prototypes to be sent in advance of negotiations. Also be wary of requests for cash for an event to be held or for future travel expenses.

Members of the WTO meet in sessions called "rounds" to negotiate agreements. Unlike a square dance round, a WTO round can last for years. WTO negotiations center on topics related to service industries, investments, government procurement policies, research subsidies, patents and other intellectual properties, and telecommunications.

Want to read what this trade policy says? Point your web browser to: www.wto.org/english/docs_e/legal_e/gatt47.pdf.

warning

"Intellectual property" refers to patented, trademarked, or copyrighted products. Books, music, and inventions are only a few examples of products protected by law. You can't import this merchandise without permission any more than you can sell U.S. intellectual property.

Free Trade Frenzy

The last two decades have seen the adoption of many free trade agreements (FTAs). The following is information about the main agreements involving the U.S.

North American Free Trade Agreement (NAFTA)

If you've been adult, conscious, and living in the U.S. within the last 20 years or so, you've heard at least something about NAFTA, the North American Free Trade Agreement. This plan to phase out all barriers to trading goods and services among Canada, the U.S., and Mexico took effect amid much fanfare on January 1, 1994. A similar agreement between Canada and the U.S. had already been in operation since 1989.

NAFTA's prime directives are to eliminate barriers to trade, promote fair competition, increase investment opportunities, and provide adequate protection for intellectual property rights. It specifically establishes trade rules for textiles and apparel, automotive goods, agricultural products, and energy and petrochemicals. It also defines standards for technical information and transportation among member nations.

Over 20 years later, NAFTA has resulted in positives and negatives, depending on who you ask. As regulations change, it is always difficult to determine which results are the fault of the regulatory changes and which are due to various economic shifts and unrelated factors.

Over the years, NAFTA has decreased tariffs, made it easier for U.S. citizens to purchase goods from Canada and Mexico, and increased trade between the three countries. However, Mexican workers have benefitted less than anticipated because of work going to other ethnic groups. In addition, despite lifting tariffs, many custom regulations have remained in place and in some cases have become stricter.

► Duty Free

Thanks to NAFTA, much of the merchandise traded between the U.S., Canada, and Mexico is duty free. With a few exceptions, this no-tariff status applies only to goods that originate in the NAFTA region. What exactly does that mean? Well, according to Article 401 of the agreement, the term "originate" is basically defined as:

- ► Merchandise entirely obtained or produced in the territory of one or more NAFTA parties

- ► Unassembled merchandise that hasn't been entirely obtained or produced in the NAFTA region but contains a 50 percent (if using the net cost method) to 60 percent (if using the transaction value method) regional value content

If you play around with your officially originating goods—if you transport them outside the NAFTA region and do anything more than unload or reload them for safer shipment—you lose the originating status.

Also, you can't try to beat the system by bringing a nonoriginating product into a NAFTA nation and then "transshipping" it on (see Chapter 5). It won't qualify as a duty-free NAFTA product. To ease your mind and confirm all the down-and-dirty details of origination, learn more about NAFTA at www.export.gov.

According to the Office of the U.S. Trade Representative, "On May 18, 2017, following consultations with relevant Congressional committees, U.S. Trade Representative Robert Lighthizer informed Congress that the President intends to commence negotiations with Canada and Mexico with respect to the NAFTA. Through these negotiations, the U.S. seeks to support higher-paying jobs in the U.S. and to grow the U.S. economy by improving U.S. opportunities to trade with Canada and Mexico."

Where does NAFTA stand today and how does it impact today's international traders? Find out by pointing your web browser to: https://ustr.gov/trade-agreements/free-trade-agreements/north-american-free-trade-agreement-nafta.

U.S.–Korea Free Trade Agreement (KORUS FTA)

KORUS FTA (https://ustr.gov/trade-agreements/free-trade-agreements/korus-fta) is the largest bilateral trade initiative since NAFTA, and it has been almost as controversial. This agreement entered into force on March 15, 2012. Under KORUS FTA, almost 80 percent of U.S. exports to Korea are now duty free. Many remaining tariffs will be eliminated in the coming years.

Although there is general consensus that the KORUS agreement will increase U.S. exports to South Korea, economists disagree on other ramifications of the agreement. Some point out that in the first year after ratification, the U.S. lost 40,000 jobs and showed a sharp increase in its trade deficit with South Korea. Other economists argue that because not all aspects of the agreement are yet in force, and because companies require time to adjust to new rules and to expand their sales networks within South Korea, it is too early to tell what the overall effect of KORUS will be.

Other Free Trade Agreements

The U.S. has bilateral FTAs in place with numerous countries, including: Australia, Bahrain, Canada, Chile, Colombia, Costa Rica, Dominican Republic, El Salvador, Guatemala, Honduras, Israel, Jordan, Korea, Mexico, Morocco, Nicaragua, Oman, Panama, Peru, and Singapore. To read these FTAs and see firsthand what they entail and how they might impact your import/export business, visit: https://ustr.gov/trade-agreements/free-trade-agreements.

stat fact

Consider Korea a major player. It is the sixth largest goods trading partner with the U.S. According to the Office of the U.S. Trade Representative, "U.S. goods and services trade with Korea totaled an estimated $154.8 billion in 2017. Exports were $72.5 billion; imports were $82.3 billion. The U.S. goods and services trade deficit with Korea was $9.8 billion in 2017."

African Growth and Opportunity Act (AGOA)

While it's not a free-trade treaty, the African Growth and Opportunity Act (AGOA) offers incentives to African nations to create free markets and open their economies. Signed into law in 2000, this act opens American markets to eligible countries. Eligibility is determined annually, and there are currently 42 AGOA-eligible countries.

Nigeria and Angola are the largest exporters under AGOA, while South Africa's exports are the most diverse. According to the U.S. Department of Commerce, sub-Saharan Africa is "poised for tremendous growth."

For more information, visit: https://ustr.gov/issue-areas/trade-development/preference-programs/african-growth-and-opportunity-act-agoa.

Wartime Challenges

Generally, war is not so great for international trade. In fact, wartime can challenge even the hardiest of traders, causing hiccups (sometimes lasting decades) to everyday trade functions and operations.

Keep in mind, a war does not have to be in or with your home country for it to negatively impact your bottom line. If, for example, you trade with two countries that are at war, this puts you in the middle of a battle on the world stage. Try as you might to keep your two trading worlds separate, the import/export world is getting smaller every day, and your clients may find out about other deals and question your loyalty to both them and their adversary.

War also can halt production of your import goods. What if you have a trade partner in a country where all metal resources are now required to go to the production of munitions? So much for the metal wind chimes you were buying by the gross. Your beautiful wind chimes have been melted to make the belly of an airplane.

Sanctions

One of the biggest effects war can have on your business is trade sanctions. *Merriam-Webster's Collegiate Dictionary* defines a sanction as "an economic or military coercive measure adopted usually by several nations in concert for forcing a nation violating international law to desist or yield to adjudication." That's a fancy way of saying that a country can bar imports to and exports from any country deemed to be breaking the international law.

This can be a direct result of war, a conflict, or a country's actions toward its own people that are considered cruel and unnecessary. For example, the U.S. leveled sanctions on the Ivory Coast in 2006 due to "numerous violations of human rights and international humanitarian law," according to the president's executive order. U.S. sanctions are currently in effect for several countries, so be sure to check with the Treasury Department before you start shipping those baseball caps to North Korea, for example.

Global Recession

A global recession doesn't do much for trade, either. Leading economists called the global financial crisis of 2007–2010 the worst financial crisis since the Great Depression of the 1930s. The financial impact of COVID-19 is likely to overshadow this crisis well into the next decade and beyond.

The collapse of the global housing bubble sent the values of all securities connected to the real estate market plummeting. Financial institutions failed. Available credit declined. Businesses failed. Investor confidence hit an all-time low, which in turn shook up the global stock markets.

The collapse of U.S. investment bank Lehman Brothers led to an intensified global crisis as trade finance increased in cost and became less available. World consumer wealth declined by trillions of U.S. dollars. Economies slowed worldwide and international trade declined.

Ernst & Young, a leading professional services organization, points out that while the global financial crisis significantly affected world trade, these effects were not consistent from country to country. In other words, some were hit much harder than others, and the global financial impact and fallout is still being felt today.

Global Responses to the Crisis

Within a few months of the beginning of the crisis (2007), the World Bank reported that 17 of the 20 largest industrialized nations had adopted new trade restriction measures. As overall trade volumes decreased, the complexity of conducting trade increased. Trade disputes also increased. The International Money Fund estimates that from 2008 to 2009, global trade fell by 12 percent. Between the spring of 2008 and spring 2009, U.S. international trade in goods and services decreased by 17 percent.

Fortunately for international trade, governments of the major world economies soon realized that protectionist measures (all too common during the Great Depression) were not the way to go. In addition to enacting national stimulus packages and institutional bailouts at home, the international community responded to the crisis with several measures.

Members of the World Trade Organization's G20 held a 2009 London Summit to plan a coordinated response to the global economic crisis. They agreed to refrain from enacting any new trade barriers or export restrictions. They also agreed not to constrain capital flow and to commit to the conditions of the Doha Round, which would boost world trade by $150 billion annually. An additional action was the adoption of the G20 Trade Package, which provided for an injection of $250 billion in trade financing over two years.

The International Finance Corporation (IFC), a member of the World Bank group, expanded its already-existing Global Trade Finance Program (GTFP) to $3 billion. This program offered guarantees and risk mitigation to banks that finance companies operating in new or challenging markets.

The IFC launched the Global Trade Liquidity Program, a coordinated global initiative undertaken by governments, development financing institutions, and private-sector banks to provide funds for developing countries. The IFC jump-started the program with $1 billion. Public sector banks have added $5 billion.

U.S. Response

Besides providing a variety of economic stimulus packages, the U.S. government authorized its Export-Import Bank (Ex-Im) to increase direct lending to financial institutions that use those funds to finance export businesses. In addition, the National Export Initiative, unveiled in 2010, increased the budget of the International Trade Administration by 20 percent to allow it to increase efforts to advocate abroad for American companies. This initiative also called on the Ex-Im bank to increase financing for small and medium businesses.

The European Union

In general, the U.S. trades separately with European countries. However, many trade issues arise with the European Union (EU) as a block.

The EU was formed after World War II with the intent of uniting nations throughout Europe both economically and politically. Along with trying to maintain peace after the bloody conflicts between European nations during the war, the aim was also to afford Western Europe what NAFTA provides for North America—a single marketplace for the goods and transactions of its member nations.

Over the years, the EU has achieved frontier-free travel and trade, a common currency (the euro), safer food, a greener environment, better living conditions in poorer regions, coordinated action on crime and terror, less expensive phone calls, and opportunities for study abroad. There has, however, been other activity within the EU, starting with the United Kingdom leaving the EU in 2016. The initial effects of Brexit, as the UK exit was called, caused severe volatility in global stock markets, forcing a lot of business owners and consumers into changing some of their major spending plans and adopting a wait-and-see attitude before making any significant investments.

The Trade Hit Parade

Before we analyze potential trade partners and what they can do for us, let's consider what the U.S. offers as a trading nation. To put into perspective the economic statistics provided in this chapter for the various foreign countries, here are a few for the U.S.

The leading imports include crude oil, machines, electronics, vehicles, pharmaceuticals, medical equipment, furniture (including lighting), gems and precious metals, organic chemicals, and plastics.

fun fact ☺

Lists of imports and exports for a given country can often look very much the same. Categories are broad, so if a country, such as the U.S., imports motorcycles and exports cars, both items are listed as "motor vehicles." Also, countries often import an item, make some additions to it, and then reexport it.

The varied topography of the U.S. and climate zones range from permafrost in northern Alaska to tropical conditions in southern Florida. It is the fourth-largest country geographically. Its population ranks third, behind China and India.

U.S. natural resources include coal, copper, lead, molybdenum, phosphates, uranium, bauxite, gold, iron, silver, petroleum, natural gas, and timber.

With a population of 327.2 million as of 2018, the U.S. boasts the largest national economy (highest GDP) in the world. It is the world's number-two exporter and the world's top importer. High dependence on foreign oil makes it a huge importer and creates trillions of dollars in deficits with its trading partners.

Trade with Emerging Markets

According to financial investment publication *Money and Markets*, an emerging market is a foreign economy that is developing because of the spread of capitalism and has created its own stock market.

BRIC is the grouping acronym referring to Brazil, Russia, India, and China. All are highly populated, falling in the top-ten world rankings. (China and India—ranked first and second, respectively—each have over a billion people.) Challenges facing BRIC union nations, as well as those trading with them, include highly uneven distribution of wealth, government corruption, and lack of fully developed infrastructures—airports and seaports, roads, bridges, telecommunications networks, and power plants.

These infrastructure weaknesses mean that, as a trader, you'll have to pay extra attention to the nitty-gritty of production, distribution, and marketing in these countries. But they also mean that opportunities abound in infrastructure imports and in consumer goods.

Internet Securities Inc. (ISI) bases its classification on factors, including population size, infrastructure, income levels, and expansion of the middle class. The Financial Times Stock Exchange (FTSE, pronounced "footsie") and Russell Indexes (www.FTSERussell.com) use a range of criteria developed in conjunction with international investors. FTSE conducts an annual review of all markets

stat fact

When looking at data from other countries, be sure to look at the gross domestic product (GDP). It is the value of total goods and services produced within a country in a year. GDP data come in two types: nominal and purchasing power parity (PPP). These figures differ widely. GDP (PPP) reflects differences in the cost of living and is the type we use here. Achieving a PPP figure involves more estimation than using nominal data.

► Give Us the Goods

Trade statistics list capital goods, consumer goods, and manufactured goods as import/export categories:

- ► *Capital Goods*. Items used to produce other goods. Machines are a good example.

- ► *Consumer Goods*. These, as the name implies, get used directly by consumers. They fall into two categories: durable and nondurable goods. The former are items like cars, appliances, and furniture. The latter include food, clothing, and gasoline.

- ► *Manufactured Goods*. Items made using machines. This is a very broad category. Any given capital good or consumer good could very well also be a manufactured good. For example, a sewing machine that is used to produce clothing is not only a capital good (because it's used to produce clothing goods) but also a manufactured good (because it is assembled from parts made by machines).

contained in its global benchmarks. The markets are classified as *developed*, *advanced emerging*, *secondary emerging*, or *frontier*.

Advanced emerging markets (AEMs) have either upper-middle incomes with advanced infrastructure or high incomes with less-developed infrastructure. Secondary emerging markets (SEMs) have either upper-middle/lower-middle/low income with reasonable infrastructure or upper-middle incomes with lesser-developed infrastructure.

Frontier markets are equity markets in small nations that are at an earlier stage of economic and political development than larger and more mature emerging markets. These markets typically have modest market capitalization but potential growth.

Familiar Territory

As a newbie on the international scene, you should familiarize yourself with our biggest trading partners and learn what each has to offer.

tip

You can research possible trade countries on the U.S. Department of State's website (www.state.gov). Click on the Countries & Areas option near the top-center of the browser window, then click on a country you're interested in. They're listed alphabetically. You can also find out more about exporting on the U.S. Commercial Service's websites: www.export.gov/welcome and http://buyusa.gov.

► Learn About Other Cultures Before Trying to Do Business with Them

To ensure you don't offend clients and jeopardize deals, be aware of the customs and culture of the nation(s) you deal with. The saying "Think global, act local" applies! It's preferable to have a cultural native smooth the way for you.

Here are a few areas where cultures can differ significantly:

► *Business Greetings*. Some countries do not shake hands (especially if any women are involved), while others regard a handshake as obligatory. Among hand shakers, degree of firmness varies. Also, eye contact is not a universal plus. In some cultures, it indicates aggression.

► *Business Meetings*. The amount of small talk before getting down to business varies by culture. This applies to in-person meetings, video calls, phone calls, and other types of virtual or real-world gatherings.

► *Negotiation Strategies*. Expectations differ for how quickly terms should be reached. Aggressive negotiation is regarded as rude in India, but it's respected in Russia. Know in advance what negotiation tactics should and should not be used when dealing with people from a particular country. Even the slightest mistake or misstep could destroy an otherwise lucrative deal or business relationship.

► *Conversational Style*. Whether or not interruptions are tolerated is a cultural factor. Willingness to say "no" also varies. (In India, "we'll see" or "possibly" often means "no.") Don't rely on language translation programs to correctly interpret innuendos and figures of speech.

► *Refreshments*. Turning down refreshments (or accepting but not tasting) can be a major breach of etiquette.

► *Gifts*. Type and monetary value of ideal gifts varies.

► *Color significance*. In Western cultures, black is the usual color of mourning, while white is a bridal color. In Asia, white or purple signify mourning. Yellow is associated with mourning or bad luck in some countries.

► *Humor*. Even if jokes translate well (which they usually don't), they are risky cross-culturally, especially in a business setting.

Canada

One of the trading partners that's the most local and easy to visit is Canada, with a population of roughly 37.59 million people as of 2019.

Canada has the second-largest land area in the world, behind Russia, but more than 90 percent of all Canadians live within 100 miles of the U.S. border. Canada's abundant natural resources—oil, natural gas, minerals and metals, forests, wildlife, fresh water—contribute to its trading economy. Canada is one of the world's major producers of minerals.

tip

Make sure your export goods have packaging information in the language (or at least in one official language) of the target country, and the text is in the same font, size, and clarity as any other language on the box.

Although its population is about one-tenth the size of the U.S., Canada is very much like the U.S. in terms of its environment and marketplace. Pair this with the fact that most of its citizens are native English speakers, and you have an ideal jumping-off point for the newbie exporter.

Annual trade with the U.S. typically accounts for about 75 percent of Canadian trade. Canada and the U.S. are each other's top trade partners. To learn more about Canada's importing and exporting activities, visit: https://oec.world/en/profile/country/can.

Mexico

Mexico is, obviously, the other most direct country in which to consider trading. With over 129.2 million people as of 2017, Mexico's population is roughly one-third of the U.S. Typically, Mexico's economy will move in the same direction as the U.S., but their needs will differ, with the U.S. trading more technical goods and Mexico trading products they grow or mine. To be most effective trading with Mexico, you should learn some Spanish and take some time to visit and learn all about the nontourist areas of the country.

Tricks
of the Trade
for Startups

Aside from money, you'll need to invest a great deal of time, energy, and emotional intensity to get your business off the ground. You'll need to get people interested in your service, persuade manufacturers or artisans to work with you, then find foreign contacts to securing financing. Going over all the details—especially the financial ones—with a magnifying lens and a critical eye is crucial to your success.

That old refrain "The best things in life are free" does not apply when you are starting a business. Fortunately, an import/export company is typically not at the expensive end of the startup costs spectrum. At the same time, you don't want to cut corners to save money initially.

Keep in mind, you'll likely need to invest money in your education and training, above and beyond the core startup costs for the business. Until you've acquired the necessary training and you're confident that you have the knowledge needed to pursue running an import/export business, don't move forward or you could wind up losing a lot of money and making some major mistakes. There are many ways to obtain the international trade training and experience you need. One option is to spend some time gaining real-world experience by working for another company before launching your own business venture.

In this chapter we help you figure out what you'll need in your office and what you can expect to pay for it. The second part of the chapter gives you a preview of the tasks you'll need to accomplish to legally set up your business.

Should You Work from Home?

One of the many advantages of an import/export business is that the startup costs can be comparatively low. You have the advantage of initially or permanently operating from home, if you want to. This strategy cuts office lease expenses down to nothing. Unless you're starting as a distributor, you can get away without purchasing inventory, which means no outlay of funds for pretty doodads to grace display spaces, since you'll have no display spaces. Your major financial outlay will go toward office equipment and market research expenses. If you are like many people, you already have the most crucial piece of office equipment: a computer with internet access.

The following is a breakdown of everything, from heavy investment pieces to flyweight items, you'll likely need to get up and running:

- ▶ Desktop computer (Windows PC or an Apple iMac)
- ▶ Laptop computer and/or tablet
- ▶ Laser printer
- ▶ Copier/fax/scanner (or all-in-one)
- ▶ High-speed and reliable internet
- ▶ Email. Includes business email accounts that end with your company name/domain name (e.g., Username@YourCompanyName.com). Using a free email account from

Google, Yahoo!, or Apple, for example, is unprofessional. Your website domain name registrar or website hosting service should be able to provide you with personalized email accounts for your business (for an additional monthly or annual fee).

▶ Website, which includes the design, maintenance (updating), and hosting of your company's website. While maintaining a presence on social media (e.g., Facebook, LinkedIn, Twitter, and Instagram) is free, you may wind up wanting to hire someone to manage your company's social media presence and website.

▶ Software, including a wide range of specialized and general business software, such as word processing, spreadsheet management, customer/client relationship management (CRM), and bookkeeping.

▶ Market research and trade leads

▶ Smartphone with calling, text, and cellular data service

▶ Voicemail

▶ Letterhead and matching business cards

▶ Office supplies

▶ Postage, which includes the monthly fee for a postage machine or the ability to create postage from your computer

▶ Travel expenses for conducting market research on foreign turf

▶ Office furniture, including a full-size desk, comfortable desk chair, office phone equipment, and filing cabinets

You can add many goodies (of varying degrees of necessity) to this list, and we'll cover more options in Chapter 10.

But let's consider you are starting from absolute scratch. You can always set up your computer on your kitchen table or on a card table in a corner of a bedroom. You can stash files in cardboard boxes or plastic crates. It's not glamorous, but it will suffice until your business becomes profitable.

Computing Computer Costs

A computer with high-speed and reliable internet access should be at the top of your list when it comes to "must have" office equipment. Your computer will allow you to access the myriad trade leads and market research materials available online, plus allow you to communicate with potential and established customers, as well as vendors worldwide, all via email.

That same computer can be used to generate invoices, certificates, and forms quickly, easily, and inexpensively, plus handle your company's bookkeeping, scheduling, internet-based voice and video calls, and help you maintain detailed information about your customers and clients (using specialized customer/client relationship management software). As you'll discover, there are also highly specialized (vertical market) software applications designed for use by import/export businesses.

To help reduce your physical paperwork and traditional filing needs, digitizing and scanning forms, documents, and files, and storing them electronically on your computer's hard drive or within the cloud, is a viable option—and one that helps the environment too!

Many people today, especially in a field that requires a lot of traveling, use a laptop computer and/or tablet as their main computer. You may also opt for a desktop computer for your office, but ensure that all your data, documents, and files automatically sync between your computers and mobile devices (via the cloud).

For a basic, Windows 10-based desktop computer (including keyboard and monitor) that can have you surfing the internet shortly after you buy it, you should allocate funds in the $800 to $2,500 range.

You'll typically pay a bit more for an Apple iMac, but there are distinct benefits of using Apple equipment, such as the company's superior AppleCare technical support and the fact that Macs are much less susceptible to viruses and malware than Windows PCs. We will go over the various permutations in Chapter 10, but this will give you a figure to pencil in for starters.

While the import/export business has been slow to adapt to new technology, the past decade has shown that the once tech-shy industry has embraced technology in a big way—and so should you!

Fax Facts

Although you technically don't need a stand-alone fax machine, because it's quickly becoming outdated technology, your life as an international trader will run much more smoothly with one since overseas businesses continue to use them. You'll use a fax machine to shoot off and receive hard-copy materials to and from clients, representatives, and distributors instead of waiting on both U.S. and foreign postal services.

Sending a pro forma invoice, for example, has a lot more impact on a potential customer when it directly follows a request for information. You can purchase a basic plain paper fax machine for as little as $100. If you spend a little more ($150 to $250), you can get a combined fax/printer/copier/scanner.

You can also set up your computer (or even your smartphone or tablet) to work as a virtual fax machine, complete with a dedicated phone number. Check out services like eFax (www.efax.com), Ring Central (www.ringcentral.com), and MyFax (www.myfax.com).

▶ Use Your Smartphone or Tablet as a Fax Machine

Thanks to its built-in rear-facing camera and internet connectivity, using an optional mobile app, such as Fax Pro, FAX, iFax, or Easy Fax, it's possible to "scan" paper-based documents, then send them as a fax to any fax machine in the world using your mobile device's internet connectivity.

You'll find the appropriate faxing apps at the App Store (iPhone/iPad) or the Google Play Store (if you're using an Android-based mobile device). Plan on paying either a per-page fee or a monthly fee for the ability to send and receive unlimited faxes from your mobile device.

With some services, like eFax (www.eFax.com), you only have to set up and pay for one account, but you're able to send and receive faxes from your computer(s), smartphone, and tablet— virtually anywhere you have internet connectivity.

Once printed (paper-based) documents are scanned into your computer or mobile device, you can use a separate app, such as PDF Expert (www.pdfexpert.com), to edit them before sending. PDF Expert can also be used to digitally sign electronic documents or contracts, which you can then electronically fax or email to another party.

A Reliable, High-Speed Internet Connection Is a Must

With the power of the internet at your command, you can go anywhere on the globe instantaneously—access trade leads as soon as they're posted, communicate with clients and client wannabes with a few keystrokes, and garner market information from worldwide sources while seated at your desk. If you're using a notebook computer or tablet, this is work you can also do from bed, while sitting on a couch, or even while basking in the sun by a pool or beach.

The average cost for high-speed cable, DSL, or FIOS (fiber optic) internet service runs between $25 and $100 per month, depending on your location, the service provider, whether you bundle the internet with other services (such as cable TV or a VoIP phone line), and the speed of the internet connection. In addition to a modem, you'll also need a wireless router to establish a wifi internet connection in your home or office.

Since most cable TV providers dominate geographic regions, you are usually at the mercy of whichever provider is in your area. Most offer bundled packages for phone, television, and internet service. Depending on your desired TV channel lineup and extra services (such as a digital video recorder connected to your cable box or a wireless router to establish wifi in your home), your monthly bill could come to $100 to $250 per month for all three.

The Skinny on Software

Software prices can vary radically, depending on which programs you buy and from whom. You'll want a good word processing program, an accounting/bookkeeping program, a spreadsheet management program, and a customer/client relationship management program. Again, this is a subject that will be covered in greater depth in Chapter 10.

Many popular applications, like Microsoft Office 365 (which includes Microsoft Word), QuickBooks accounting, and most CRM programs allow users to pay a low monthly subscription free (often less than $10 per month) for full access to the software, instead of forcing customers to purchase it outright (and then pay for updates separately).

Purchase Leads Online

Like just about everything else in the international trader's world, the amount you'll pay for market research and trade leads is a variable, almost entirely dependent on you and your personal style. If you choose to go with the Commercial Service's trade leads and other market research information, you can pencil in at least $75 per month or $200 (or more) per year.

tip

You can find free office software, which is fully compatible with Microsoft Office (Word, Excel, PowerPoint, Outlook, etc.), at www.openoffice.org. Meanwhile, Apple offers Mac users its iWork applications (including Pages for word processing) for free (www.apple.com/iwork), and Google offers the Google G Suite applications (including the Docs word processor) for free to Windows and Mac users, and iOS and Android mobile device users (https://gsuite.google.com).

save

You can save big money on leads. The International Trade Administration offers leads and market information for the best price of all—free. Just point your web browser to: www.export.gov.

Back to the noncommercial Commercial Service, the Gold Key Matching Service program (www.export.gov/Gold-Key-Service) can provide a lot of help. It's hard to pin a price tag on their program because costs vary with the countries involved and the number of matches and meetings, but as a thumbnail, you can figure between $950 and $3,500.

As you surf the internet, you'll find other trade lead services and sources of market research, including LinkedIn.com, that may cost more or less, or nothing at all.

Phone Service

If you're using a landline at home, you already know that your cost depends at least partly on the different calling features you choose. If you don't already have a landline for personal use, you should install at least one dedicated line for your business. For the purpose of startup budgeting, let's allocate about $50 per line. You'll also need to add the phone company's installation fee, which will vary.

You may also want to obtain a toll-free 800 number for incoming calls. Although most 800 numbers only work when receiving calls from within the U.S., they give your business additional credibility.

Mobile Phone Service

In today's business world, a smartphone is a must-have business tool for making and receiving voice and video calls, sending and receiving text messages, accessing the internet while on the go, managing your email accounts, and more. If you're already using Apple equipment, go with an iPhone. However, if you're already accustomed to using an Android-based mobile device, that will work just as well.

All smartphones come with an assortment of built-in applications, at least one front-facing and two (sometimes three) rear-facing cameras, and a wide range of other technologies that allow the smartphone to handle many tasks while you're on the go. Plus, thanks to the millions of optional, third-party apps from the App Store (iOS) or Google Play (Android), you can customize your mobile device with a suite of useful apps that can help you become more productive in virtually every aspect of your personal and professional life, from communications and scheduling to information management.

In conjunction with your smartphone, you'll need to sign up with a cellular service provider to give your phone calling, texting, and wireless (cellular data) internet capabilities. In the U.S., there are several major cellular service providers. Each offers many different plans, some of which include unlimited calling and texting throughout the U.S. Others offer unlimited service throughout the U.S., Canada, and Mexico, or offer various international calling plans for calling from the U.S. to other countries (or for calling anywhere in the world while you're traveling abroad).

Since you'll likely be doing a lot of international travel, choose a cellular service provider with competitive international calling and roaming packages. Especially if you'll be doing a lot of international calling and travel, check out the Google Fi cellular phone service (http://fi.google.com). It's extremely inexpensive (less than $50 per month) and works with almost any smartphone, nearly anywhere in the world.

Brand Your Business to Enhance Its Image

Business stationery and matching business cards are as important to a savvy international image as a well-answered phone and a professional-looking website. To create a brand identity that will help sell your product or service, you'll need letterhead, envelopes, and business cards.

You can have a set of stationery and business cards inexpensively printed for you at a local quick print shop, such as FedEx Kinko's or through an office supply superstore's in-house printing service. Visit your local Staples, Office Max, or Office Depot, for example. Either way, you should allocate $100 to $300 for the printing services, as well as a bit extra for the one-time design fees (which might include the creation of a company logo).

There are also countless online-based print shops that will help you design and print letterhead, business cards, invoices, and other business-related documents. Check out the offerings from companies like:

- ▶ 48HourPrint.com: www.48hourprint.com
- ▶ Moo: www.moo.com
- ▶ PrintRunner: www.printrunner.com
- ▶ Vistaprint: www.vistaprint.com

Don't forget you'll also need office supplies—pens, pencils, paper clips, mailing envelopes, reams of blank paper for your printer, a stapler with staples, tape, and printer cartridges. Plan on initially spending at least $200 to nicely equip your home office.

Mailing Matters

Your startup postage costs will be fairly low, but you will need to tally them. How much you spend depends a great deal on how much material you are mailing out and where on the globe you are sending it. Clearly, mailing price sheets or brochures will be much pricier than sending email price quotes or listing your prices on your company's website.

Given current initiatives to reduce paper usage, not to mention recent hikes in postal rates, you will probably want to concentrate your promotional efforts online. This is even truer if you are positioning your company as environmentally responsible. That being said, if you plan to participate in in-person meetings, trade shows,

tip

When you travel abroad on trading trips, bilingual business cards are a much-appreciated gesture in some countries—and a necessity in others. Do your homework! You might also want to set up local (virtual) phone numbers within the countries you plan to do business with, so (prospective) customers and clients can make a local call but still reach you back in the U.S.

or business conferences, you'll likely want professional-looking printed materials to share with prospective customers and clients that support the content that you've previously emailed (although these materials can also be provided in electronic form via a flash drive, for example).

Services like Stamps.com and Endicia (www.endicia.com) allow you to generate and print postage stamps directly from your computer and printer, so a separate postage machine (or constant trips to the post office) is not required.

Traveling Trader

This category, too, will vary tremendously according to how you choose to tailor your market research, your startup costs, and, ultimately, your business life. Some traders are on the road often, while others are armchair travelers. Of course, when you do travel, your costs will vary depending on where you go, for how long, and whether you choose to spend your nights at a five-star resort hotel or a local Airbnb (www.airbnb.com).

You may find that you can conduct all of your market research from your computer or tablet, or you may discover that for your particular product category, you need to study the market up close and personal by traveling to that country.

Expenses Add Up, So Be Prepared

Other expenses you'll need to plug into your startup expenses chart are business licenses, business insurance, legal advice, utility fees, and accounting/bookkeeping fees—the costs intrinsic to any company's startup and subsequent operation.

Calculate Your Business Startup Costs

Use the Startup Costs Worksheet in Figure 4–1 on page 48 to calculate your company's startup costs.

The Trader's Trunk

This part of the chapter explores the bottom of the trader's trunk, those features that form the basics of the business, from company name and legal structure to permits.

Name Your Business

Every business, like every child, has to have a name. You should devote (almost) as much thought to choosing your company's name as you would for your offspring. After all, you

Startup Costs Worksheet

Costs	Your Company
Rent	$
Office equipment & furniture	
Market research/trade leads	
Software	
Smartphone and cellular phone service	
Landline phone service (including 800 number and/or fax number)	
Utility deposits/fees	
Employee payroll	
Business-related advertising and promotions (online and in the real world)	
Legal services (including business licenses)	
Postage	
Internet service and online security (such as anti-virus and malware protection software, and a virtual private network for secure internet connectivity)	
Website design, domain name registration, and hosting	
Stationery and business card printing	
Insurance	
Travel	
Office supplies	
Company logo and branding design (including copyright and trademark filing fees, if necessary)	
Email account(s)	
Accounting/bookkeeping service	
Miscellaneous expenses (add roughly 10% of total)	
Total Startup Costs	$

FIGURE 4–1: **Startup Costs Worksheet**

plan to have your business around for a long time. You want a name you can be proud of, one that identifies your business—and by extension, you—as worthy of your clients' confidence.

Because import/export is a more serious business than, say, pizza delivery or greeting card design, you should probably rule out names like Thyme to Trade (even if you specialize in herbs and spices). Instead, your name should call attention to your expertise and efficiency. The terminally creative, however, can take heart. Noncutesy doesn't mean dull. Your name can—and should—deliver a snappy punch.

One trader attacked the name problem from the standpoint of his vision of the company. "With Global Partners," said Wahib Wahba, "we wanted to say that we're all partners, me and my clients and manufacturers. We all have to be partners to make it work."

When brainstorming your company name, keep in mind that, with a few exceptions, the people you'll target won't be using English as a native language. So take care with the expressions you choose. Colloquialisms and slang words sometimes aren't clear even to people in different parts of the U.S. Don't make things more difficult by pressing them on non-Americans. Everyone in the industry, on the other hand, easily understands international trade buzzwords, like "global" and "overseas."

Many importers and exporters incorporate the name of the region with which they trade into their business moniker, for example, Far East Imports or Amazon Traders. Or you might want to incorporate a geographic feature of your own region, such as Desert Traders if you live in Palm Springs, or Sea-to-Sea Exports if your office is near a seaport.

warning

When brainstorming a business name, be careful not to fence yourself in with a moniker that may limit you later. If you're starting out importing Mexican pottery, for example, you may not want to call your company Mexican Pottery Imports. Unless you're certain that's the country and product category you'll stick with for the life of your business, give yourself some room for growth and expansion with a less restrictive name.

You might even decide on a variation of your own name. Lloyd Davidson, owner of LND Export Management, used his initials as the basis for his company name. Sam Nelson, owner of Nelisco Inc. in North Carolina, also used part of his name.

Whatever you go with, remember that you will be repeating your business name every time you answer the phone. Sound out the title before you settle on it. Some names look great in print but are difficult if not impossible to understand over the phone. M&A

▶ Talking Trade

Here's a list of buzzwords you can use to help brainstorm a company name that has global appeal:

Abroad	Global	Pacific
Atlantic	Inter-Continental	Passport
Caravan	International	Seven Seas
Cargo	Hemisphere	Trader
Compass	Mediterranean	Tropical
Earth	Overseas	Worldwide

Associates, for example, may seem like a perfectly reasonable name for partners Marty and Andrea, but when spoken, it sounds like MNA.

Most callers rate about a C-minus in listening comprehension. No matter how clearly you enunciate, they aren't going to understand M&A. So save yourself hours of telephone frustration and choose something simple.

For a list of some words that might help get your creative gears cranking, check out the international lexicon in "Talking Trade" (see above sidebar). Next, use the brainstorming worksheet in Figure 4–2, page 51, to help craft your business name.

Newly Registered

After you've decided on a name, you'll need to register it. Basically, registering your name means that you notify the proper authorities that you're doing business under a name other than your own. This lets the public know that Tropical Trading Partners is owned by you, professional exporter.

The process varies in different regions of the country. In Florida, for example, you access the state government website and click around until you finally call up the page about fictitious business names. You'll fill out a series of forms, swear you are who you say you are, and enter your credit card number. Eventually, you'll receive a letter confirming that you registered your name with the state. If you want a nice little certificate to frame and hang on your wall, you need to shell out extra bucks.

In California on the other hand, you file an application with the county clerk, then advertise your name in a "general circulation" newspaper in that county for four weeks.

Business Name Brainstorming

List three ideas based on the geographic area you plan to trade with (i.e., Into Africa, European, Down Under):

1. _____

2. _____

3. _____

List three ideas based on the types of products you plan to trade, remembering not to limit yourself to one product alone (i.e., Arts and Antiques, Gourmet Goods, Image Imports):

1. _____

2. _____

3. _____

List three ideas based on a local feature (i.e., mountain, seaside, or historical reference like Alamo, or even a botanical feature, if that's what your area is known for or you like, such as magnolia, rose, or chaparral):

1. _____

2. _____

3. _____

After you've decided which name you like the best, do the following:

❑ Say it aloud to make sure it's easily understood and pronounced. (Has it passed muster with your family? Have you had a friend call to see how it sounds over the phone?)

❑ Do a search for it online to make sure the same or a similar name is not already used.

❑ Verify that it's available as a domain name (www.register.com, www.godaddy.com, and www.squarespace.com are good places to check).

❑ In most parts of the country, you'll want to check with your local business county clerk's office to make sure it's available. You can use a website such as Legal Zoom (www.legalzoom.com) to register and check your business name.

FIGURE 4–2: **Business Name Brainstorming**

► Make Sure the .Com Website URL Is Available

Once you decide on a business name, visit any website domain name registrar (such as godaddy. com), and make sure the dot-com domain name is available.

There are a lot of domain name extensions available, such as .info, .biz., and .org, but you must own the domain name for your business that ends in ".com." This is what most web surfers type when using their web browser, even if they're told to use a different domain name extension.

Also, make sure your company name and website domain name are easy to spell and remember, and won't get easily confused with another business or competitor.

For example, if your business name is ABC Imports, you should register the domain name www. ABCImports.com. If you don't have the .com extension, chances are whoever does will wind up receiving a large chunk of your website traffic, which means lost business.

Make sure your website domain and company name do not violate another company's copyrights or trademarks. Then at the same time you register your website domain name, obtain business email addresses that end with the same extension, such as Username@YourCompanyName.com.

Once that's all said and done and you've paid the fee, you receive your statement of registration. Check with your city, county, and state government to find out what the story is in your state.

Structurally Sound

To appease the IRS, your business must have a structure. You can operate it as a sole proprietorship, a partnership, or as some type of corporation. Many international traders go with the simplest version, the sole proprietorship. You'll probably be starting out on your own, so there's no need to get complicated or expensive. You can always switch to another business structure later if you take on partners and/or employees.

The differences in business structures center primarily on legal liability, taxes, and paperwork/bureaucracy. Be sure to check with your attorney and accountant before making a final decision about how you'll structure your business from a legal standpoint.

Beyond the basic structure for your company, various other international trade configurations exist. There's the joint venture, which is a sort of marriage or partnership between two distinct and separate companies, for example, yours and one in a foreign country. There's also the strategic alliance, an agreement between your company and another one to work toward a common goal.

Why would you want to form a venture with an overseas company? One reason is to get around trade barriers. If your company is part domestic in whatever country you're working with, you can skim around prohibitive tariffs and quotas. Another reason? You can form a team or network with an in-country company that already has effective trade channels in operation. A third reason is to get into government-controlled infrastructure-type projects, like power plants or telecommunications.

Then there's the wholly owned subsidiary or branch, in which your company or your client's company becomes owner of a firm. You can encounter a spider's web of entanglements in international arrangements of this type because the host country often sets up all sorts of special rules, such as how long a "foreign" company (that's you) can own property or how much profit you can collect.

tip

Find everything you need to know about small-business tax issues by visiting the IRS's website (www.irs.gov/businesses/small-businesses-self-employed). From deductible business expenses to applying for EINs (employer ID numbers), the IRS has you covered. When it comes to filing the correct paperwork, a fee-based company, like LegalZoom.com, can be helpful.

So why would anybody want to open a subsidiary or branch abroad? In a word: profit. To vitalize their own economies by creating jobs and cash flow for their people, emerging nations often offer hefty incentives to businesses from more developed countries. If you do your homework and check out every permutation of foreign business ownership laws, you're less likely to get stung by unpleasant surprises.

There's also the licensing or franchising type of business. With licensing, you give a foreign company or licensee permission to sell your, or your client's, trademarked product and in return, they pay royalties on their sales. Everybody recognizes the world's preeminent licensing products: anything stamped with the likeness of Mickey, Minnie, or their Disney cohorts. You might develop a gold mine in licensing characters developed by a client with loveable little chaps just waiting to be discovered.

With a franchise, you give your or your client's foreign buyer permission to sell your licensed products with your special sales or service techniques.

The ultimate franchisor, known around the world, is McDonald's. American food franchises traditionally do very well abroad, but there are many other franchises available or that you can put together yourself. All you need is your imagination and some attention to detail.

Trading Places

Where should you locate your business? You have a lot of choices. Because most of your business will be conducted long-distance via email, phone, and mail, you won't need to be available at set hours as you would if you were running a retail establishment or restaurant. Because you will rarely have clients dropping in, you will not need a receptionist, a lobby, or even meeting rooms. You also won't need signage or substantial client parking.

tip

Delve into Entrepreneur's annual online resource for franchises at www.entrepreneur.com/franchises/500. You'll find lots of information on each company listed, including their respective financials.

For these reasons, many of the traditional (and more expensive) options aren't the best choice. Instead of paying for retail or office park space, consider a warehouse, if you anticipate having a lot of inventory or a home office.

If you plan to work from home, you should check into zoning regulations. A small international trading company is not likely to attract much attention from local authorities, but you should still play it safe. Find out from your local city or county government whether any permits are necessary. While you're at it, check to see if you'll need a business license, which is usually an official-looking piece of paper you get in exchange for a nominal annual fee.

Attorney with ELAN

Attorneys are like plumbers; you don't want to think about them until you need one. As a business owner, however, you should have a good, trustworthy, and responsive attorney on call. Make sure it's someone who knows and has experience with international trade.

You'll want your lawyer to look over any contracts you write or receive, relating to working with manufacturers, representatives, or distributors, for example, and to advise you on the fine points of foreign trade law. You likely won't need to call them every week, or even every month, but there's no point waiting until you have a pressing problem before you establish a relationship with a lawyer.

To get you off on the right foot and to answer any startup questions, the SBA and the Federal Bar Association have developed The Export Legal Assistance Network, otherwise known as ELAN. As an enticement to the red-tape-phobic would-be trader, the ELAN folks will sit you down with a volunteer trade attorney who'll answer all your questions—for free! After the initial consultation, you can either sign on with the volunteer as your permanent trade attorney or take your newfound knowledge and hit the road without a backward glance.

You can also find a reliable import/export attorney by asking for referrals from associates in the field or your international banker, but with the ELAN program, what have you got to lose?

Contact the Export Legal Assistance Network at www.exportlegal.org, or through the SBA's Small Business Answer Desk at (800) U-ASK-SBA. You can also check out www.lawyers.com or LinkedIn.com when seeking an import/export lawyer.

aha!

The Commercial Service people and their compatriots at your local Export Assistance Center (www.export.gov/locations) can help you set up a joint venture program.

Details, Details

Remember, expenses, licenses, and fees can crop up and add up quickly, depending on what you're importing and exporting, to where and from whom. Do your homework! The more you know about running an import/export business, the better a trader you'll be.

► Get the Legal Help You'll Need

The Export Legal Assistance Network (ELAN) is a jumping-off point for traders with legal questions. According to ELAN's National Coordinator, Judd Kessler, "Fear is one of the greatest obstacles for people interested in becoming a professional importer or exporter. One cause for this fear is lack of familiarity with legal issues."

A service of the Department of Commerce, ELAN has over 250 legal counselors in 70 cities who provide import/export legal service in addition to their daily legal pursuits. Since 1984, the group has performed free initial legal counseling sessions for both new and established traders.

You only get one call, so do your homework first. Know your product(s), your target market(s), and your representatives, as well as how you'll be paid. "Above all else, have a business plan," added Kessler.

The ELAN lawyers hear many kinds of issues on the phone, from questions about foreign trade agreements to how to avoid risks, customs concerns, trademark registration, and more. Kessler advises traders to be conscious of export regulations and terrorism concerns. Make sure you check that your product(s) and target market are not on the US's forbidden list. ELAN has advised exporters of products ranging from liquid-dispensing and bottle-filling equipment to scrap metals.

Daily
Operations

N ow that you're versed in the ins and outs of import and export in general, let's take a closer look at business-related operations. In this chapter, you'll discover what an international trader's daily work life is often like, including what sorts of tasks need to be performed on a routine basis and how these responsibilities typically get completed.

Trading Particulars

Most beginning traders do not have it in their budgets to sail off to Africa in search of the latest handcrafted items or the wherewithal jet off to France each November to sample the fresh bottles of Beaujolais Nouveau. Most traders starting out do their research using the internet, so plan on spending a lot of time online.

What you'll be doing online during your peak hours and beyond will depend upon how you have structured your services. Some traders act only as sales representatives, finding buyers and taking commissions. They choose to steer clear of the shipping, documentation, and financing aspects of the deal. Others are happier offering a full line of services, buying directly from the manufacturer and taking on all the responsibilities of the transaction, from shipping to marketing. These traders often specialize in either import or export and stick to the merchandise industry they know best.

The Exporter at Work

In a nutshell, your most basic tasks will typically involve obtaining merchandise, selling it, transporting it, and getting paid for it. Exporting is usually considered to be easier than importing due to less red tape, so that's what we'll focus on first. Keep in mind, however, that exporting and importing are two sides of the same coin.

The Export Path

Let's discuss what the export process is for products in general. Once you've found a buyer for your merchandise, here's what you'd typically do:

1. Generate the pro forma invoice. We have provided a checklist of what the pro forma invoice should include in Figure 5–1 on page 59, and we will also go over it in detail in the next section. Give the importer a quote on your merchandise; negotiate if necessary.

2. Properly classify merchandise with the correct Harmonized Tariff Schedule (HTS) code. (See Chapter 6.)

3. Determine if your merchandise has an Export Control Classification Number (ECCN). (See "Export Control 101" on page 66.)

4. Screen merchandise against U.S. Export Administration Regulations (EAR) to determine if it requires an export license. (See "Export Control 101" on page 66.)

5. Screen all parties in your export transactions against the various governmental Restricted or Denied Parties lists to ensure you're not shipping to someone you

shouldn't be. (Once again, see "Export Control 101.")

6. Receive the letter of credit (L/C) from your bank.
7. Fulfill terms of the L/C.
   a. Manufacture the merchandise if necessary.
   b. Make shipping and insurance arrangements.
   c. Pack the merchandise.
   d. Transport the merchandise.
   e. Collect shipping documents.
8. Present shipping documents to your bank.
9. Collect your payment.
10. Return to step 1 and repeat, potentially with different products and customers/clients.

The Pro's Pro Forma

Let's say you've noticed on your trips through Italy that while the Italians are the original experts on gourmet

warning

Make sure to check that your proposed goods to export don't require an export license. Also remember that comprehensive U.S. embargoes prohibit persons from engaging in trade, commercial, or financial transactions involving Crimea (region of the Ukraine), Cuba, Iran, North Korea, Sudan, and Syria.

Pro Forma Invoice Particulars

Here's a review of a pro forma invoice's main ingredients. For your first few efforts, you might make copies of this list and check off the items as you go. Use the blank invoice form in Figure 5–3, page 62.

❑ Product description

❑ Price

❑ Terms of sale (How is your merchandise going to be picked up or shipped? When will ownership—or title—change hands?)

❑ Terms of payment (How are you going to be paid? L/C, prepayment, 90-day time?)

❑ Length of time prices are valid

❑ Length of time necessary for shipping

Remember to check shipping dates and prices and special documentation questions with your freight forwarder before you issue the pro forma invoice.

FIGURE 5–1: **Pro Forma Invoice Particulars**

coffee drinks, nobody takes their beverages "to go." After doing some culture research to make sure Italians don't hate everything to do with drinking on the run, you've decided that "go cups," those ubiquitous insulated mugs, would go over well in Italy.

You've contacted a Miami manufacturer and gotten their OK to represent their product (which we'll now call "yours"). Then you've contacted an Italian company and sent them your brochure and price list and, when they asked for it, a sample. They love it! They then email you with a request for a pro forma invoice.

The pro forma invoice is a quotation—an invoice that the buyer gets to approve before it becomes fact. Keep in mind, however, that once your buyer accepts it, you're stuck with it, too, so think it through carefully. It contains a lot of information, including the following:

warning

Get quotes from your freight forwarder *before* you send out your pro forma invoice. If you guesstimate that it will cost you $200 to ship the cups to Rome, but later find out the cost is $2,000, you'll lose your profit.

- ▶ Price
- ▶ Shipping date and terms
- ▶ Letter of credit information, including bank to be used and expiration date
- ▶ Necessary documents
- ▶ Packing or labeling requirements

Check out the sample pro forma invoice in Figure 5–2 on page 61. The From, To, and Date sections should be self-explanatory. Below the date is your quote for the number of cups you understand the importer wants and the amount you're charging per cup. USD is international code for U.S. dollars. (For other currency codes, see Chapter 12.) Because Canada, Australia, and other countries also use dollars, quoted with the $ sign, the use of "USD" makes a clear reference to U.S. currency.

The term EXW on the next line means "Ex Works," or at your works—your (or your customer/manufacturer's) shop, warehouse, or factory. This tells the Cappuccino Imports people the price for 5,000 go-cups if they arrange to pick up the shipment at your place. The term CIF on the next line is import/export shorthand for cost, insurance, and freight. This is your price—after adding in freight costs—if you pay for shipping the 5,000 go-cups, insured, to Rome, which, of course, will make it much easier for the Cappuccino Imports people to pick them up.

You won't see the little numerals in the Terms & Conditions section on most pro forma invoices. We've put them in to make it easier to explain each point. So, are you ready? Follow along on the sample in Figure 5–2 on page 61:

Sample Pro Forma Invoice

From: Coffee Holic Exports
                   123 Cafe Street
                   Berry, FL 30000, USA

To: Cappuccino Imports
                   456 Via Espresso
                   Ostia Antica, Italy

Date: June 4, 20XX

For: 5,000 (five thousand) Coffee Go-Cups, Style A
                   @ USD 3.00

Shipping Terms: EXW Miami, Florida, USA   USD 15,000.00

                   CIF Rome   USD 16,000.00

Other Terms and Conditions:

1. Sight letter of credit in U.S. dollars on a U.S. bank

2. 2% additional discount from EXW cost ($300.00) for advance payment in U.S. dollars (check payable at a U.S. bank)

3. Our bankers: The Bank of Berry, Berry, Florida, USA

4. Export packing included

5. Prices good for 90 days

6. Shipment: within 60 days after receipt of check or letter of credit; please open letter of credit for 90 days total

Thank You!

FIGURE 5–2: **Sample Pro Forma Invoice**

Pro Forma Invoice

From: _____

_____

_____

To: _____

_____

_____

Date: _____

For: _____

_____

Shipping Terms: _____

_____

Other Terms and Conditions: _____

_____

_____

_____

_____

_____

Thank You!

FIGURE 5–3: **Pro Forma Invoice**

1. A sight letter of credit means a letter of credit, a sort of bank draft, paid as soon as you've fulfilled the conditions spelled out in it. This contrasts with a time or term letter of credit, which gets paid after a period of time.

2. The 2 percent discount is an incentive for the Cappuccino Imports people to pre-pay, but it's not something they have to do. You can make the discount, assuming you want to offer it, any amount you like.

3. This item is a hint: Italians, it would be nice if you opened the letter of credit at The Bank of Berry. As the exporter, you can specify that it must be opened at your own bank, but here we're giving them an option.

4. This is another little courtesy. It will save the Cappuccino Imports people some money and, in this case, won't cost you a whole lot more. Again, though, make sure you've figured your packing costs properly before offering the quote. When you're shipping items like fine china or crystal, packaging and packing is going to be a much bigger issue than it would be for plastic cups. When you're shipping steak or seafood, it's also going to be a big issue, so get in the habit of checking this stuff out before you open your pro forma mouth and insert foot.

5. This protects you from the buyers' hemming and hawing until sometime next year or the year after when it might cost you more to obtain the go-cups.

6. This item gives you time to have the cups manufactured, packed, and shipped before the letter of credit runs out. You don't have to stipulate this amount of time; pick what's comfortable for you and your supplier. Keep in mind that you may need to have the cups specially labeled or include some kind of user information, such as whether they are dishwasher safe or contain hot beverages that may burn, and that this will have to be translated into Italian. All this can take extra time. Also be sure to allow for plenty of shipping time. There's nothing worse than finding out that the ship your cups are booked on sails one week before they're ready to go.

At the bottom of your invoice, don't forget the "Thank You!" People the world over appreciate courtesy.

Documentation

There's one other item to think about on a pro forma invoice: *special documents*. Some countries require certification for certain items—for example, food and pharmaceutical goods. Other countries, particularly those in Latin America, the Middle East, and some Sub-Saharan countries, tend to require legalization or consularization of documents, which is another way of saying they like to have a special fee paid for the privilege of stamping the document "legal." Many countries have abolished this requirement, as the process makes it extremely difficult (if not impossible) to document via electronic methods.

Frequently, your customer will inform you of this requirement when they ask for your pro forma invoice. But don't assume. Do your homework. Check with your freight forwarder. If they think special documentation will be required and your customer hasn't asked for it, make sure your invoice says, "Price does not include legalization," or whatever the documentation may be. Bring the issue up again in the cover letter you send with the pro forma invoice.

Take a Letter

Your cover letters are also an important aspect of your correspondence. Its tone and professionalism, not to mention its friendliness and content, can set you apart as the kind of company potential importers will want to work with (see Figure 5–4, page 65).

The first paragraph speaks for itself: It thanks your customer for their order, reiterates what they're purchasing, and indicates that you plan to work with them over the long haul. You want to ensure the reader that you're not a fly-by-night operator.

Paragraph two offers two important points. It asks whether the order will be prepaid by check or whether the customer plans to pay by letter of credit (otherwise known as an L/C). The opening bank is the customer's bank. This bank cannot issue a letter of credit number until the letter of credit itself has been issued. So, what you're saying here is, "Tell me the L/C is on its way."

The last paragraph is essentially used to once again thank the customer or client and reiterate that you appreciate their business.

Anyone who's had the experience of sending a "wish you were here" postcard from a foreign country knows you usually arrive home long before the postcard does.

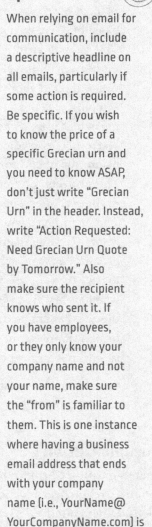

tip

When relying on email for communication, include a descriptive headline on all emails, particularly if some action is required. Be specific. If you wish to know the price of a specific Grecian urn and you need to know ASAP, don't just write "Grecian Urn" in the header. Instead, write "Action Requested: Need Grecian Urn Quote by Tomorrow." Also make sure the recipient knows who sent it. If you have employees, or they only know your company name and not your name, make sure the "from" is familiar to them. This is one instance where having a business email address that ends with your company name (i.e., YourName@YourCompanyName.com) is worthwhile.

Sample Pro Forma Invoice Cover Letter

Coffee Holic Exports
123 Cafe Street • Berry, FL 30000 • USA
(305) 000-0000 • (305) 000-0000
email: CoffeeHol@Holiday.com

June 4, 20XX

Sr. Antonio Franco
Cappuccino Imports
456 Via Espresso
Ostia Antica, Italy

Dear Signore Franco:

Thank you for your order of our Coffee Go-Cups! Please find herewith our pro forma invoice. We believe your customers will love the cups, and we look forward to a long and mutually prosperous relationship with you and your firm.

Please advise either when payment is to be sent or the name of the opening bank and letter of credit number.

Again, we thank you for your order and look forward to hearing from you soon.

Very best,

Charlie Holic

Charlie Holic
Coffee Holic Exports

FIGURE 5–4: **Sample Pro Forma Invoice Cover Letter**

Mailing documents to other lands is not a speedy process. In some third world countries with shaky infrastructures, it can be downright miraculous if your mail arrives at all.

Many international traders rely on the fax machine, but with more countries becoming computer savvy, email (and services like What's App) tends to be a preferred method of communication (but this varies by country or region).

You'll probably do a lot of your preliminary negotiations by email. However, you may decide that a faxed pro forma invoice, a sheet of paper your customer can hold in their hand, lends a more formal note, provided your customer has a fax machine. The most expensive option is to use a service like FedEx that has reliable international delivery options that are trackable. This option allows you to send paper-based documents, with original signatures, to and from your customers or clients.

tip

Using the FedEx website (www.fedex.com) or the FedEx mobile app on your smartphone or tablet, it's possible to process and track shipments with ease—anytime and from anywhere. Of course, there are plenty of other express courier/shipping services that have global reach, like DHL and UPS, so compare services and prices.

You could spend upwards of $50 to send a standard FedEx envelope to someone in another country via its overnight, two-day, or even three-day delivery service. However, if you're dealing with a contract that's worth tens or hundreds of thousands of dollars, a service like FedEx may be the most reliable way to go.

Export Control 101

All items exported from the U.S. must have an Export Control Classification Number (ECCN). This is a five-character code. Take, for example, 4B994. The first digit refers to one of ten different broad classifications for items. In this case, the 4 indicates a computer-related item.

How do you come up with the ECCN number for your product? There are three ways:

1. *Determine it yourself.* You can look at the alphabetized index for the Commerce Control List (CCL) on the U.S. Export Administration Regulations (EAR) website (https://www.bis.doc.gov/index.php/regulations/commerce-control-list-ccl). Select "Commerce Control List (CCL) Index" to download the appropriate PDF file.

2. *Go to the source: the manufacturer.* Often manufacturers know the ECCN. They may also know what countries require a license for that product.

3. *Submit a classification request online through the Simplified Network Application Process Redesign (SNAP-R).* Go there via www.bis.doc.gov and select "SNAP-R" under "Licensing."

The BIS and EAR websites will also provide you with information about whether your items need an export license. In addition, you can find the Restricted or Denied Parties lists there.

Let's Talk Shipping

Now that you've gotten a feel for the pro forma invoice, let's focus on shipping terms. Remember that your price quote will vary depending on how you or your customer decide to send the merchandise. In the coffee go-cup order, for example, there's a $1,000 difference between the price if the customer arranges for the order to be picked up or if you send it to Rome for them. Your freight forwarder can make all these arrangements for you and carry them out, but you need to understand them to quote your prices profitably.

International shipping terms are sometimes referred to as "Incoterms" (short for international commercial terms) and are published by the International Chamber of Commerce (ICC). Incoterms is a worldwide standardization of definitions that are used in shipping documents. Most shipping terms can be used interchangeably for air, sea, and ground transportation. In Figure 5–5, page 68, you'll find a handy list of common shipping terms.

Ex Works (EXW)

This is where the merchandise is picked up at your "works"—your shop or warehouse, or your supplier's warehouse or factory. The unstated agreement here is that you'll have the product ready to go, properly packaged for shipping, stacked on a shipping pallet (if necessary), and properly banded and labeled. You'll also have the merchandise ready and waiting at the time the customer has specified for pickup.

In an EXW transaction, your responsibility for the merchandise ends when the customer or their representative picks up the goods. At that point, they've taken legal possession or title. If the go-cups are lost at sea in a freak storm or are blasted out of the sky by aliens, you're off the hook and still get paid under the terms of the letter of credit.

Free Carrier (FCA)

This is the same thing as EXW, except it means you'll load the truck or minivan or whatever carrier the customer sends to pick up the goods. Because this is basically a courtesy, you should plan on charging the same price for FCA as you would for EXW. You won't see this term used for ground transportation—when you're shipping by truck or rail—because in this case, it's basically the same thing as FOB, which is described later.

Shipping Terms on Parade

Terms of Sale	Exporter's Job and Responsibilities	Buyer Takes Title At
EXW—Ex Works	Pack and label merchandise; have it ready for loading	Exporter's facility
FCA—Free Carrier	Pack and label merchandise; have it ready for loading; load truck	Exporter's facility
FAS—Free Alongside Ship	Ship to port or airport; pay truck freight	Ship or plane, departure city
FOB—Free on Board	Ship to port or airport; have loaded; pay freight forwarder	Ship or plane, departure city
CFR—Cost and Freight	Ship to destination port or airport	Destination port or airport
CIF—Cost, Insurance, and Freight	Ship, insured, to destination port or airport	Destination and port or airport
CIP—Carriage and Insurance Paid To	Ship, insured, to destination port or airport; then have delivered by ground transport	Importer's facility
CPT—Carriage Paid To	Delivers goods to a mutually agreed upon location	Mutually agreed upon location
DDP—Delivered Duty Paid	Ship, insured, to destination port or airport; then have delivered by ground transport; pay customs duties	Importer's facility
DAP—Delivered at Place	Deliver to the place buyer designated	Designated place of arrival by buyer
DAT—Delivered at Terminal	Delivers to the terminal and unloaded	Designated terminal or location within
DPU—Delivered at Place Unloaded	Delivers to a specified location and unloaded	Designated location

FIGURE 5–5: **Shipping Terms on Parade**

Free Alongside Ship (FAS)

This means that you, as the exporter, will have the merchandise delivered, just as it sounds, right alongside the ship (or air carrier). In other words, instead of just having the goods ready for pickup, you'll deliver them to the ship or plane to be loaded. "Ship" can also mean a warehouse in the port area where the steamship line will later pick up the go-cups and whatever other merchandise is waiting for pickup and take it all to the ship.

In this situation, you pay for transportation to the ship or ship's warehouse, whichever your customer has specified, and you have responsibility for the cups until the shipping line representative signs for them and takes over the title. If the coffee cups meet with a nasty accident on the freeway in this instance, it's your responsibility. You'll have to replace them if you want to receive payment.

How much you should charge for FAS delivery is up to you. If you live near the point of delivery and the load is light, you'll probably hop into your car and deliver them yourself. Another option is to call UPS or a local delivery service.

Free on Board (FOB)

This term means that you not only have the merchandise delivered to the port, but you also see that it's loaded on board the ship or vessel. Here you're taking on several additional responsibilities and expenses. For starters, there's the transportation fee to the port. There are also the terminal receiving charges (TRC), or wharfage, which the shipping line charges to load your merchandise onto the ship, and then there's the freight forwarder's fee.

In this instance, your responsibility does not end until the merchandise is safely loaded onto the ship and signed for by the captain or his representative. You can charge what you like for the added responsibility.

Be sure you check with your freight forwarder before committing yourself to an FOB price quote. Steamship line prices can vary among ports. Also, trucking or common carrier prices will vary among cities and can change with fluctuations in fuel prices. You'll want to double-check the matter of legalization or consularization fees, because if they're necessary, you'll have to supply your importer with a certificate of origin, packing slip, and invoice stamped by somebody in the importing country's local American embassy.

FOB prices are usually requested and quoted with the port of departure listed, as in FOB airport, Seattle; or FOB vessel, Panama City, Florida; or just FOB Panama City, Florida, without the words "vessel" or "airport."

Cost and Freight (CFR)

Here you're taking on even more responsibility. This means you'll not only transport the packaged merchandise to the port or airport and load onto the ship, but you'll also pay the shipping charges. You might see CFR written as C+F or C&F, but these are dated references that have mostly been retired from service.

Cost, Insurance, and Freight (CIF)

You might recognize this one from the pro forma invoice. It means that you're paying to ship the merchandise, and you're also paying the insurance to cover its safe arrival. Marine insurance usually includes transportation to the port as well as on board the ship, so if something hideous happens anywhere en route, you're responsible, but you're also insured.

Again, as in every example discussed within this section, you can tack on whatever fee you like, but you want your pricing to remain competitive. CIF prices and quotes are written with the destination listed, as in CIF Rome. The seller will have to contract for insurance to cover buyer's risk against loss or damage to the goods.

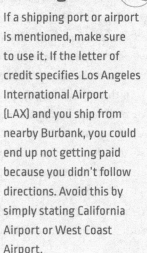

warning

If a shipping port or airport is mentioned, make sure to use it. If the letter of credit specifies Los Angeles International Airport (LAX) and you ship from nearby Burbank, you could end up not getting paid because you didn't follow directions. Avoid this by simply stating California Airport or West Coast Airport.

Carriage and Insurance Paid To (CIP)

This option tacks on one more stipulation. You'll arrange and pay for having the merchandise insured, trucked to the port or airport, shipped or flown to its destination, and then delivered directly to your customer's door (or other specified location) by local ground transportation. Of all the shipping terms, this is the only one you won't see applied to air freight as well as ocean, because CIF and CFR will cover your shipment. You also won't see this term used for ground transportation. The seller will have to contract for insurance to cover buyer's risk against loss or damage to the goods.

Carriage Paid To (CPT)

In this case, you arrange to sell the goods and deliver them to either your customer or someone else as determined by the buyer (your customer) at an agreed-upon location. For instance, the buyer might have a specific warehouse in which you both agree the merchandise should be delivered. The seller is responsible for paying the costs of the carriage necessary to transport the goods to the agreed-upon destination.

Delivered Duty Paid (DDP)

Not to be confused with DDT, DDP is like CIF, except that besides having the merchandise insured and shipped, then delivered to your customer's door, you also pay all customs duties. This is not ideal for you as the exporter, although you'll do your homework before you agree so you know how much money to tack onto your invoice.

If you're the importer, especially a newbie, it's a nice way to have someone who knows the ropes take on more responsibility. You should be aware that DDP is not the most common way for the exporter to ship, so don't expect to have it handed to you without some negotiation.

Delivered at Place (DAP)

In this scenario the seller will deliver the goods and place them at the disposal of the buyer on the arriving means of transport. The goods should be ready at the designated place of destination. At this designated place, the risk transfers from the seller to the buyer.

Delivered at Terminal (DAT)

In this case the goods are delivered and unloaded from your means of transport and placed at the terminal of the arriving seller. A terminal can be a warehouse or anyplace else the buyer designates and that you both agree upon in advance. Make sure you know where the buyer wants you to go. At the designated location, the risk shifts from the seller to the buyer.

Delivered at Place Unloaded (DPU)

In this situation the goods are delivered to a location that's predetermined and specified and then loaded from the means of transport. Once the unloading task is completed, the risk is transferred from the seller to the buyer.

Carrying the Day

There are three types of ocean carriers on which you can place your merchandise:

warning

The insurance granted by an airline's waybill is not the same as the insurance certificate that may be required on your letter of credit. Make sure you've got the real thing, or you may not be in compliance with the L/C, which means you may not get paid.

1. *Conference lines.* This is an association of carriers that join together in ocean freight conferences to establish common shipping rates and conditions. They offer two fee schedules—the regular one and the lower one they'll give you if you sign a contract to use only their ships during the contract period.

2. *Independent lines.* These lines operate on their own and usually offer rates that are about 10 percent lower than their conference competition. So why wouldn't you just go with them and forget the conferences? Because the independents' space is based on availability and there isn't always room for your goods.

3. *Tramp vessels.* These ships can be conference or independent, but they're called tramps because instead of operating on a fixed schedule, they tramp around the world, seeking out whatever bulk cargoes might be available at the last minute.

Just Say No

Keep in mind, it's not always in your best interest to let the exporter ship their merchandise CIF (cost, insurance, and freight). Having them pay the freight and insurance, plus handle all the paperwork may sound wonderfully simple (and it is), but you'll ultimately pay for this additional service.

Do your homework. Ask for the weight and dimensions of the shipping containers and how many containers there will be. Next, contact your customs broker and get your own price quotes. If you discover that you can do better than what the exporter has quoted, renegotiate. If you want your goods shipped EXW (ex works), FCA (free carrier), or FOB (free on board), make sure the letter of credit specifies your preferred carrier.

On the other hand, if you're a newbie importer and you decide that the difference in price between the exporter's quote and the ones you've received is minimal, it might be worth it to let them carry the ball—at least for your first few forays until you learn the shipping ropes.

The Import/Export Referee

Now that you know how to get your merchandise shipped, let's focus on you getting paid. Over the centuries, international traders have devised the letter of credit (L/C) as an honorable and safe method of ensuring that the importer gets the goods they've paid for in the manner they want them shipped from an exporter who could be halfway around the world.

At the same time, the letter of credit assures the exporter that they will get paid for their merchandise once it has been sent across international borders to someone the seller may never have met.

The letter of credit does this by acting, with the help of the bank, as a sort of import/export referee, making sure that the exporter has carried out the importer's instructions before it hands over payment. For the exporter's peace of mind, the letter of credit guarantees that their payment is already in the bank and that once they've carried out the instructions embedded in the L/C, they'll receive the money. A letter of credit (sometimes called a *documentary credit*), is often abbreviated as L/C.

Letters of credit can take on various "looks," from the flowery formal business letter to the snappy let's-get-to-the-point list to the generic fill-in-the-blanks form, depending on the issuing bank's modus operandi. But whatever the style, each L/C will contain the same information and will be used the same way.

Exporter's Letter of Credit Checklist

As the exporter, there are a number of items you'll need to know or negotiate before the importer sends you the letter of credit (L/C). Here's a handy checklist to help you make sure you've covered all your bases. You might want to make copies of this list and check things off as you go.

❑ Which will be the advising bank (i.e., your bank)? _____

❑ How much time will you have to ship your merchandise after you receive the L/C? _____

❑ How much time will you have to get your documents to your bank? _____

❑ Will the L/C be irrevocable? The answer should be yes. _____

❑ Is the L/C payable at sight (when you present the done-deed documents, not after another 30, 60, or 90 days)? The answer should be yes. _____

❑ Will you pay your bank charges, and will the importer pay his? _____

❑ What will your bank charges be? _____

❑ Are there any special requirements? If so, what are they? _____

❑ Remember: When the L/C is opened, get the name of the opening bank and the L/C number.

FIGURE 5–6: **Exporter's Letter of Credit Checklist**

Figure 5–6 provides a checklist summarizing the preliminary considerations an exporter needs to make to obtain an L/C; for importers, look at the checklist in Figure 5–7, page 74. Next, check out Figures 5–8 and 5–9 on pages 75 and 78, respectively, to get an idea of what typical L/Cs look like.

Tale of an Importer

Signore Franco of Cappuccino Imports zips down to his bank, the Banco della Roma, and applies for a letter of credit in the amount of USD 16,000, the amount needed for the exporter, Coffee Holic, to send him 5,000 coffee go-cups CIF Rome. (CIF is cost, insurance, and freight paid to Rome.) The bank checks Sr. Franco's account to make sure he has USD 16,000 available. The bank may (or may not) freeze this sum until the letter of credit becomes payable.

As the importer, Signore Franco could be called either the applicant or the opener, since they're the person applying for, or opening, the L/C. The exporter (in this case, Charlie) is called the beneficiary because he ultimately will receive the deposit into his account.

Importer's Letter of Credit Checklist

When you're the importer, you'll need to ascertain a number of points before issuing your letter of credit (L/C). Here's a handy checklist to help you make sure you have everything present and accounted for.

❑ Will the L/C be confirmed? _____

❑ What will your bank charges be? _____

❑ Is the L/C payable in the exporter's desired currency? What is that currency (U.S. dollars, Mexican pesos, etc.)? _____

❑ How much time do you want to allow for shipment? _____

❑ How much time do you want to give the exporter to get his documents to the bank? ____

_____

❑ What documents will you need? _____

❑ Is everything in the L/C on the pro forma invoice? _____

❑ What are your shipping requirements? _____

❑ What about insurance? _____

Remember: Notify the exporter of your bank and L/C number, and be sure to get the loading date and other information so you can file your ISF form on time (see Chapter 6).

FIGURE 5-7: **Importer's Letter of Credit Checklist**

You should note that the Banco della Roma is an international bank and is familiar with L/Cs. If Sr. Franco had gone to a smaller bank, without an international department, then either he'd have been bundled out the door to find another bank to work with or his bank would have found an international affiliate to help it through the ropes. But in this instance, it's not a problem.

Sr. Franco tells his bank exactly which documents he'll want from the Coffee Holic people. In this case (see Figure 5-8, page 75), he's asked for the following:

▶ Full set of clean, on board air bills of lading, issued "to order"
▶ Commercial invoice, original and five copies
▶ Packing slip, original and five copies
▶ Insurance certificates

Sample Letter of Credit #1
The Bank of Berry
Specialists in Small-Town & International Banking
Berry, Florida 30000, USA

July 2, 20XX

Coffee Holic Exports
123 Cafe Street
Berry, FL 30000, USA

Dear Sirs:

Our correspondents, Banco della Roma, request us to inform you that they have opened with us their irrevocable letter of credit in your favor in the amount of maximum Sixteen Thousand and 00/100 ($16,000.00) United States Dollars by order of Cappuccino Imports, 456 Via Espresso, Ostia Antica, Italy.

We are authorized to accept your 90-day sight draft, drawn on us when accompanied by the following documents, which must represent and cover full invoice value of the merchandise described below:

1. Signed commercial invoice in original and five (5) copies
2. Full set of clean ocean bills of lading, dated on board, plus one (1) non-negotiable copy, if available, issued to the order of Banco della Roma, notify: Cappuccino Imports, 456 Via Espresso, Ostia Antica, Italy, indicating Credit No. 0123
3. Insurance certificates in duplicate, in negotiable form, covering all risks, including war risks, strikes, and mines, for the value of the merchandise plus 10%

    Covering: Coffee Go-Cups, Style A
                     As per pro forma invoice dated June 4, 20XX
                     CIF Rome
    Merchandise to be forwarded from Miami to Rome
    Partial shipments prohibited
    Transshipments prohibited

The above-mentioned correspondent engages with you that all drafts drawn under and in compliance with the terms of this credit will be duly honored on delivery of documents as specified, if presented at this office on or before October 1, 20XX. We confirm the credit and thereby undertake that all drafts drawn and presented above will be duly honored.

Jennifer Schneider Jordan

for The Bank of Berry

FIGURE 5–8: **Sample Letter of Credit #1**

Sr. Franco's bank neatly condenses all this into L/C format and sends the letter of credit to the Coffee Holic people's bank in Berry. When The Bank of Berry receives the L/C, it sends it on to Charlie Holic, the exporter. Again, if Charlie's bank is small and doesn't know how to deal with L/Cs, it will either send him packing or find an international bank to help with the transaction and charge a fee for doing so. But, as in Rome, this bank can deal with letters of credit.

The importer's bank is called the opening, originating, or issuing bank, while the exporter's bank is known as the advising bank because it advises the exporter of the L/C.

Now the ball is in Charlie's court. It's up to him to carry out every detail of the letter of credit exactly as it's spelled out. This includes using a particular ocean carrier or sending the merchandise from a particular port, if that's what's specified. Here, Charlie has it easy. He can ship from any East Coast port on any carrier, so long as the merchandise ends up (in one piece) at its destination on or before October 1, 20XX.

warning

Unless otherwise stated, a letter of credit is irrevocable. This means that once it's been opened, neither the importer nor the exporter can change their mind about anything in it without a tremendous amount of hassle. Whether you're acting as importer or exporter, make sure you know, understand, and can carry out what you're committing to.

Once the merchandise has made it to Rome, Charlie takes a trip to the bank with all the documents—including the bills of lading (which are the documents that establish the terms of a contract between a shipper and a transportation company, which the shipper pays for), the commercial invoice with all its copies, the packing slip with all its copies, and insurance certificates—proving that he's done his job as set out in the letter of credit. The bank people, in their capacity as "import/export referee," check over all these documents and assure themselves that everything is fine. Then they have Charlie's payment, which has been waiting in Sr. Franco's account at the Banco della Roma, transferred to Charlie's account.

Meanwhile, back at the FedEx counter, all the documents Charlie (or his freight forwarder) assembled in the course of shipping the merchandise is sent to the bank in Rome to be handed over to Sr. Franco.

End of transaction.

Not Everyone Is Honest

All letters of credit are generated through banks. Usually, the importer will arrange for your bank to be the advising bank, but occasionally they'll use another American bank. If this is OK with you, go for it. If not, ask that your bank be included in the loop. You'll have to pay its fees on top of whatever other bank charges you're committed to, but you'll have the security of knowing that the bank representatives you're familiar with are on the job.

If you ever receive an L/C directly from an importer, be on guard! Letters of credit can only come from banks, so an L/C generated by any other entity is a major indicator that something isn't right. Turn the letter of credit over to your international banker and let them take it from there.

The L/C Revue

Now that you understand why and how a letter of credit works, let's go over each item in the L/C one step at a time. Feel free to follow along using the Sample Letter of Credit provided in Figure 5–9 on page 78.

1. This gives the basic information—who the L/C is from, who it's written to, how much money it's for, and in which currency. It's also important that it states this is an irrevocable letter of credit. This is standard operating procedure, but worth repeating. Never accept a revocable letter of credit, because that would mean the importer could back out of the deal at any time. This section also gives the information that this L/C is available at sight. As you already know, this means the money will be paid as soon as the terms of the L/C are met; it's not a time draft to be paid out over a designated period.

2. This section spells out that the merchandise is to be sent CIF (cost, insurance, and freight) by sea. How do you know this? Because it calls for a full set of clean on board bills of lading, for starters. Bills of lading are forms issued by the sea, land, or air carrier to verify the merchandise they're transporting. The term "on board" is used by steamship lines to indicate that the merchandise is on board the ship, as opposed to sitting on the dock. This way, the exporter knows his product

warning

Customs doesn't inform importers of shipment arrivals. This is the responsibility of the shipper or some other designated party. If you're the importer of merchandise arriving at an American port, find out in advance the scheduled loading date at the foreign port and the scheduled arrival date. Then follow up. If the paperwork isn't presented to customs within 15 days of arrival, the goods will be transferred to a warehouse, and you'll pay for storage.

Sample Letter of Credit #2

The Bank of Berry

Berry, Florida, USA

Opening Bank L/C No.: 0123   Our Reference No.: 0456D

July 2, 20XX

1. By order of Cappuccino Imports, Ostia Antica, Italy, we advise this irrevocable Documentary Credit No. 0123 in favor of Coffee Holic Exports, Berry, Florida, USA, in the amount of USD 16,000.00 (Sixteen Thousand and 00/100 United States Dollars) available at sight, against your drafts, accompanied by the following documents:

2. Full set of clean on board bills of lading issued to order of shipper, marked notify applicant, freight prepaid

3. Beneficiary's signed commercial invoices in original and five copies

4. Packing slip in original and five copies

5. Insurance policy in negotiable form issued to our order and showing claims payable at destination for the full invoice amount plus 10% covering all risks, SRCC, and war clause

6. For: 5,000 Coffee Go-Cups per pro forma invoice dated June 4, 20XX

7. Shipment from: East Coast port

8. Shipment to: Rome, Italy

9. Shipment not later than: September 1, 20XX

10. Date of Expiry: October 1, 20XX

11. Part Shipments: Prohibited

12. Transshipments: Prohibited

13. Documents must be presented within ten days after shipment

14. Banking charges in the United States for the account of beneficiary

15. Applicant's bank: Banco della Roma

16. We hereby confirm this letter of credit.

Jennifer Schneider Jordan

for The Bank of Berry

FIGURE 5–9: **Sample Letter of Credit #2**

is underway and not baking in the sun waiting for the next available ship to come along.

Full set is another term used exclusively by steamship lines and refers to the three original bills of lading traditionally issued and signed by the captain or one of his subordinates. This is how you know the order is to be sent by sea. The steamship line people, who enjoy getting repeat business, will provide you with as many copies, marked non-negotiable, as you need.

To order of shipper means that the merchandise is consigned to the steamship line and not to the importer, although the shipper will turn the goods over to the importer when they reach their destination. The applicant, to be notified when the merchandise reaches its destination, is the buyer (in this case Cappuccino Imports). Finally, this section clearly says freight prepaid—and that's how you know that the merchandise is being sent CIF.

3. This sentence says that the beneficiary (the exporter) must provide not a pro forma invoice, but the familiar, ordinary one they use for routine transactions, signed in their own hand, along with five copies.

4. The packing slip called for here (like its compatriot the invoice), is an everyday packing slip with copies that Charlie Holic uses all the time.

5. An insurance policy for your merchandise is a must and is not difficult to obtain. Your freight forwarder can make all the arrangements. The acronym SRCC (or SR

▶ Applying for the Letter of Credit

As the importer, you get to apply for the letter of credit. Your bank will provide you with a form on which to submit all the necessary information. (See the sample in Figure 5–10, page 80, to see what the finished product will resemble.)

If you don't already have an account with an international bank, you will be required to place all the funds guaranteed by the L/C into the institution's coffers. If you're already a customer with a gold star next to your name, the bank will set you up with a L/C against your account. Either way, the bank sets the L/C funds into a sort of escrow account and holds them for you until the close of the transaction.

Aside from the money you need to pay the exporter, there are various bank fees for L/C transactions. These include advising, assignment, payment, and transfer fees. The exact charges will depend on the bank, but you can expect to pay between $1,000 and $1,500 for a $50,000 transaction. Talk to your banker before you embark on a project.

Sample Request to Open L/C

Request to Open Documentary Credit
(Commercial Letter of Credit and Security Agreement)

To: Banco della Roma   From: Cappuccino Imports

Please open for our account a letter of credit in accordance with the under-mentioned. We agree that, except so far as otherwise expressly stated, this credit will be subject to the Uniform Customs and Practice for Documentary Credits, ICC Publication #500. We undertake to execute the bank's usual form of indemnity.

Type of Credit: Irrevocable
Method of Advice: Fax, full details
Beneficiary's Bank: The Bank of Berry
In Favor of Beneficiary: Coffee Holic Exports
                          123 Cafe Street
                          Berry, Florida 30000, USA
Amount or Sum of: USD 16,000.00
Availability: Valid until October 1, 20XX

This credit is available by drafts drawn at sight, accompanied by the required documents.
Required Documents:
1. Invoice in original and five copies
2. Full set of clean, on board bills of lading to order of shipper, marked notify applicant, freight prepaid
3. Packing slip in original and five copies
4. Insurance policy in negotiable form showing claims payable at destination for full amount plus 10 percent covering all risks, SRCC, and war clause

Quantity & Description 5,000 Coffee Go-Cups, Style A, per pro forma invoice of Goods:
                        dated June 4, 20XX
Price Per Unit: USD 3.00
Terms & Port: CIF Rome
Ship From: East Coast port
Special Instructions: Part shipments prohibited
                        Transshipments prohibited
                        Documents must be presented within 10 days after shipment
                        Banking charges in the U.S. for the account of beneficiary

FIGURE 5–10: **Sample Request to Open L/C**

& CC) means strikes, riots, and civil commotion. The importer wants the merchandise covered for all potential risks.

warning

Be sure your insurance covers your merchandise from your driveway to the importer's door. Don't leave gaps in the coverage area. Strange and unexpected things can happen on piers or in air cargo bays.

6. These are the 5,000 go-cups precisely as spelled out in the pro forma invoice. Type in this same phrase describing your merchandise per pro forma invoice dated (whatever) on every document you ultimately hand over to the bank.

7. Remember that "East Coast port" gives Charlie Holic the freedom to choose any East Coast port he wants to ship from.

8. The destination port

9. This is the absolute latest date for the carrier to leave port with the merchandise on board—the last possible date Charlie Holic can send his coffee cups off to Rome. One day later and he runs a serious risk of not getting paid because he's violated the stipulations in the letter of credit.

10. The date of expiry is the date the letter of credit expires. Like time and tide, the L/C waits for no one. If you aren't at the bank by the date of expiry with all your documentation in hand and correct, you don't get paid.

11. Part or partial shipments are those sent in batches rather than as a complete set. Cappuccino Imports might want Coffee Holic to send a part shipment if it planned to sell only, say, 1,000 go-cups at a time and didn't want to warehouse the entire 5,000-cup order. In this case, though, the importer is eager to get all the merchandise at once. They don't want to pay the extra expense of multiple shipments.

12. Transshipment is the cargo opposite of nonstop. In other words, it means that the merchandise is off-loaded somewhere en route to the final destination, new bills of lading are issued, and the whole process starts over again. Not nonstop and not fun to keep track of.

13. This section spells out how long the exporter has to get the shipping documents (bills of lading, invoices, and packing slips) to the importer so that they have them ready to show their home-turf customs people when the merchandise arrives. It's not good to make people wait for the documents because if the goods arrive before the documentation, they'll have to leave all those eagerly awaited coffee cups sitting in a warehouse and pay storage fees. Sending documents ASAP will ensure you have a customer for life and that you get paid ASAP! *Note*: If the L/C doesn't specify how much time you have to send your documents, then you have 21 days.

14. This means that the beneficiary, or exporter, will pay his own bank's L/C charges and the importer will pay the fees charged by his bank. Occasionally, either exporter or importer will pay all fees. Your bank usually deducts the charges from your L/C payment before it turns the funds over to you.

15. This, remember, is the importer's bank.

16. When your bank confirms the letter of credit, it is saying that, so long as you conform to the terms of the L/C, it will pay you, come hell or high water.

tip

Some exporters who deal with importers in volatile areas, like parts of Africa or the Middle East, arrange for a bank in a stable country to confirm the L/C so that they're guaranteed payment.

The Negotiator

A negotiable bill of lading is like a signed check with nobody's name on the "pay to the order of" line. The shipper can give it—and thus the merchandise it describes—to anyone they choose. So if something goes wrong with the letter of credit after your shipment has already arrived on foreign shores and your customer won't accept the merchandise, you can hustle and find someone else to buy it.

A non-negotiable bill of lading, on the other hand, is like a check made out to a specific person. Only that person (or company) can take receipt of the merchandise; if something goes wrong after it arrives on foreign shores and you want to sell the goods to someone else, you'll have to start the whole shipping document process over.

What Happens When Mistakes Are Made?

Life is full of surprises. Someday something will go wrong with the letter of credit transaction—and it's best to be prepared.

First, keep your wits about you and call your bank. Your bank will then contact the importer and explain the problem (euphemistically called a discrepancy). For example, the air carrier screwed up and delivered the

tip

Ask your international banker for a copy of UCP 600, otherwise known as ICC Uniform Customs and Practice for Documentary Credits. The latest version is from 2007 (it is only updated every few years). It is published by the International Chamber of Commerce, and copies can be ordered through various sites online. This must-read document sets forth the guidelines for all letter of credit transactions.

▶ A Day in the Life

What does a trader's day really look like? What do they do in between preparing pro forma invoices, requests for letters of credit, and shipping documents?

Here's a behind-the-scenes peek, courtesy of Michael Richter, an international trade consultant in Germany:

- ▶ First hour. Read statistics printed overnight by the computer to see if each representative/agent has fulfilled their plans, and initiate changes if necessary.

- ▶ Work on the internet for one or two hours to see what inquiries have come in, then answer them personally or forward them to past or present clients who may be interested.

- ▶ Have a short meeting with colleagues to see if assistance is needed, then support them or troubleshoot.

- ▶ Look at the day's newspapers (in print or online) to see whether there's any movement within the industry that requires immediate action. Signing up for a service like Apple News (Apple News+) or Google News allows you to create a customized newsfeed on your computer or mobile device that caters to your areas of interest.

- ▶ Take a coffee break.

- ▶ Look at the mail and check your email to handle or forward items.

- ▶ After lunch, take time to reflect on what has and what should have happened.

- ▶ Discuss problems and/or chances for the future with prospects and/or business partners.

- ▶ Look again at email and the internet for any news or try to find new opportunities.

- ▶ At the end of the day, there should be about an hour to discuss again with colleagues how the day went and/or problems that came up.

- ▶ One or two evenings each week, attend business events or meetings with partners for discussion.

merchandise 30 miles from where it should have landed, or because of icebergs, the ship is still in the North Atlantic, 500 miles (and two days) from where it's supposed to be.

At this point, the importer could either forgive the transgression and agree to pay you anyway, or they might decide not to accept the whole shebang, and the letter of credit is immediately rendered null and void. In this case, all your documents get returned to you. So, what happens to your merchandise? If you can't come to an agreement and save the deal, you can store the merchandise in a warehouse while you find a new buyer. You'll have to start all over again with a new letter of credit and new shipping documents, but you can still potentially sell those goods to somebody else.

Another option is to ask the importer for an amendment to the letter of credit. After your bank contacts the importer's bank, which then contacts the importer, they may agree to extend your deadline. You might, however, be penalized because the importer could require you to lower your price. It's then up to you to decide whether to accept the deal.

Here's what you do if you don't like the amended letter of credit: Head to your bank, hand over the L/C along with a letter stating that you are rejecting the deal, and ask for a receipt. Next, send a letter to the importer telling them why you've rejected the amended L/C. Hopefully, they'll generate another amendment, and you can get your deal back on track.

Cash Is King

Although the letter of credit is the safest way to ensure payment (especially for newbies) and is a common method of payment, there are other ways to negotiate an international trade transaction. Here's a list of other potential payment options:

tip

The best and brightest way to avoid the whole L/C discrepancy mess is to give yourself a little more time than you think you'll need when you quote time periods in your pro forma invoice. Build in a 10 to 20 percent margin of safety.

- ► Cash in advance
- ► Open account
- ► On consignment
- ► Collection draft

Cash is always good, so you might think the cash in advance option is always the best. But keep in mind that the other options have their benefits too. Let's go over each transaction in more detail.

Cash in Advance

The importer pays for the merchandise before it's even shipped. With this method, the buyer must implicitly trust the exporter to follow through on the deal. You might see it used in a strong seller's market when demand for a product is high or for small deals (where both parties agree that the cost in time and money isn't worth investing in a method such as a letter of credit).

As a variation on a theme, sometimes when a manufacturer needs a lot of upfront money, he may demand partial cash in advance, such as 25 percent, to offset their costs.

▶ What Is the Berne Union?

The Berne Union (www.berneunion.org) was founded in 1934 by private and state export credit insurers from France, Italy, Spain, and the UK. Following the meeting in Berne, Switzerland, the members decided to call the newly minted union the Berne Union.

Their mission has not changed in over 80 years:

▶ To actively facilitate cross-border trade by supporting international acceptance of sound principles in export credits and foreign investment.

▶ To provide a forum for professional exchange among members.

Open Account

The buyer has an account with the exporter. When they receive the merchandise, they send payment to the seller. In essence, the exporter is offering credit to the buyer. This can be risky! As with the cash-in-advance transaction, this type of account is typically used when the exporter feels comfortable with the buyer. However, where cash in advance puts all the risk on the importer, open account puts all the risk on the exporter's shoulders.

tip

Air waybills (bills of lading from air carriers) are never negotiable.

Another tack that's gaining popularity is to use an open account, but at the same time, buy credit insurance in case the deal goes bad. This payment method is cheaper than an L/C: $250 or so vs. the $1,000 to $1,500 for a letter of credit.

On Consignment

The seller ships their merchandise without any sort of payment and doesn't get paid until the importer sells the goods in their own country. This system is by far the riskiest! It is not advisable for any deal, because if the buyer can't liquidate the product, they'll return it without payment, thus sticking the exporter with unnecessary shipping costs.

Collection Draft

This transaction, often called a *cash against documents transaction*, is similar to the letter of credit in that the bank acts as the go-between for buyer and seller. In a collection draft transaction, the exporter ships the merchandise. Their bank then sends the bill of lading and other specified shipping documents (which are necessary to collect the goods down

► On the Road

What does a trader do when they're traveling? Here's another behind-the-scenes peek, courtesy of Jan H., the Belgian tire trader. Note that Jan's day, in typical European fashion, evolves through a 24-hour clock, or what we think of as military time.

Day in Belgium

07:00–09:00: Office work, emails, faxes offers, mail, etc.

09:00–12:00: Drive to airport, meet customer from Finland; back to warehouse, customer chooses products

12:00–13:00: Lunch with customer, general discussions

13:00–18:00: Visit with a customer from Nigeria; long discussion, haggling over prices, payment terms, etc.; supervise loading of containers bound for the U.S.; phone calls, faxes, email; arrival of a customer from France, discussions

18:00: Quick trip home to change and shower

19:00–??: Pick up French customer at hotel for cocktails, dinner, and more negotiations

Day on the Road in Germany

05:00: Leave home for 400-km drive

08:00: Arrive at first supplier; discussions and purchase of goods

10:00: Leave for next supplier

11:00: Next supplier; discussions without any result

12:00: Visit customer, make a sale

13:30: Visit another supplier; more discussions

15:00: Leave for another 300-odd-km drive

18:00: Arrive at hotel; check email on laptop, phone calls

19:30: Sauna and swim in hotel pool

20:30: Dinner with supplier, then to bed!

Day in Miami

07:00: Swim in hotel pool; breakfast, phone calls, and faxes

08:30: A good friend, customer, and supplier picks me up; go to his office, business discussions

13:00: Free afternoon; go to shopping mall and hotel pool; check emails, make a few phone calls

19:00: Dinner and a show with friend

23:00: Bed

at the dock) to the importer's bank, which keeps a tight grip on the documents until the importer coughs up the exporter's payment. Once payment has been extracted, the bank releases the documents to the importer, sends the funds to the exporter, and everybody is happy.

A Draft Is a Buyer's Order to Pay

To complete the collection draft, or cash against documents, the exporter has to draw up the draft part of the deal, which is basically the buyer's order to pay. There are three types of drafts:

1. *Sight draft.* This requires payment before the importer can get their hands on the goods. The exporter retains title until they've reached their destination and are paid for. It's called a sight draft because as soon as the merchandise has arrived and is theoretically "in sight" of the dock, or unloaded from an airplane, the draft is payable. The risk here is that the buyer may change their mind while the merchandise is in transit and decide to forget the whole deal. Then it's the exporter's responsibility to pay return passage for their stuff.

fun fact

Lots of international banks have accounts at American banks. That way, you can be paid in your dollars or by wire transfer. Working in reverse, if you're the importer, you can have the exporter paid in their native currency.

2. *Time draft.* The exporter extends credit to the importer. The importer has a certain amount of time, say, 30, 60, or 90 days from the moment they pick up the merchandise and accepts the draft, to make payment. With some time drafts, payment is due within a specified number of days after "sight," or arrival of the goods. In this case, the draft is called a date draft.

3. *Clean draft.* The shipping documents are sent to the importer at the same time as the merchandise. This is basically the same as sending the goods on open account and is extremely rare. Again, it's used only when the exporter has extreme confidence in their customer.

Signing Off

Now that you've had a look at some of the forms and letters needed to satisfy clients, it's time to check into the demands of government entities. These are the topics of the next chapter.

Rituals and Red Tape

Thus far, you've learned a bit about how to ship your merchandise and how to get paid once the goods arrive. Moving forward, there's still a lot you need to understand about all the required paperwork and documents involved in making each transaction happen.

This chapter focuses on the documentation needed to get the merchandise the rest of the way into the importer's hands. You'll also learn more about what the importer (or the importer's representative) needs to do with these documents to get the merchandise through customs.

In Great Form

The easiest way to get the forms you'll need is to use the internet. Using your favorite search engine, such as Google or Yahoo!, a simple search for "Export Forms" will result in many options—everything from government agency example forms to software you can purchase to generate customized forms yourself.

Certain Documents Are Equivalent to Cash

Most shipping records are known as collection documents and in some ways are the same as cash. Once you present the documents to a bank, demonstrating that you've fulfilled the conditions of the L/C, the bank issues payment.

You can have your freight forwarder handle all the paperwork so all you have to do is visit your bank with the completed documents in hand. However, as the exporter, you need

▶ The International Organization for Standardization Will Impact Your Work

As a trader, you should become familiar with the ISO 9000, or the International Organization for Standardization (ISO). This organization defines, establishes, and maintains an effective quality assurance system for manufacturing and service industries.

You'll also want to know the QS 9000 and the ISO 14000. These are the quality management standards devised by the International Organization for Standardization in Geneva, Switzerland.

If the product you're representing has an ISO 9000 certification, it can hold its head up among its competitors. It's been manufactured with quality, customer service, and business efficiency in mind.

A QS 9000 certification is the next step up (the "more mature version," according to the ISO 9000 Network, a commercial certification group) and relates specifically to the automotive industry, while the ISO 14000 focuses on management of the environment.

For more information, visit www.iso.org, or check with the National Institute of Standards and Technology's website: www.nist.gov.

to understand how each link in the chain functions. You also need to understand these documents when you're the importer, because either you or your customs broker will use them to claim your cargo once it arrives at the harbor, loading dock, or airport.

Here's a listing of the most common documents you'll need to become well-acquainted with:

▶ *Bill of Lading.* "Lading" means freight or cargo, so a bill of lading is basically a receipt from the cargo handler—the steamship, air, or truck line—showing that it's got your goods. To make things official, the document is signed by the captain (on a ship) or other agent of the transporter as binding evidence that the merchandise has been shipped. There are various permutations of the bill of lading, including:

- *Clean or Clean on Board.* This means the transport company has not noted any irregularities in the packing or the condition of the goods. In other words, it has a clean bill of health. This is the standard bill of lading.

- *Foul.* A foul bill of lading is the opposite of a "clean" one. It indicates, for example, that the transport company has discovered something sticky leaking from those boxes marked "blood byproducts." If your bill of lading gets marked "foul," you'll want to exchange the bum container for a "clean" one and have the shipment relabeled before it's presented to the importer.

- *On Board.* This confirms that the cargo has been placed on board the vessel and carries no other guidelines or stipulations. It's an elderly shipping term and isn't used much these days.

- *On Deck.* This is relevant only if the goods, such as livestock, must be transported on the deck of the ship.

- *Order.* This is a negotiable bill of lading that must be endorsed by the shipper before it's handed over to the bank for collection. An order bill of lading is usually made out to the bank or customs broker, or it can be left blank, like a blank check.

- *Order Notify.* This is like the order bill, except that the consignee (the buyer) and sometimes the customs broker must be notified when the ship reaches port. This is particularly nice if you're the importer because the shipper will notify you in advance when the vessel will arrive.

- *Straight.* This one is non-negotiable, like a check with the name of the payee filled in. It spells out to whom the merchandise is consigned. Because it prohibits release of the goods to anyone but the person specified on the documents and thus offers the most protection, the straight bill of lading is usually preferred by newbie importers.

- *Through Bill of Lading.* This is the "pass it on down" bill used when several carriers are involved if, for example, the merchandise needs to go by rail or truck to the port and then by ocean, or vice versa. It allows the transportation of goods both within domestic borders and through international shipment.

► *Certificate of Manufacture.* Used when the buyer pays for the goods before shipment, this document verifies that the merchandise has been manufactured and fulfills the general product requirements (see Figure 6–1 for a sample and 6–2, page 93, for a form you can use). This document provides proof that the goods are on hand and ready for shipment.

► *Certificate of Origin.* Some countries require a separate certificate of origin (see Figures 6–3 and 6–4, pages 94 and 95), even though this information is provided on the commercial invoice. The certificate is especially important when you're importing goods that require regulatory approval, such as medical equipment or food. Our own Food and Drug Administration, for example, requires a certificate of origin for every imported product. Some countries will count a piece of paper with your signature below the statement, "I certify that these goods were manufactured in the United States of America," as acceptable. Others want the statement notarized, on a form from your local chamber of commerce or on a special form for that particular nation.

Sample Certificate of Manufacture

From: Coffee Holic Exports
123 Cafe Street
Berry, FL 30000, USA

To: Cappuccino Imports
456 Via Espresso
Ostia Antica, Italy

Date: July 15, 20XX

Opening Bank: Banco della Roma

L/C or Other Reference No.: 0123

Merchandise: 5,000 Coffee Go-Cups, Style A

We hereby certify that the above-described merchandise has been manufactured as of July 30, 20XX, and is available for shipment as of August 1, 20XX.

By: _____
(signature and title)

FIGURE 6–1: **Sample Certificate of Manufacture**

Certificate of Manufacture

From: _____

_____

_____

To: _____

_____

_____

Date: _____

Opening Bank: _____

L/C or Other Reference No.: _____

Merchandise: _____

We hereby certify that the above-described merchandise has been manufactured as of
_____, and is available for shipment as of _____.

By: _____
   (signature and title)

FIGURE 6–2: **Certificate of Manufacture**

▶ *Commercial Invoice.* The commercial invoice is the same as any invoice used by a domestic company and is essentially a finished version of the pro forma invoice. You can make up your own commercial invoice on your computer or buy preprinted blank forms with carbon copies at an office supply store. When you fill in those blanks, you'll want to be sure you've added the same particulars you have on your pro forma invoice and the L/C number, if you're using an L/C. Plus, you'll need to add the terms of the sale (e.g., FOB or DDP) and a statement certifying the goods were manufactured in the U.S., followed by your signature. This will help skate the merchandise through customs. Check out Figure 6–5 for a sample commercial invoice on page 96 to get an idea of what yours should look like, and Figure 6–6, page 97, for a form you can adapt for your own business.

warning

Some countries require more information on shipping documents than others. Be sure to check with your customs broker to make sure the forms you're using cover everything.

Sample Certificate of Origin

I, <u>Charlie Holic</u>, <u>Owner</u> of <u>Coffee Holic Exports</u>, declare that the

   (name of person)   (title)   (name of company)

goods described herein are the product of the United States of America.

Marks & Numbers	No. Containers	Gross Weight or Quantity	Description
As Addressed 1 thru 50	50	5,000 pieces	Coffee Go-Cups

Certified by: _____ Date: _____

          (signature of person named above)

This space for notary, if required:

The <u>Berry</u> Chamber of Commerce, a recognized chamber of commerce under the laws of the state of <u>Florida</u>, has examined the manufacturer's invoice or shipper's affidavit on the above-described goods and, to its best belief, certifies that the merchandise originated in the United States of America.

By: _____

       (signature and title)

FIGURE 6–3: **Sample Certificate of Origin**

Certificate of Origin

I, _____, _____of _____, declare that the
    (name of person)   (title)   (name of company)

goods described herein are the product of the United States of America.

Marks & Numbers	No. Containers	Gross Weight or Quantity	Description

Certified by: _____   Date: _____
          (signature of person named above)

This space for notary, if required:

The _____ Chamber of Commerce, a recognized chamber of commerce under the laws of the state of _____, has examined the manufacturer's invoice or shipper's affidavit on the above-described goods and, to its best belief, certifies that the merchandise originated in the United States of America.

By: _____
     (signature and title)

FIGURE 6–4: **Certificate of Origin**

Sample Completed Commercial Invoice

Date: July 15, 20XX

From: Coffee Holic Exports
               123 Cafe Street
               Berry, FL 30000, USA

To: Cappuccino Imports
               456 Via Espresso
               Ostia Antica, Italy

Merchandise Ordered: 5,000 Coffee Go-Cups, Style A

On Order or L/C No.: L/C 0123

Shipping Terms: CIF Rome

Price: USD 16,000

We hereby certify that these goods were manufactured in the United States of America and that this is a valid, true, and correct invoice.

By: *Charlie Holic*_____   Title: *Owner*_____
              (signature)   (title)

FIGURE 6–5: **Sample Completed Commercial Invoice**

Commercial Invoice

Date: _____

From: _____

_____

_____

To: _____

_____

_____

Merchandise Ordered: _____

On Order or L/C No.: _____

Shipping Terms: _____

Price: _____

We hereby certify that these goods were manufactured in the United States of America and that this is a valid, true, and correct invoice.

By: _____   Title: _____
        (signature)   (title)

FIGURE 6–6: **Commercial Invoice**

▶ Living in a Dangerous World

Although you don't need a license to export most merchandise, you'll need a validated export license to ship goods that the U.S. government wants to control, such as articles of war, advanced technology, and products in short supply.

Obtaining a validated license can be time consuming, costly, and in some cases, impossible. If you're an export novice, you should probably leave exporting sensitive materials to somebody else, but if you simply must send sensitive materials, be sure to contact the Department of Commerce first. It can tell you if your potential export is on the CCL (you read about this in Chapter 5, remember?), which means it needs a validated license.

▶ *Consular Invoice.* Not every country will demand one of these—the ranks are mostly filled by emerging nation types. Basically, a consular invoice is one in which you fill out a form available from the local consulate office here in the States, pay a nominal sum, and go on your merry way. Certified by a consular official of the foreign country, it is used by the country's customs officials to verify the value, quantity, and nature of the shipment. The presumed idea behind the invoice is to ensure that overpriced or underpriced goods don't enter the country, but in actuality it's a sort of collection plate for the national economy.

▶ *Dock Receipts.* This receipt is used if the importer is responsible for shipment from a U.S. port. It verifies that the merchandise has indeed made it as far as the dock.

▶ *Inspection Certificate.* The importer may request one of these to certify the quantity, quality, and/or conformity of the product. Suppose you are bringing in cookie-making equipment. You may want to have an inspector check the machines to make sure they're in good working order before you take title. You can elect a standard export inspection, which is done by a standard inspector nominated by the exporter or shipping line, or you can hire a specialized private company to

warning

Do you need to submit an SED (Shipper's Export Declaration) for shipments to and from U.S. territories and possessions? The answer depends on where you're shipping to and from. Check with your freight forwarder, a customs broker, or the Foreign Trade Division Regulations people (www.census.gov/foreign-trade/index.html). Click on "Regulations."

do the job. Inspection certificates are often obtained from independent testing organizations.

▶ *Insurance Certificate*. This confirms that marine insurance has been provided for the cargo and indicates the type and coverage. Insurance is covered in greater detail within Chapter 9.

▶ *Packing List*. The packing list or packing slip is a sort of shopping list of the merchandise in the shipment, along with information on how it was packed, how the various items are numbered, the serial numbers, if applicable, and weight and dimensions of each item. The packing list is an important ingredient in the L/C because it (again) verifies the shipped goods and shows to whom they're consigned. You'll find a sample packing list in Figure 6–7, page 100, and a form you can adapt for your business in Figure 6–8, page 101.

▶ *Shipper's Export Declaration (SED)*. This is required by the U.S. government on all exports in excess of $2,500 or that require an export license. The reason behind it is to give the folks down at the Census Bureau fodder for their statistics (which you, for one, will probably want to take advantage of during your market research phase), and it gives all the usual information, including product descriptions, value, net and gross weight, and license information.

The Importer at Work

You've found the merchandise you want to buy and then resell as an importer. Here's what happens next:

1. Receive pro forma invoice, the exporter's quote on the merchandise; negotiate if necessary.
2. Open a letter of credit at your bank.
3. Receive confirmation of the deal and a schedule for loading and arrival of the goods.
4. File an electronic Importer Security Filing (ISF) form at least 24 hours prior to merchandise loading at the point of origin.
5. Verify that the merchandise has indeed been shipped.
6. Receive documents from the exporter.
7. See merchandise through customs.
8. Collect your merchandise.

We've already covered the pro forma invoice, the request to open a letter of credit (L/C), and the L/C itself in Chapter 5, but here's what else you need to know.

Sample Packing List

From: Coffee Holic Exports

123 Cafe Street

Berry, FL 30000, USA

To: Cappuccino Imports

456 Via Espresso

Ostia Antica, Italy

Date: July 15, 20XX

Per your order __No. L/C 0123__, the following merchandise has been shipped to __Rome__, departing __August 3, 20XX__, by ship.

Item Number	Quantity Ordered	Quantity Shipped	Description
Style A	5,000	5,000	Insulated Plastic Coffee Go-Cups

No. containers & type: _50 cardboard boxes_

Weight per container: _4 kilos_

Dimensions of each container: _3.5 x 3.5 x 3.5 meters_

Containers numbered: _1/50_

Marks: _Cappuccino Imports_

Ostia Antica, Italy

Boxes 1/50

FIGURE 6–7: **Sample Packing List**

Packing List

From: _____

_____

_____

To: _____

_____

_____

Date: _____

Per your order _____, the following merchandise has been shipped to _____, departing _____, by ship .

Item Number	Quantity Ordered	Quantity Shipped	Description

No. containers & type:_____

Weight per container: _____

Dimensions of each container:_____

Containers numbered: _____

Marks: _____

_____

_____

FIGURE 6–8: **Packing List**

The Importer Security Filing (ISF)

As an importer/exporter, you'll likely need to develop at least a basic understanding of the maritime shipping regulations that the Customs and Border Protection (CBP) agency enforces. Before going into the details, let us first say that these regulations affect only non-bulk goods arriving by sea to a U.S. port. If your merchandise is flown into the U.S. or shipped to Mexico or Canada, and then trucked or railed into the U.S., it (and you) are exempt from these requirements. Bulk cargo (e.g., grain, coal, oil) is also exempt.

The Importer Security Filing (ISF) regulations require carriers and importers to provide the CBP (www.cbp.gov), via a CBP-approved electronic data interchange system, with information to assist the agency in identifying high-risk shipments to prevent smuggling and ensure cargo safety and security.

Importers and carriers must submit specific information before the cargo is brought into the U.S. by vessel in accordance with specified time frames.

For security purposes, ISF (more commonly called ISF 10+2) requires containerized cargo information to be transmitted to the agency at least 24 hours before goods are loaded onto an ocean vessel headed to the U.S.

The goal of the measure is to ensure supply chain security back to the point of stuffing (i.e., packing) the shipping container. The information provided on the ISF form is used only for security purposes. It is not a substitute for the entry documents.

Due to the Additional Carrier Requirements, the ISF is known as ISF 10+2 because importers are required to electronically file 10 (actually, 11, but we'll get to that later) data points about the shipping containers' contents, and carriers (i.e., shipping companies) are required to file an additional two pieces of data. Even though you're not responsible for the last two, we'll cover them in the next section.

So, what are the 10 data points? They include the following:

1. *Seller's name and address.* This refers to the exporter, as listed on the commercial invoice.
2. *Buyer's name and address.* This is the importer from the commercial invoice.
3. *Importer of record number/foreign trade zone applicant identification number.* This is the importer's IRS, EIN, Social Security, or importer's ID number. If you're having the goods stashed in a foreign trade zone (FTZ), you must also provide an appropriate number.
4. *Consignee number(s).* This is the IRS (or other, see above) number of the individual on whose account the cargo is shipped. This number will often be the same as item 3.
5. *Manufacturer (supplier) name and address.*

6. *Ship-to name and address.* This is the information for the person who will physically receive the goods.

7. *Country of origin code.* This is the code for the country of manufacture, growth, etc., of the goods, as used by U.S. Customs.

8. *Commodity Harmonized Tariff Schedule (HTS) number—first six digits.* The HTS is the primary resource for determining tariff (customs duties) classifications for goods imported into the U.S. Because of the ISF requirement, goods must now be pre-classified instead of simply being classified upon arrival at customs. Because classification is still part of the entry process, however, we'll discuss it later in the "Entry" section of this chapter (see page 105).

9. *Container stuffing location.* This is the location where the goods were put into the containers. Since this can sometimes change at the last minute, customs gives importers more time to file this information.

10. *Consolidator's name and address.* This is the information about the individual who stuffs the container. Often, this, too, can't be determined much in advance, so importers are given extra time to submit this information as well.

As for that previously mentioned 11th data point, let's focus on the master bill of lading (B/L) number. We discussed the bill of lading at the beginning of the chapter. You must file these data points well in advance of the goods' arrival in the U.S. In fact, the first eight must be filed no later than 24 hours before loading the cargo. If the ISF information is not filed, the cargo will not be loaded.

Sometimes changes to the data occur in transit. For example, if the ship-to party changes or the cargo containers ended up being stuffed somewhere other than where you indicated, you must update your ISF filing with these changes before the goods arrive in the U.S.

Besides completing the ISF filing, importers (or their representatives) are required to post bond. The bond assures customs that the ISF will be timely, accurate, and complete—in other words, not a headache or time-sink for customs.

Automated Manifest System

The Automated Manifest System (AMS), which is used for the processing of electronic air manifests, is now governed by U.S. Customs and Border Protection. The purpose of AMS is to provide:

► Increased validation of submitted data to ensure compliance with established standardized requirements. Data elements, subject to increased validation, necessary for successful processing include:

- Header format must comply with published Implementation Guide in Appendix D of the Customs Automated Manifest Interface Requirements (CAMIR).
- Consignee country codes must be entered and valid.
- Shipment weight values must be numeric and greater than zero.
- Bonds must be on file and valid.

▶ New system validations providing more descriptive language for error codes

warning

If you fail to submit an ISF and your cargo is inadvertently loaded anyway, it's likely to be off-loaded at another port of call before reaching the U.S. This will create a logistical problem—and considerable expense—for you.

If you are using the AMS or the Automated Commercial System (ACS), which is also referred to as the Automated Broker Interface (ABI), you must complete the process no later than 24 hours prior to loading of the goods at the foreign port. This means that the importer must stay "up to speed" on when the goods are to be loaded and when they are scheduled to arrive in the U.S.

According to the U.S. Customs and Border Protection's website, "The Automated Commercial System (ACS) is the system used by CBP to track, control, and process all commercial goods imported into the United States. ACS facilitates merchandise processing, significantly cuts costs, and reduces paperwork requirements for both CBP and the trade community." More information about ABI can be found by pointing your web browser to: www.cbp.gov/trade/acs/abi/contact-info.

Note that noncompliance with the ISF filing requirement results in fines, usually 20 percent of the dutiable value of the goods. Keep in mind, the ISF 10+2 electronic filing requirement applies only to non-bulk goods arriving by sea to a U.S. port.

You can be fined up to $5,000 by the local port for each violation related to not properly utilizing AMS or ACS. So, it's important that you carefully review the ISF 10+2.

If your head's spinning right about now, or you're worried about completing your ISF filing successfully, take heart. You can (and probably should) have a representative do it for you. Also, a quick Google search of "ISF 10+2" will produce links for numerous logistics and regulatory compliance companies that will handle the filing for you.

Understand Who Is Responsible for Handling Specific Requirements

While the goods are in transit, the shipping company is responsible for completing the "+2" part of the equation, aka the Additional Carrier Requirements. These two submitted data points are the following:

1. *Vessel stow plan.* This indicates how the container is stowed on board.
2. *Container status.* This is a confirmation that the container remains secure.

Both data points must be submitted no later than 48 hours after departure.

If a voyage is shorter than 48 hours in duration, the CBP must receive the stow plan before the vessel arrives at the first port in the U.S. If the vessel is carrying "bulk and break" goods (also known as "general cargo") that need to be individually loaded and are not in bulk, such as grain, or in intermodal containers, they are exempt from this requirement.

You've Arrived

When the goods arrive, the importer takes over. The first task is to move the new arrivals through customs. This is usually managed by a customs broker. In fact, unless you have an import license (for which you have to take a government-administered test), you typically can't take your own merchandise through customs.

Still, it's important to know how your merchandise gets imported. The more you know, the better you'll be able to help your customs broker—and yourself. There are four basic steps to taking your goods through customs:

1. *Entry.* Deciding where and how you'll enter your merchandise
2. *Examination and valuation.* Determining the legality and tariff or duty value of your goods
3. *Classification.* Determining the percentage of tax that will be charged on the value of your merchandise
4. *Payment and liquidation.* Coughing up the cash to pay the tariff or duties

But let's take this one item at a time.

Entry

There are eight main types of import entry into the U.S.:

1. *Consumption entry.* Merchandise to be offered for sale
2. *Formal entry.* Goods worth more than $2,500
3. *Informal entry.* Goods worth $2,500 or less
4. *In-transit entry.* Goods moving from the port of unloading to the port of destination
5. *Mail entry.* Items sent by another country's mail system
6. *Personal baggage entry.* Goods arriving in a passenger's suitcase
7. *Transportation and exportation entry.* Goods arriving at a nondestination country's port and passing through to the destination country

8. *Warehouse entry.* Goods sent to a bonded warehouse or a foreign trade zone

tip

In the event of a change in the party receiving the goods, a negotiable bill of lading or document can be used to claim title to the merchandise; a non-negotiable one cannot.

While it's good to know about these entry types, the most common distinction is between informal and formal entry and involves the value of the goods. Some informal entries can be made without a customs broker, if the merchandise is imported by an individual for personal use or sale in the individual's shop and the merchandise is worth $2,500 or less. Merchandise imported by a trader, no matter how small its value, must be handled by a customs broker.

Because this book is all about the business of being an international trader, we're going to go with the formal entry version of the customs game. This means you'll need a customs broker to handle the entry for you.

Special Operations

There are a few circumstances that don't fit the usual import scenarios. For example, what do you do if you want to travel abroad with your sales samples so you can show them to prospective buyers?

You could go through the whole complicated import process in each country. Or you can take your samples on the Grand Tour duty-free with an ATA carnet. ATA is an acronym for the combined French and English "Admission Temporaire" or "Temporary Admission." It means exactly what it says, in whichever language you choose. The carnet is also known as a Merchandise Passport for the goods that will be imported for a limited time. It is an international customs document that gets the merchandise into certain countries without any duties paid until they're returned to home port. The ATA carnet is:

► valid for one year;
► good for as many international stops as you care to make with it during that year, and
► used not only for commercial samples but advertising materials and professional equipment as well.

Currently over 85 countries and territories recognize the ATA carnet. Visit www.atacarnet.com for a complete list. If you're trading with Taiwan, you'll need a TECRO/AIT carnet (www.atacarnet.com/advisory/tecroait-carnet-taiwan). It is the only country that accepts this type of carnet.

Another possible scenario involves bringing items into the U.S. temporarily for purposes, including (but not limited to) samples, display items, emergency use, and products for fairs or exhibitions.

If you need to import vehicles for building, bicycles for an international race, fine art or theatrical materials for show, merchandise samples for pre-selling, or a host of other possibilities, you can bring them into the country (duty-free) with a Temporary Importation Under Bond (TIB).

With a TIB, you post a bond for double the estimated duty amount, thus assuring the customs people that you'll cover the import fees should you fail to return the samples to their country of origin within one year. This period may, with the grace of the district or port director, be extended for up to three years.

You can obtain a carnet in four simple steps:

▶ Gather information listed on the application checklist.
▶ Register for an online account.
▶ Log in to complete and submit the online carnet and bond application.
▶ While logged in, provide payment method and method of overnight delivery.

Customs Limbo

According to U.S. Customs, goods brought into the country are in a sort of import limbo—not considered legally entered—until after the following actions have been taken:

▶ Shipment has arrived within the port of entry.
▶ Delivery of merchandise has been authorized.
▶ Customs duty has been paid.

When your merchandise arrives at the U.S. port of entry (the dock, airport, or border), the carrier submits the bill of lading or air waybill to the on-site customs office. This document is now known as evidence of right to make entry.

The shipper notifies your customs broker—and the clock starts ticking. Your broker has 15 days to provide the necessary documents to get your goods out of hock. You and your broker will probably already have a fair idea of when your merchandise is due to arrive because the exporter will have notified you of its ETA and the vessel it's coming in on.

warning

If you don't file for entry of your merchandise within 15 days, customs considers it abandoned and puts it into a bonded warehouse of its own under general order, otherwise known as G.O. After a six-month holding period, G.O. goods are sold at public auction unless they're perishable or explosive, in which case they get dealt with a lot sooner.

Released from Custody

Next up is entering your merchandise. The most common type of entry is called entry for consumption. This, of course, is consumption as in "to be consumed" (i.e., used or sold), and the customs people have handily broken down this stage of the process into two parts:

1. Filing the documents necessary to determine whether merchandise may be released from customs custody
2. Filing the documents that contain information for assessing duty and for statistical purposes

Here's a list of the entry documents your customs broker will need:

- ▶ Entry manifest (also known as Customs Form 7533) or Application and Special Permit for Immediate Delivery (aka Customs Form 3461)
- ▶ Bill of lading or air waybill (also known as the evidence of right to make entry)
- ▶ Commercial invoice or pro forma invoice if the commercial one can't be produced
- ▶ Packing lists
- ▶ Certificate of origin, if necessary
- ▶ Customs bond (which is posted by your broker and assures customs that it will get the duties, taxes, and any penalties out of you one way or another)

You can see why it's so important to do your homework and make sure the exporter sends you copies of all documents ASAP.

Your Merchandise Is About to Be Released

After customs has gone through all these documents, accepted the bond, and decided that everything's legal and up to snuff, the merchandise is released. You could say, however, it's out on bail, pending the last two phases of the customs game.

The first of these is the entry summary documentation. Now your broker has ten days to deposit the estimated duties and file the necessary documentation, namely:

- ▶ Entry summary (also known as Customs Form 7501)
- ▶ Any other invoices and documents necessary for the assessment of duties, collection of statistics, or other determination that you've met import requirements

Warehousing (Storage) Options

Just because your merchandise has arrived at the port of entry doesn't mean that you have to rush home with it right away. In fact, you don't even have to enter it immediately. You can choose instead to stash it in a bonded warehouse or transport it to a foreign trade zone.

A bonded warehouse is a yard, shed, storage area, or warehouse within customs territory where you can store your imported merchandise for up to five years without paying duty. While your goodies are in the bonded warehouse, you can clean, sort, and repack them, but that's it. You can't assemble them or attach them to something else and create a new product in the process. It's called a bonded facility because the owner has to post a bond with customs.

A foreign trade zone, or FTZ, is a secure area under control of the U.S. Customs and Border Protection (CBP) that is generally considered outside CBP territory upon activation. They are typically found near CBP ports of entry and are often in the form of a warehouse.

An FTZ is the U.S.'s version of what is known internationally as a free trade zone. You can use an FTZ to store and process your imported goods without having to pay duties or jump through the usual customs hoops. Although it sounds like it might be a chunk of foreign land floating somewhere above the surface of American soil, an FTZ is much more prosaic.

Unlike the bonded warehouse, the FTZ allows you the freedom to assemble or manufacture your goodies into any product you choose. Local governments set up FTZs to promote international trade, which, in turn, stimulates economic growth. What the FTZ means to you is savings.

If you plan to export the merchandise immediately and you're only holding it in the U.S. for a short time, you get away with not having to pay customs duties. If you're going to enter the products into the country, you can alter or modify them to lower the import costs.

For example, you might bring in fancy sequined fabric squares from Thailand and sew them onto American-made cushions to create decorator throw pillows. When you're ready to bring them out of the FTZ, you pay duties on the throw pillows. If duties on throw pillows are cheaper than those on the sequined fabric squares, the FTZ saves you money.

Another FTZ bonus is that you can get around the import quota issue. If U.S. Customs allows only so many straw hats, for example, per year, and that quota has already been filled, you might hold onto your hats in your FTZ space until the next quota period rolls around.

tip

In special cases, such as with perishable items, customs will issue a permit for immediate release of goods. (After all, customs isn't stupid; it doesn't particularly want 500 kilos of fish sitting on its dock for five days or more.) You can't make up your mind at the last minute, however; you must apply for the permit before your merchandise has arrived.

You would probably use the bonded warehouse when planning a quick in-and-out entry for your merchandise, while you'd use the FTZ when you need to manipulate your products as we've explored. As always, the best way to choose which to use is to consult your customs broker or freight forwarder.

We are not the only country with foreign trade zones. Every country uses a different term, but the idea is the same. As an exporter, you can use these zones to receive goods that will be reshipped in smaller lots to customers in the region.

Earlier in this chapter we mentioned eight main types of customs entry. It's worth saying a little more here about the three you're most likely to deal with.

1. *Consumption entry.* You already know this one. It's used when the merchandise is intended for immediate resale. This type is the most common.

2. *In-transit entry.* This is used when you want the goods whisked to another location within the U.S. for customs clearance. For instance, you may have arranged to have them brought in by ship to New York, but you want to store—and assemble—them in an FTZ in Ohio.

3. *Warehouse entry.* This is sort of a layaway plan. You leave your imported goods in a customs-bonded warehouse and withdraw them in portions. Each time you make a withdrawal, you pay duty on that part.

Examination and Valuation

After you've decided to enter your merchandise, customs personnel will inspect your shipment to make sure it can legally enter the country and to determine its tariff or duty value. Why do they want to dip into your goods? They're checking to verify the following:

▶ The merchandise is marked with the country of origin.
▶ Any required markings or labels are clearly displayed.
▶ The merchandise is correctly invoiced.
▶ The merchandise quantity matches the quantity on the invoice.
▶ The shipment contains no prohibited articles.
▶ The shipment contains no illegal drugs.

They're also checking the dutiable status and value of your goods. The value is the price you've paid for the merchandise, plus any added amounts, if not included in the price. These added amounts include the following:

▶ Packing costs incurred by the importer

▶ The value of any assists (which can be a tool, die, mold, engineering drawing, or artwork; in other words, something that assists in the assembly and sale of the product)

▶ Any selling commission incurred by the importer

▶ A royalty or license fee required from the importer as part of the sale

▶ The proceeds accrued by the exporter of any subsequent resale, disposal, or use of the imported goods

You can see why it's important to make sure everything is listed on the commercial invoice!

Classification

The Customs Service classifies goods according to tariff schedules. Different types of goods are assigned different percentages on which they're taxed. The amount of duty varies dramatically depending on what the products are and what they're made of. Cotton knit shirts, for example, may be taxed at 17 percent, while woven (nonknit) cotton shirts might be taxed at only 8 percent.

▶ Last Person in America

U.S. Customs insists that each item imported into the country be marked or labeled with the country of origin. The marking must be clearly visible to the ultimate end user, which refers to "the last person in the U.S. who will receive the article in the form in which it was imported."

In other words, if you're importing ceramic pigs from the Emerald Isle, each little porker must be stamped or labeled "Made in Ireland" on its underside so the last person in the U.S. can tip over the little chap and read where he came from. You can't settle for a "Made in Ireland" marking on the box in which a dozen pigs are shipped, because the ultimate consumer will probably only be buying one piglet at a time.

There are, of course, exceptions to this rule, and they're rather eclectic. Because you can't know and probably could never guess the extent of all these exceptions, it's best to check with your customs broker while you're still in the final negotiations stage with the exporter.

You don't want someone shipping you 1,000 bales of barbed wire you can't use because it's unmarked. Nor do you want to pay extra for marking 5,000 ceramic bricks from Mexico when it's unnecessary.

During the classification step, the customs people will decide which category your merchandise falls into. Their decision is based on an extremely complicated set of rules called the Harmonized Tariff Schedule of the United States (HTS).

The word "harmonized" refers to the fact that it harmonizes with, or matches, the tariff schedules of the rest of the industrialized world. The harmonized schedule comes in a book big enough to serve as a booster chair for a hefty three-year-old and is jam-packed with enough classifications, subclassifications, and sub-subclassifications to satisfy even the most nit-picking person on earth. You can access the most up-to-date version at: www.usitc.gov/tata/hts/index.htm.

aha!

Another way you can find Harmonized Tariff Schedule (HTS) numbers online is by going to: http://findhts.com.

Cotton fabric, for example, is classified by whether it's bleached or unbleached, printed, composed of yarns of a different color or dyed, whether it's pure cotton or a mix of fibers, the number of single threads per square centimeter, yarn sizes in the warp, whether the fabric is or is not napped, etc. Even fish livers must be classified by how much oil, fat, or grease they contain. Now you see why you need a customs broker!

As mentioned in the "Adding 10+2" section of this chapter, if your goods are non-bulk items and are arriving in the U.S. by sea, pre-classification of the goods is required before they're even loaded onto the ocean carrier. Any classification disagreement that might arise is handled at entry.

If, however, your goods are not arriving by sea or if they are bulk items like grain or oil, classification will be handled at entry. Note that the broker, while versed in the harmonized system and armed with the basic HTS number for your merchandise, is not the one who hands down the final classification decision. This falls to the customs officer. Teams of customs inspectors rove each port of entry, with various inspectors specializing in different types of goods.

Payment and Liquidation

Now that your merchandise has been classified, it's on to the exciting phase of paying the piper, or in this case, the customs person. As with many assignments under government aegis, this is not always a simple, cut-and-dried operation.

It can be, of course. Your entry summary and documentation can be accepted as submitted without any changes. In this case, you simply hand over a check for the amount of duty, or tariff, owed, and your merchandise or entry is entered as liquidated. This means done, over, finished, complete. You and customs have figuratively shaken hands and closed the books.

In other cases, however, customs may send you notification that the classification is not correct and cannot be liquidated as entered after all. If the revised classification results in a tariff change in your favor, they'll send you a refund. Like their compatriot, the IRS, however, they can also decide on a change in their own favor, in which case you need to send them money.

If you don't agree with the change, you have 90 days to file a protest, which then goes on to review or, in some cases, to court. The entry is not considered liquidated until the final ruling.

A Happy Ending

Nothing makes customs inspectors happier than a shipment they can go through easily. Suggest that your exporter follow these customs tips:

- ▶ Invoice merchandise in a systematic manner.
- ▶ Show the exact quantity of goods in each box, bale, case, or other package.
- ▶ Number each package (e.g., box three of four).
- ▶ Put these numbers on the invoice next to the itemized goods in each package.

Once you have your happy ending, with your goods safely in your possession, you can get to the fun part: selling! Provided, of course, you know who you're selling to. The next chapter covers this topic, among others.

warning

Don't wait for a last-minute shocker when you learn the import tariff. Make sure you've checked with your customs broker for an idea of what the HTS number for your products will be before you bring them into the country. Don't leave it to customs to decide this number; there's a fee for that!

Market Research

I n order to prosper, every business needs consumers for its products and services. Now that you know what running an import/export business entails, you need to plan, or target, your market. In other words, determine who your potential clients will be, which geographic areas you'll draw from, and what specific products or services you'll offer to draw them in.

The proper market research can help boost your trading company into a true profit center. The more research you do and the better prepared you are before you officially open your doors, the less floundering you're likely to do.

This chapter focuses on providing market research tips and techniques for the newbie importer/exporter. Ultimately, you'll want to do some in-depth investigation into each of the following areas:

aha!

Trade shows, art festivals, crafts shows, internet searches, and small shops (that specialize in locally made goods) are all good venues for spotting the perfect international trade product.

▶ The product or service you plan to sell
▶ The end user you'll aim for (mass-market consumer, heavy industry, light industry, medical or hospital use, government, business, professional, etc.)
▶ The country or countries you'll export to or import from
▶ The trade channel(s) you'll use (direct sales, representative, distributor, or commission representative)

See Figure 7–1 for a product market research worksheet to help you make all these important decisions.

Product Market Research Worksheet

Use this worksheet for each product or service you're considering. Give each product a grade: Fantastic ("A"), Has Potential ("B"), or Not Such a Good Idea ("C"). When you've completed several sheets, compare them, weed out the "C's," and start working on the "A's." Keep the "B's" in mind for future reference.

1. Name or description of product _____

   _____

2. What are the product's selling features? _____

   _____

3. Are there competitive products? If so, list them: _____

   _____

FIGURE 7–1: **Product Market Research Worksheet**

Product Market Research Worksheet

4. What are their selling features? _____

_____

5. What is the sales potential of the product or service in my target market? _____

_____

6. What are comparably priced goods going for in my target market? _____

_____

7. Who will be the end user of the product? _____

_____

8. Who are your customers for this product, and how well do you know them? _____

_____

9. Is the population of potential end users large enough to have substantial sales? _____

_____

10. Can I expand the market, or is there limited space in the current market for expansion?

_____

11. Which elements have the most influence on potential customers or clients? Price, quality, brand name, "imported" cachet, service, credit terms, delivery terms, advertising, or marketing assistance? _____

_____

12. Where can I buy this product at a reasonable price? _____

_____

13. Will I need to have it manufactured, and how much will it cost? _____

_____

14. If I can afford to have it manufactured, what is the turnaround time for the product? Will the quality be good enough to garner a decent price? _____

_____

FIGURE 7–1: **Product Market Research Worksheet,** continued

Product Market Research Worksheet

15. What will be my cost for the product? _____
_____

16. What will my markup be? _____
_____

17. How will I market the product without spending a fortune? _____
_____

18. What variables will affect pricing (special packaging or marking requirements, special shipping requirements as for perishables, other variables)? _____
_____

19. What are the potential problems that will contribute to my price, such as end user unfamiliarity with the product or service? _____
_____

20. What are the potential benefits that can contribute to my price, such as high demand for the product or service? _____
_____
_____

21. What is the potential for licensing? _____
_____

22. Are there any add-ons I can market with the product? _____
_____

23. Is the product a fad or a trend, or is there potential market stability? _____
_____

24. Do I have ideas for follow-up products that will appeal to this same audience? _____
_____
_____

FIGURE 7–1: **Product Market Research Worksheet,** continued

Product Market Research Worksheet

25. If the product doesn't do as well as expected, do I have a backup plan for selling the goods elsewhere or at a discount where I will get some return on my investment?

_____

The Prospective Product's Final Grade: _____

FIGURE 7–1: **Product Market Research Worksheet,** continued

Manufacturer or Artisan?

Your target market, the customers you are aiming for, can encompass any product or service you can think up. Any manufacturer, supplier, importer, exporter, artisan, crafter, or retailer is fair game. You can go after companies that deal in heavy construction equipment or delicate jewelry, gourmet goodies or pet food, telecommunications or toys. The only essential requirement is that they want to sell their merchandise or buy someone else's.

Targeting by definition means finding your key demographic audience. Through due diligence, you can find the age group, gender, economic group, region of the country, and so much more about your potential sales market. You may also find out if the market is over-saturated or in need of your product. Doing this will help you decide whether to change products or how to move along quickly while the need remains.

If you have previous experience in a field, you should seriously consider targeting that market first. You'll feel comfortable with the jargon and procedures, so your sales pitch—and your initial sales—will go more smoothly and easily. As a bonus, you may already have contacts in the field who can either become your first clients or steer you toward colleagues in that area.

If you have a passion for an industry but are not yet the expert, take some time to study the field and seek a mentor.

Sometimes you can find a mentor at SCORE, a nonprofit organization that is supported by the SBA. SCORE has been helping entrepreneurs get started and

tip

Need information about a country? Get connected with every national embassy in Washington, DC, through http://embassy.org.

You can also get country-by-country statistics and other information through the World Bank at: http://data.worldbank.org.

grow their businesses for over 50 years. To learn more and to potentially find a mentor, point your web browser to: www.score.org.

Wahib Wahba began in a field he knew well—runway and navigational lights. Then he moved on to other international construction projects. His company exports railroad and telephone pole materials and construction services, as well as other heavy equipment materials.

Where in the World?

Besides deciding what products you'll specialize in, you'll want to think about what countries you'll work with. Some traders start with a part of the world they already know; others let their products be their guide.

Wahib Wahba, raised in Egypt, found exporting to Egypt a natural. North Carolina exporter Sam Nelson began his trade with Africa, where he had contacts. He now also exports to the Middle East and Europe, among other places.

In Brazil, John Laurino works mostly with Brazilian companies locating and developing international business opportunities. Searching for leads for these clients takes him around the globe. "I have business relations throughout the entire world, except places very poor in foreign trade," he explained.

In Germany, Michael Richter counts only one area of the world where he hasn't done business. "[I have dealt] with all internationally interesting markets worldwide," he said, "except South America, as I don't speak Spanish."

Check out Figure 7–2, page 121, for a worksheet to help you determine your best market.

What's Your Niche?

Now that you've narrowed the list of products you'll target, it's time to figure out your niche, the unique angle that will set your business apart from—and above—the competition.

This is where you should let your creativity shine. In addition to importing the goods, you can decorate them, package them together, or, depending on the items, offer them for an exclusive price (e.g., unique, high-end goods at a discount).

There's a market for almost everything; you just have to find it and see if there is enough markup for you to make it worthwhile after buying the product and importing it. Conversely, you'll have to export goods with the same mindset.

If your buyers know they cannot make a profit after buying from you and paying to import the product, they will go elsewhere. Sources for finding import/export customers

Country Market Research Worksheet

Once you've done your product market research (or at the same time, if your market is intrinsic to product sales), move on to this worksheet. Make copies and use one for each country you're considering. Then give each one a grade: "A" for Fantastic, "B" if it has Potential, or "C" if it's Not Such a Good Idea. When you've completed several sheets, compare them, weed out the "C's", start working on the "A's," and keep the "B's" on file for future reference.

1. Why does this country have potential for my product or service? _____

   _____

2. How can I gain exposure in this country? _____

   _____

   _____

3. Will I need to travel abroad to find markets, conduct research, and find distributors, or can I do this at home via the internet and phone calls? _____

   _____

   _____

4. Will I encounter language barriers or difficulties? _____

   _____

5. What cultural differences will I need to account for? _____

   _____

6. How will I handle them? _____

   _____

7. What is the economic climate (on a national level—unemployment rates, inflation, or depression; on a personal level—disposable incomes, spending patterns)? Has the economy been stable or volatile over the last five, or even ten years? You don't want to enter a country that has had significant economic changes. _____

   _____

   _____

FIGURE 7–2: **Country Market Research Worksheet**

Country Market Research Worksheet

8. What is the sociological climate (urban and rural populations, literacy and educational levels, any special religious considerations)? _____
   _____

9. What is the political climate? Has it been stable in recent years? _____
   _____

10. Will I experience any special shipping or handling problems because of geography or local customs? If so, what? _____
    _____

11. What trade channel will I use (direct sales, representative, distributor, commission representative)? _____
    _____

12. How will I locate my trade channel people? _____
    _____

13. What will contribute to my price, such as quotas, tariffs duties, or specific country regulations? _____
    _____

14. What are the country-specific benefits that can contribute to my price, such as duty-free or low trade barriers? _____
    _____

Final Grade: _____

It's important to remember that if you fill out these pages but don't take action within a year or so, you should go back and do some research since a lot can change, such as a country's politics and economy.

FIGURE 7–2: **Country Market Research Worksheet,** continued

are abundant. But as an international trader, the trick lies not merely in what information you can find, but in what you do with it.

You may decide to start as an export management company (EMC), seeking buyers for domestic manufacturing firms, or as an export trading company (ETC), finding domestic sources willing to export. Alternatively, you might want to stick with the more typical formula of importing and exporting on your own as an import/export merchant. Or you could structure your business as an EMC for a particular type of merchandise or for a particular country.

In Florida, Lloyd Davidson positioned his company as both an EMC and ETC, depending on his clients' needs. "[As an EMC, we] work directly for a manufacturer, or his exclusive distributor/manager for international sales, as a marketing and screening provider," Lloyd explained. "We will search for and locate overseas buyers-for-resale and/or qualified distributors/sales representatives. [Our] objective is to function as an extension of [our] principal's in-house export sales efforts."

Under its ETC hat, Lloyd said, "My company performs in a fashion similar to that previously described, except for a diminished principal relationship, and business is typically conducted on a case-by-case or ad hoc basis. It is more a sourcing function for the buyer and the seller."

John Laurino in Brazil also has structured his business from the viewpoint of assisting clients rather than selling products. "My company is an international business services provider. We assist companies in locating and developing worldwide business opportunities," he stated.

In Germany, Michael Richter described his company's role as "a worldwide consultancy to SMEs [small- and medium-size enterprises] that wish to increase their sales and profits by using the available world markets more successfully."

In France, Bruno Carlier works with a broad range of merchandise. "We export a wide range of products, from protection and security products to computing products," he said. "We also export products such as plastic films and bags and some ferrous and aluminum products."

Sam Nelson, in North Carolina, sells medical equipment manufactured in either the U.S. or China to companies in both developing nations and highly industrialized countries. "We trade all over," he explained.

These strategies are all excellent examples of finding a unique angle.

Another good strategy might be to consider worldwide social movements that appear to be gaining momentum and could provide good trading opportunities. Presently, we can identify two: sustainable growth and fair trade. We discuss these in the next few sections. But be forewarned that trends and social movements change often, so be alert.

Give Old Products a New Purpose

"Reduce, Reuse, Recycle" is a popular slogan. It's not a bad idea for trading either, especially if you want to export to countries less wealthy than the typical highly industrialized nations.

In Belgium, Jan Herremans specializes in the worldwide import and export of new and used tires, secondhand vehicles and machinery, and secondhand clothing.

Secondhand items are a good example of the "reuse" philosophy. If you're considering exporting secondhand items, give emerging market countries a closer look.

Like small, high-growth companies, emerging markets are characterized by high potential—and high risk. The Pacific Rim markets, for example, grew rapidly, then collapsed in 1997 and 1998. Use the phrase "emerging markets" in any search engine to find articles and listings of countries that fit the emerging markets category. The concept of emerging markets and what constitutes an emerging market are covered in Chapter 1.

Many emerging market countries are good candidates for the following secondhand items:

tip

Used clothing is graded from AAA (highest quality) down to B (lowest quality), with AA, A, and A-B in between. Sold wholesale in 1,000-pound or 100-pound bales with typical minimum orders of 20,000 pounds and prices ranging from $.15 per pound to $2.25 per pound, used clothing comprises everything from suits to swimwear. Check out online information and videos at sites like: http://bestusedclothing.com.

- ► *Clothing.* The U.S. generates 1.4 tons of used clothing annually. According to numerous online sites dedicated to used clothing exporters, 800,000 tons of used clothes are exported from the U.S. each year.
- ► *Designer clothing and accessories* (e.g., hats, purses, belts). Eastern European countries, with their increasing exposure to Western fashion but lack of corresponding wealth, may be good markets for these items.
- ► *Jewelry.* Eastern European countries as well as developing nations in Asia and Africa are good possibilities.
- ► *Household goods.* All the countries listed for items above are good candidates.

One way to recycle is to create something new with discarded material. "Generally, I think new products made from recycled materials is a wide-open field," said industry expert Wendy Larson. "Consumers all over the world could respond to that message."

A variety of online services focus on high-end used clothing, fashion accessories, and household items, such as Poshmark (www.poshmark.com), TheRealReal (www.therealreal.com), Tradesy (www.tradesy.com), and FashionPhile (www.fashionphile.com).

Organically Yours

Another aspect of the environmentally conscious sustainability movement is organic products. Wendy Larson, member of the Organic Trade Association (www.ota.com) and manager/CEO of a marketing cooperative, noted double-digit growth in the past and predicts a strong future for the organics industry.

"The newest generation of consumers is eager to do better in caring for our environment," she explained. "Consumers realize that the choices they make with their buying dollars have longer impact than just today's comforts."

Your choices in organic exports are enormous. Nuts, grains, dairy products, meat, fruits, vegetables, and frozen foods are just a sampling. Other possibilities, especially for emerging markets, include agricultural goods like organic seeds and fertilizers.

Fair and Square

You could also decide to specialize in Fair Trade goods. The World Fair Trade Organization (WFTO) has a directory where you can find supplier sources for giftware, household goods, furniture, and clothing. Find them online at: www.wfto.com.

The Fair Trade movement is an organized social movement to help producers in developing countries get higher payments for their goods. Proponents of the Fair Trade movement include organizations like Serrv International, Oxfam International, and Amnesty International.

WFTO's website lists its ten principles of fair trade:

tip

According to the International Centre for Trade and Sustainable Development, sustainable practices can lower costs and make U.S. exports more competitive. Check out this organization at: www.ictsd.org.

1. Operations for disadvantaged producers
2. Transparency and accountability
3. Fair trade practices
4. No child labor/no forced labor
5. Fair payment
6. Good working conditions
7. No discrimination/gender equality/freedom of association
8. Capacity building
9. Promote fair trade
10. The environment

My Mission: Trade

As an import/export newbie, you may start by simply selling your clients' products in foreign markets. Acting as their representative, you'll transact business in their name for a commission, salary, or retainer and commission.

Again, you need to research your market, find out what sorts of buyers are available, and know the types of goods they're buying. This is an extremely important step in setting up your international trade business, one you cannot afford to overlook.

As long as you're hoping to export goods out of the U.S., an array of resources are available. Because exports give the economy a big charge, government agents are happy to help you sell just about anything to foreign markets.

Arguably the largest clearinghouse of information for finding foreign buyers is the International Trade Administration (ITA), a division of the U.S. Department of Commerce.

► Support Services EMC

As your niche, you might specialize in smaller manufacturers that haven't considered exporting or maybe providers of services—everything from bridge building to telecommunications—that have no idea how to go about it. For these people, you might promote yourself as a sort of support services EMC, a full-service company offering everything for the international product wannabe. Consider doing any—or some combination of—the following:

- ► Finding, evaluating, and appointing dealers, distributors, and commission representatives in foreign markets

- ► Providing all promotional support: advertising, marketing, and trade show exhibitions

- ► Translating documents and correspondence

- ► Preparing all foreign distributor agreements

- ► Preparing all acceptances and approvals

- ► Arranging financing

- ► Overseeing all order-processing correspondence

- ► Managing all shipping and documentation

- ► Providing all after-market assistance

Keep in mind, the ITA's Commercial Service is always willing to help you. Its only mission is to help you develop and flex your export wings, which it does by providing some phenomenal services—everything from country-specific market analyses to trade leads to setting up and chaperoning personal meetings between you and interested foreign businesspeople. The Commercial Service is one place you can see your tax dollars at work, seemingly just for you.

According to the Commercial Service website (www.trade.gov/cs) the organization's mission is: "To create prosperity by strengthening the competitiveness of U.S. industry, promoting trade and investment, and ensuring fair trade and compliance with trade laws and agreements."

The group employs trade specialists in more than 107 cities and more than 75 countries to help you meet your importing/exporting goals. Services include, according to the website, market research, export counseling trade leads, trade complaint filing, introductions to buyers and distributors, and advocacy services.

Unfortunately, if you're hoping to sell foreign-made merchandise in the U.S., you'll have to find this information without help from the government. Don't despair. There are still plenty of sources for market research. See the "Stay Up-to-Date by Reading Trade Publications" section on page 129.

Take Advantage of Export Market Research That's At Your Disposal

USA Trade Online (http://usatrade.census.gov) is a terrific source for export market research. Provided by the Foreign Trade Division of the Census Bureau, it is a comprehensive website that offers international trade data, profiles of companies, and much more.

A Ton of Research Is Just a Few Clicks Away

Panjiva (https://panjiva.com) is a company that helps people involved in international trade. It opens the door to finding companies with whom they want to do business.

Panjiva works with businesses in virtually all industries. Founder and CEO Josh Green explained, "If you're involved in international trade, it is likely we have the data you're looking for. We have many government sources, and governments are very good at seeing what crosses their borders. Many countries make the data about their shipments available. In fact, we get 35,000 shipping records every day, and we associate the shipments with the companies that are involved. That lets us tell a story that explains what each company is all about."

What that means to you as an importer is that if you are looking for a supplier of patio furniture, you can find out which companies are involved with patio furniture, and you can evaluate the companies to determine whether they are the ones you with whom you want to do business.

In business since 2006, Panjiva has played a role in thousands of trades. They've also seen the industry change. "Ten years ago when we walked into someone's office and told them that we could help them make decisions about where to do business, people in the industry would say, 'I've got relationships. I know somebody in China, I know somebody in Vietnam.' The import/export industry was largely a relationship business," explained Green.

"Today, the business has grown as people recognize it's a vast world of opportunities and that data needs to be part of their decision process," he added.

Technology is a tool that is helping importers and exporters find opportunities in places they had never dealt with in the past. Relationships are still important, but if, for example, your contact in China is forced to raise prices, you can find someone to work with in Korea or perhaps Cambodia or another country.

The Panjiva website has a ton of information that is available for free to the public, which helps people learn about their services. "Chances are if you do a search for a particular factory, the Panjiva review will probably come up high on the list," added Green. People can also pay for access to more detailed data if they find a business with whom they might want to make deals.

Where to Turn For Additional Guidance

U.S. Export Assistance Centers (USEACs) are, as their website explains, "The point of entry for U.S. businesses to receive trade counseling, advocacy, market intelligence, and business

---

▶ The ITA Is Also a Valuable Resource

The U.S. government's International Trade Administration (ITA) is on a mission—to help American businesses compete in the world marketplace by:

▶ Promoting and assisting American exports (and exporters)

▶ Assuring American businesses equal access to foreign markets

▶ Empowering American businesses to compete against unfairly traded imports

Among the many services for companies, the ITA U.S. Commercial Service offers trade counseling, market intelligence, business matchmaking, and commercial diplomacy. Visit: www.trade.gov/cs/services.asp

matchmaking services from the U.S. Commercial Service." This is a market research tool to make startup entrepreneurs in other industries start salivating with envy.

USEACs offer front-line outreach and service operations for U.S. exporters from international trade specialists working in over 100 locations in the U.S. and Puerto Rico. To find contact information and to schedule a meeting with a trade specialist, visit: http://2016.export.gov/usoffices/index.asp.

Stay Up-to-Date by Reading Trade Publications

You can find out a lot on your own by reading local, national, and international newspapers and trade publications—either in printed or online form—as well as by surfing international trade sites on the internet (see the Appendix for a list).

Individual importers and exporters are not quite as accessible as professionals in some other industries. They're often abroad on business, and when they're in the office, they're on overload with catch-up work. But if you present yourself in a pleasant and courteous manner, they may share their expertise with you.

You'll find international traders in online directories or in various industry associations (check out our Appendix for a list). If you plan to conduct a phone or in-person interview, be sure you call first to schedule a short meeting at a convenient time to your interviewee.

If you're approaching your subject via email, write a short note explaining that you'd like to conduct a "mini-interview online" or by phone and would like the opportunity to talk. It's professional courtesy to presume (correctly) that other people have busy schedules. Let your subject know the reason for the interview, about how much of their time you expect to take, and possibly even divulge a few of the questions you'll be asking. This will put them at ease about the interview and get them thinking ahead.

Most people, once you get them going, are happy to talk about themselves and their businesses. Take advantage of this to learn what you need to know, but don't monopolize a trader's time or personal space. Courtesy will get you further than you might imagine!

Now, with all these caveats firmly in mind, check out the "International Trader's Interview" in Figure 7–3 on page 130. Make copies and use it for phone or personal interviews, or use the questions for your email interview.

Consider checking out the Commercial Service's Matchmaker Trade Delegation program, the ultimate in "dating services" for the export-ready trader. For this one, you'll need to have your merchandise market research complete and be ready to implement sales.

Simply contact the Matchmaker people and they do everything necessary to introduce you to the right business contacts at trade delegations that target two or three countries with strong sales potential for American products.

International Trader's Interview

Company name: _____

Name and title of contact person: _____

1. What does your company do? Import, export, or both? _____
   _____

2. What types of products do you deal with? _____
   _____

3. Which products have you had the most success with and why? _____
   _____

4. Which products have you had the least success with and why? _____
   _____

5. What type of competition do you face? _____
   _____

6. What countries do you work with? _____
   _____

7. Where and how do you find most of your customers? _____
   _____

8. What is your trade channel? Do you use direct sales, sales representatives, distributors, or commission representatives? _____
   _____

9. Could you explain why? _____
   _____

10. What methods of transport do you prefer? _____
    _____

FIGURE 7–3: **International Trader's Interview**

The U.S. Department of Commerce staff will have completed all the legwork by the time you arrive in the country. The hotel reservations, meeting facilities, interpreters, and appointment schedules are all arranged for you. All you have to do is arrive ready to interview your potential business prospects.

As a Matchmaker delegate, here is what you get:

▶ Market analysis of your merchandise or service
▶ Two days of prescreened business appointments in each country
▶ In-depth market and trade finance briefings by both American government and local experts
▶ "Logistical support," including hotel reservations, interpreters, and meeting rooms
▶ Embassy receptions and site visits (with selected Matchmakers)
▶ Counseling and follow-up from your local Export Assistance Center

To learn more, use your favorite search engine (such as Google or Yahoo!) and enter "Commercial Services Matchmaker Trade Delegation."

Get Personalized Service from the Commercial Service

The Commercial Service offers its "Gold Key" program for exporters who want more personalized service. While the Matchmaker service sends you globe-trotting with 10 to 20 other company representatives and sets you all up with a booth and display, the Gold Key option finds potential partners for you and you alone—in the country you want. (With the Matchmaker program, you must choose from preset country formats.)

The basic charge for an agent distributor search will may vary depending on the country you choose. If you want star treatment—a car, an office, a driver, and interpreter—the bills grow from there. All you need to bring is your product or service literature.

Many Additional Resources Are at Your Disposal

As helpful as the Commercial Service's programs are, they're not your only option. You can find lots of other sources for market research and trade leads simply by surfing the internet. You will find many services out there with helpful information for newbie traders. Check out the following organizations:

▶ *The World Bank* (http://data.worldbank.org). This organization is a United Nations financial institution. It provides loans to developing countries, and it also provides an enormous quantity of data useful to, among others, importers and exporters. This data, which can be viewed on a country-by-country basis, can provide good ideas for trade leads.

► What's in a Lead?

So what does a trade lead look like? A text advertisement or invitation.

Company:	Car Hop Ltd.
Contact:	Ms. Daphne Denton
Position:	Head of Export
Business:	Car pennants and other designer car accessories
Address:	No. 1 The Groves, Greater Chestershire Industrial, Estate, Chestershire
Country:	Great Britain
Phone:	011-44-181-000000
Fax:	011-44-181-000001
Email:	carhop@holiday.com

Car pennants from CAR HOP LTD. are the latest in auto accessories. Find your vehicle fast in a crowded car park with these colorful plastic banners that extend from the radio aerial. Pennants can be had in a variety of sport team logos, with city names, or personalized with your name, your girlfriend's or your dog's names. Any color, text, and graphics. Gift shops, clubs, service stations, and auto parts centers sell our products. Dealer inquiries welcome. Ask for our detailed catalog, check their website, or inquire about your own designs. Also ask about your range of related CAR HOP accessories.

Date:	17 July 20XX
From:	Spencer Avalon
Company:	Avalon Traders Ltd.
Phone:	(000) 000-0000
Fax:	(000) 000-0001
Email:	avalon@holiday.com
Subject:	Pine Furniture
No. Units:	2 x 40 containers
When:	Immediate

Buyer's Location: Asia
Seeks Products From: USA and/or Canada
Transaction Range: $50,000+
Business Activity: Resell to dedicated distributors
Frequency: 4x per year
Acceptable Terms of Sale: FCA/FOB/FAS
Acceptable Payment Terms: Letter of credit, at sight
Comments: Seller must ship within seven days of receiving letter of credit.
Contact Spencer Avalon for full details.

▶ *World Trade Point Federation* (www.exporthelp.co.za/network/wtpf.html). This is also a division of the United Nations. On this site you can post a notice saying what sort of widgets you're hoping to import or export. You may also be able to find trade partners in the countries you've targeted. The WTPF has 100 trade information and facilitation information centers. They also assist by disseminating trade information electronically to over 70 countries.

▶ *Organization of Women in International Trade* (http://owit.org). This not-for-women-only site provides networking and educational opportunities.

▶ *International Chamber of Commerce* (http://iccwbo.org). This site offers information about conferences, online libraries, information about advocacy, codes and rules, and much more.

Using your favorite search engine, try conducting a search on the country you're interested in trading with. For example, enter "France, chamber of commerce," and you should get a good start on finding market leads.

Because some of these sites are freebies while others are not, check out several before committing yourself to a fee-based service. If you decide to try a service that has a fee attached, it's a good idea to first make sure your company's budget can handle the expense. Search the internet for comments and even reviews of any pay service. Some have had very dissatisfied customers, so know before you spend any money.

Trade Dollars and Sense

I n Chapter 4 you started to calculate how much it's going to cost you to get your business up and running. In this chapter, the focus is more on figuring out how much you can expect to make. The size of your cut will largely depend on two factors: how much you charge clients, and how much you pay in expenses.

Pricing Your Products and Services

As an international trader, you are an intermediary in the buying and selling, or importing and exporting, transaction. Therefore, you have to determine not just the price of the product but the price of your services as well. These two figures are separate yet related. The price of your services needs to be added to the product price, but this could affect its competitiveness in the marketplace.

Because the fee for your services impacts the success of the product, you may ultimately decide to change your pricing structure. You don't want to undercharge your client so that you can't cover your expenses and make a profit, but you don't want to overcharge and reduce the competitiveness of your company and the merchandise you represent.

Import/export management companies use two basic methods to price their services: commission and retainer. Normally, you choose one method or the other based on how salable you feel the product is. If you think it's an easy sell, you'll want to work on the commission method. If you feel it's going to be a more difficult sell and require a lot of extra market research and effort, ask for a retainer.

A third method is to purchase the product outright and sell it abroad. This is a common scenario when you're dealing with manufacturers who would rather use you as a distributor than as a representative. You'll still market the product under the manufacturer's name, but your income will come from the profit generated by sales rather than by commission.

Commissioned Officer

Import/export management companies usually operate on a commission basis, earning about a 10 percent commission. These fees are based on the product cost from the manufacturer.

Let's say you're working with English lawn chairs, which cost you $110 each. Here's what you do: First, take the price the manufacturer is charging for the product: $110. Now multiply $110 by 10 percent, which gives you a commission of $11 per chair.

So, your product price at this point is $121 per chair ($110 + $11). To come up with the final price, you'll need to add other costs to this figure, such as any special marking or packaging, shipping, insurance, and any representative or distributor commissions that you'll pay to others in the trade channel. Once you've arrived at a final price, check it against your competitors' prices. If your product's price is comparatively low, you can bump up your commission percentage slightly.

For now, however, you can see that for every chair you or your trade channelers sell, you'll get $11. If you sell a thousand chairs, that's $11,000 for you.

Crunch the Numbers Before Agreeing to Terms

If the manufacturer can't discount an item's price sufficiently, or if you feel that the product will be a tough sell, ask for a flat retainer. You'll pass all the costs of market research along to the manufacturer. By taking a retainer, you guarantee yourself a set income rather than one tied by commission to a "problem" product.

To determine what your retainer should be, you'll need to consider three variables associated with the performance of your services:

1. *Labor and materials or supplies.* This usually includes your salary or estimated salary on an hourly basis, plus the wages and benefits you pay any employees involved in the performance of the job. To determine labor costs, estimate the amount of time it will take to finish a job and multiply it by the hourly rate of your salary and that of any employees you might use. You can compute materials as a percentage of labor, but until you have past records to use as a guide, you should use 2 percent to 6 percent.

2. *Overhead.* This variable comprises all the (nonlabor) indirect expenses required to operate your business. To determine your overhead rate, add up all your expenses for one year, except for labor and materials. Divide this figure by your total cost of labor and materials to determine your overhead rate. Or use a rate of 35 percent to 42 percent of your labor and materials.

3. *Profit.* After all labor, materials, and overhead expenses are combined, profit can be determined by applying a percentage profit factor to those combined costs.

After profit is determined, adding it to the total operating costs produces the amount of the retainer.

When determining your prices, as in most industries, you need to consider whether you are selling a product based on cost only or adding value to the transaction. Selling by price only is the most common method in trade, but it can be very competitive if your product has many traders selling.

If your competitors keep undercutting your price, you may find that you need to lower your prices to stay in the game; this becomes a race to the bottom at which point you will not see any profits.

Adding value means shipping more quickly, using better packaging, offering great customer service if there's a problem, and effectively handling the special needs of your customers. For example, can you rush a product to a customer if necessary? By adding more value, you can justify charging a little more. Do some market research through surveys and interviews with companies that could become customers. Also look for any articles that talk about customer wants and needs.

If you can be the company that is most customer-centric, and you meet their needs, you can add value and outpace your competitors even with slightly higher rates.

The Great Sock Caper

Let's say you're working with a manufacturer who wants to export self-laundering socks. Because you're not certain the world is ready for this breakthrough, you decide to take it on a retainer basis. You figure it will take you a week to complete the deal—to arrange for the export of 530 dozen socks priced at $24 per dozen. To calculate your retainer, figure your labor and materials cost. (Check out the chart in Figure 8–1 on page 139.)

Next you calculate your overhead—all the non-labor, indirect expenses required to operate your business. Divide this number by your total labor and materials number. Until you have past expenses to guide you, you can figure that overhead will cost you from 35 percent to 42 percent of your labor and materials cost. You can raise or lower the percentage depending on the workings of your own operation.

Next, add your overhead figure (in this case, it's $445.53) to your labor and materials cost, and there's your total operating expenses figure.

Most traders plan on making a net profit of 8 percent to 10 percent from their gross revenues. If you want to net 8 percent before taxes from the self-washing sock sales, multiply your total operating expenses by a profit factor of 8.7 percent. This produces a profit of $131.05, which is then added to the total operating expenses figure to produce the retainer. If you consult the chart in Figure 8–1, you will see that the retainer you should charge is $1,637.38.

> **tip**
>
> Your profit factor should always be larger than the net profit you're aiming for. If you want to net an 8 percent profit, for example, set your profit factor between 8.7 percent and 9 percent.

Remember, if you can add value by being the fastest, the most flexible, or anything else, you could charge $1,800, and customers will pay because they know you are the best at giving them what they need.

Competitive Pricing

How you price your products is extremely important. The price has to be high enough to generate a profit, yet low enough to be competitive in the marketplace you have chosen. This makes it essential for you to do your market research!

Figuring Your Retainer

	Hours	Rate	Cost
Labor*	40	$26/hour	$1,040.00
Materials (2% of Your Labor)			20.80
Total Labor & Materials			**$1,060.80**
Labor & Materials			$1,060.80
Overhead (42% of Labor & Materials)		445.53	
Total Operating Expenses			**$1,506.33**
Total Operating Expenses			1,506.33
Profit Factor of 8.7%			131.05
Your Net Profit—Retainer			**$1,637.38**

*Labor cost is based on temporary help. If your employees are part time, add 15 percent for payroll taxes, workers' compensation, and other necessities. If your employees are full time, add 30 percent. (Be sure to confirm these percentages with your accountant.)

FIGURE 8–1: **Figuring Your Retainer**

Determine the typical price range for selected merchandise in your target market, then compare it against the manufacturer's price. You'll then need to determine whether that price is competitive in the marketplace. If it's not, do one of the following:

▶ Ask the manufacturer or supplier for a better price. Negotiate!
▶ Operate on a retainer-only basis with no commission.
▶ Reconsider doing business with that manufacturer or supplier.

Once you have determined the average price range for comparable products and decided that you can add commissions and other markups to the manufacturer's price and still be competitive, start seeking a buyer.

Keep in mind that pricing is often a case of trial and error. Persevere until you come up with the magic number for both profit and salability.

Seek Out the Best Deals and Terms

The retainer is a smart way to ensure an income on problem products. If you do your job well and the product takes off, generating tons of sales, the manufacturer may start resenting having to pay you merely to arrange sales, which becomes rather easy. (After all, the manufacturer is supplying the product and paying all the costs to develop the market.)

In the end, the manufacturer may decide to cut you out of the deal by selling direct. Remember maintaining a good rapport with suppliers, which includes manufacturers, goes a long way.

If, however, you've been working all along on a commission basis instead of on retainer, the manufacturer will probably view your commissions, which are costing less than the retainer would, as fair compensation.

Being the Distributor Could Pay Off

Occasionally, you'll want to, or be asked to, act as a distributor for the merchandise. This means that you'll purchase the product from the manufacturer—usually at net wholesale prices, less a percentage for the manufacturer's sales overhead—and sell the merchandise abroad.

When you're wearing your distributor cap, every product you purchase from the manufacturer should be priced to cover the following:

- ► Its wholesale cost
- ► Handling costs (shipping, cargo insurance, tariffs, freight forwarder fees, sales rep commissions, and any other special costs the project or product requires)
- ► A proportionate share of your overhead
- ► A reasonable profit for you

To accomplish this, you have to apply a markup to the cost of the product, and this gives you your selling price. If the cost of the product, for example, is $5 and your selling price is $10, then your markup is $5 (100 percent).

warning

Never underestimate the value of a good supplier who can help you learn more about the business and even provide advice. Too many people think of the supplier as someone you haggle with—a good supplier (whom you trust) can make a huge difference. Once you establish a good rapport, they can help you with pricing and even think ahead and be ready with what you need even before you ask for it. Be respectful and try to build a good, long-lasting relationship with your supplier(s).

Do Research Before Setting Your Prices

Let's say you are working with decorative frog and flower porch lights that you have bought from a company in Taiwan. You know they'll sell like crazy all over the U.S. The manufacturer is charging you $5 per light (unit). Check out the chart in Figure 8–2 and you'll see that your costs to bring the lights stateside are $6.47 per unit. If you double this, selling each light for $12.94 at a markup of 100 percent, you'll be making $38,820 on the deal. This is potentially a good situation.

Remember, however, that you'll be selling the porch lights to retailers, who will also need to add their markup to make a profit. There's no point in pricing yourself right out of the ballpark. If you add a 100 percent markup and the retailer does the same, each light will now cost the consumer $25.88. This price might now be too high to be competitive.

tip

Find a customs broker or freight forwarder you will be comfortable with. Look online or ask other international traders for recommendations. Check references from people who have worked with the customs broker before. Ultimately, you want to pick someone who is friendly, knowledgeable, and experienced.

Figuring Your Markup

Manufacturer's Cost for 500 Dozen Frog-and-Flower Porch Lights	$30,000
Customs Broker's Fee	280
Inland Freight from Factory to Port	600
Marine Insurance	340
Ocean Freight from Keelung, Taiwan	6,000
Import Tariffs/Taxes	1,590
Total	**$38,810**

Divide your total costs of $38,810 by 6,000 (500 dozen) units.
This gives you a per-unit cost of $6.47.

FIGURE 8–2: **Figuring Your Markup**

► Don't Forget to Calculate in Applicable Broker Fees

One type of cost you'll likely incur are broker fees. The customs broker is the professional who guides your goods through customs. There is no one-size-fits-all fee structure for this service. It's all based on what's involved with each shipment.

Expect to pay more if your shipment is subject to restrictions. If you have a food shipment, for example, your broker will have to deal with the Food and Drug Administration. If you're bringing in transmitters, the Federal Communications Commission will be involved. If your cargo consists of several different types of furniture, like tables and chairs, each distinct piece will have to be categorized. If other agencies get involved, the charges increase.

Thus, you might want to lower your markup. If you make it 50 percent, your per-unit cost drops to $9.71, but you still make $19,410 on the deal—not too bad.

Projecting Profits Can Be Tricky

It's much more difficult to determine a set yearly income for an import/export business than for many other types of companies. If you're in the car wash business, for example, you're dealing with a predetermined service—cleaning vehicles—and while you can add or subtract waxes, vacuums, and air fresheners, the main thrust of what you're selling is not going to change. In import/export, however, there are no fixed boundaries. Your profits and expenses will be different for each project.

Baseline Expenses

Don't forget about your fixed expenses—ones that will form the baseline of your business and that you'll always have, no matter what you're importing or exporting. These, subtracted from your projected gross income, will tell the true tale of how much your company will be making.

We'll assume once again that you'll be homebased, so we won't worry about expenses for office rent or utilities. We do, however, need to consider the following expenses:

tip

Here are good questions to ask prospective customs brokers and freight forwarders: Do you specialize in these transactions? How long have you been in operation? How many offices does your firm have, and where are they located? Ask for references and confirm those references.

▶ Freight Forwarders Have Fees Too

The freight forwarder's fees, like those of the customs broker, are not cut and dried. Prices are based on product, origin, destination, size, and weight. Air rates are usually based on either a per-pound or per-kilo weight, or on dimensional weight, whichever is greater.

Dimensional weight is figured by multiplying length by width by height in inches, and then dividing by 166 to arrive at the number of pounds. The air carrier is compensating for the fact that a 48-inch square box of feathers, while weighing little, will take up more room than a 48-inch box of bricks.

Ray Tobia, president of Air Sea International Forwarding, emphasizes that it's difficult to give ballpark estimates. This is especially true in an era of rapidly changing freight charges. However, as you can imagine, air charges from Newark, New Jersey, to London will be considerably less than charges for sending the same consignment from Los Angeles to London.

Freight forwarders' ocean rates usually run per 20-foot or 40-foot container or, for loose freight, on a weight/measure basis—per cubic meter or per 1,000 kilos, whichever is greater.

- ▶ Smartphone and cellular service
- ▶ Landline phone service
- ▶ Postage
- ▶ Stationery and business card printing
- ▶ Office supplies
- ▶ Computer and printer supplies
- ▶ Travel
- ▶ Internet service
- ▶ Website maintenance and hosting
- ▶ Loan repayment

Phone It In

As you know, phone service of some sort is a must in the import/export business. Whether you'll need or want a traditional landline depends on your business. Email, texting, or using WhatsApp are often the methods of choice for communicating with customers. You'll learn about WhatsApp and similar communications tools in the upcoming sidebar.

"We used to communicate by fax, because it was very expensive to conduct business over the phone," said Wahib Wahba in Maryland. "Now we use the phone all the time because it's more affordable than it was before."

save

Look into the Google Fi cellular phone service for low international rates (https://fi.google.com). It works with any smartphone and can be used in almost any country around the world for a flat monthly rate that's less than $50.

If you choose the good old-fashioned method of picking up the phone for your international dealings, your charges may be much higher than if you send emails (depending on the service you use to make the calls). Of course, you can also use VoIP (Voice over Internet Protocol) for making low-cost internet-based voice calls, which is significantly less expensive than traditional long-distance (international) calls. Check out VoIP apps, such as Skype (www.Skype.com) or WhatsApp (www.whatsapp.com) for your internet-based international calling needs.

For international travels, you'll likely need an international cellular service plan through a U.S. carrier to keep you connected via your smartphone. Each cellular service provider offers slightly different pricing and coverage options when it comes to international roaming and usage. The key is meeting your own needs.

When roaming outside of the U.S., there are three main options:

1. Purchasing a supplemental international plan from your home cellular service provider.
2. Using a local (pre-paid) SIM card for each country you visit. If you Google pre-paid SIM cards that work throughout the world, or in specific countries you'll be traveling to, you'll discover a wide range of options and prices. Part of your choice should be based on how many countries you will be visiting and whether you'll require a lot of cellular data usage.
3. Acquiring a personal internet hotspot that works almost anywhere in the world, then relying on a VoIP calling service to make and receive calls via the internet. Skyroam (www.skyroam.com) offers a low-cost personal wifi hotspot that works in many countries around the world.

Send Sales Materials via Mail or Email

Your ongoing postage charges will also vary, depending on how much you rely on mail rather than phone or email, and where in the world you are sending materials. Some of the printed materials you're likely to send include catalogs from exporters, your own catalogs, brochures, price sheets for importers, introduction letters, and pro forma invoices. Of

▶ What's the WhatsApp?

While not as popular within the U.S., many people who live overseas rely on WhatsApp to make and receive internet-based voice calls, video calls, and text messages. In fact, unlimited use of WhatsApp is bundled with many cellular service plans overseas. With this in mind, consider setting up your own WhatsApp account so you'll be able to communicate with customers and clients overseas—for free.

You can use WhatsApp with your internet-connected computer or mobile device. It's similar in some ways to Skype or FaceTime. It works across all hardware platforms and has been adopted by people living in many countries (including emerging markets that are starting to get cellular phone service).

In addition to using WhatsApp to make and receive calls (and use text messaging) from the U.S. to other countries, many world travelers use WhatsApp while they're abroad to communicate in whichever countries they're visiting or to contact people back in the U.S.

Keep in mind when using WhatsApp that you can only communicate with other WhatsApp users. Regardless, people like this service because it offers a lot of easy-to-use features and functions, it's free, and it's secure.

To sign up for a free WhatsApp account, visit www.whatsapp.com using your favorite web browser, or download and install the WhatsApp mobile app onto your smartphone by visiting the App Store (iOS) or Google Play Store (Android).

course, much of this information, including catalogs, can now be offered online or emailed. For example, printed brochures and catalogs can be converted into digital PDF files, which can easily be emailed.

The U.S. Post Office (www.usps.com) has lots of other options, including Express Mail, Priority, and First-Class International mail. Its website offers an International Mail Calculator. Plug in the name of the country to which you want to send mail and the weight of your package, and the calculator will show you prices for various types of postal services, including allowable size dimensions.

Basic Office Supplies, Like Paper, Cost Money Too

Once you have made your initial outlay for office supplies, business cards, and stationery, your fixed expenses in this category should be fairly low. But you'll need to pay for paper for your printer (and perhaps your fax machine) on an ongoing basis.

However, these days, you can store numerous files on flash drives, within your computer's internal hard drive, or in the cloud to save paper—and the planet. Popular and secure cloud-based services that allow you to store data, documents, and files include Dropbox (www.dropbox.com), Apple iCloud (www.apple.com/icloud), Microsoft OneDrive (https://products.office.com/en-us/onedrive/online-cloud-storage), Google Drive (www.google.com/drive), and Box (www.box.com).

Travel Tip

Your annual travel expenses will be entirely dependent on how you structure your business. Michael Richter travels infrequently since he has built his company around consulting clients from his home country of Germany.

In São Paolo, Brazil, John Laurino travels in-country once a month and abroad once a year, spending about ten days on each trip. Meanwhile, across the Atlantic in Belgium, Jan Herremans spends three to four days a week away from home in Europe. He takes an average of eight four- to ten-day intercontinental trips per year. Base your projected travel expenses on the type and duration of travel you'll likely be doing.

Olé for Online Service

Getting comfortable using the internet to support all aspects of your import/export business is a must! In most cases, it is also a fixed expense. Internet service providers (ISPs) that provide DSL, cable, FIOS or satellite-based internet access generally charge a flat rate for unlimited monthly service.

Weaving the Web

A professional business website is a must. North Carolina trader Sam Nelson explained that many of his clients order medical supplies straight from his website. For him, as well as his clients, this is an efficient transaction method. The functionality of your website should be based on the services your company offers, as well as the needs of your customers or clients.

If you learn how to make changes to your website, you can update it yourself. However, if you are not tech savvy or scared of making mistakes, hire someone to do this for you. Either way the site must be updated regularly.

Website maintenance and content updating fees should also be fairly fixed (and dependent on the complexity of your site). Scout around for someone who can manage your website.

While you can build your own website with little or no programming know-how, you will wind up with a more professional site by working with an experienced website designer.

Use Google, or a freelance service such as Upwork (www.upwork.com), to find a reliable website designer that won't charge you a fortune. Tell them exactly what you need. Make it clear whether you want to handle business transactions (ecommerce) on the website, or if you're just planning to share information. Either way, make sure your company's contact information is clearly displayed on every web page.

Websites that are overloaded with material can load too slowly and be hard for customers to navigate. Look at other import/export sites for ideas, but don't plagiarize. Also look at examples of what the designer has done in the past. If every site in their portfolio looks the same, you may want to go with someone else who can see your vision for the site and not take a cookie-cutter approach.

Prices can differ significantly, so get quotes and references, and go with someone in the mid-range. If you're designing a new website, do not pay to have someone program your website from scratch. Consider asking them to use WordPress and WordPress templates, for example, so it will be easier to make future changes and updates. Visit www.wordpress.org for more information.

Repaying Your Lenders Is a Business Expense

Several references to a fixed expense called a *loan repayment* have been made throughout this book. If you don't borrow money to start your business, you won't need to bother with this one. If, however, you finance your startup costs through any means, you'll need to repay the lender(s). Here's where you pencil in whatever your monthly fee is, including interest charges.

Putting It Together

You may have many more expenses than the ones discussed thus far. Once you have calculated your estimated operating expenses, subtract them from your calculated earnings, and you'll have a projected income/expense total.

You can do your own projected operating income/expense statement by using the worksheet in Figure 8–3 on page 148.

tip

Carefully research your markets and products; diligently calculate all shipping tariffs, taxes, and other fees; and keep a close eye on all your documentation. This will give you the best shot at achieving your ideal operating figures.

Operating Income/Expense Statement

Projected Monthly Income	$
Projected Monthly Expenses	$
Rent	
Market research/trade leads	
Phone service (include cell phone and land line)	
Utilities	
Employee payroll	
Advertising and marketing	
Postage	
Insurance	
Internet service	
Travel	
Miscellaneous expenses (stationery, office supplies, computers, etc.)	
Loan repayment	
Total Expenses	$
Projected Income/Expense Total	$

FIGURE 8–3: **Operating Income/Expense Statement**

A Little Bit of Luck

Now that you have done all the arithmetic, determine how much you will need to get your business up and running. Consider using a spreadsheet program (such as Microsoft Excel) to help with the number crunching and to keep your financial information well organized.

As a bonus, you can present all these figures and calculations to your prospective lenders to show them that your business is a good risk and that you will be able to repay your loan without difficulty.

Romancing the Bank

You might want to consider financing through your bank or credit union. In this case, your startup costs and income figures are extremely important. The bank will want to see this information neatly laid out and carefully calculated. You'll want to show all the statistics you can gather for the bright future of your chosen product niche and the trading market(s) within which you'll be operating.

Also of great importance is your background. Do you have experience in the industry? Have you been financially responsible in your personal life? Are you in debt, or do you have a low credit rating? People invest in people, so make sure that you are the kind of person a loan officer at your bank or credit union (or whomever else you go to for funding) is impressed with, as well as your partner (or team) if you have one.

Consider Working with the Ex-Im Bank

The Export-Import Bank of the United States, located in the financial district in lower Manhattan (called Ex-Im Bank by those in the know), was born in 1934 during the dark days of the Depression, when exports were viewed as a potential boost to our economic rehabilitation. After World War II, the bank helped American exporters in the reconstruction of Europe and Asia and took on the task of promoting trade between the U.S. and the Soviet Union.

Now that these missions have been accomplished, the bank has transferred much of its attention to emerging countries whose economies are, according to Ex-Im, growing at twice the rate of the industrialized world.

One of the Export-Import Bank's ongoing goals is to help jump-start the global economy and get it moving again. An additional goal is to increase exports of the environmental goods and services that are in great demand among emerging nations.

Most consistently, however, the Ex-Im Bank is a government agency on a mission to help finance the overseas sales of U.S. goods and services. What this means to you is that

Ex-Im representatives are standing by to potentially lend you working capital (assuming, of course, that you qualify). Again, the government is eager to help you sell U.S.-made goods abroad, so if you're exporting, this is potentially a great resource for you. You can contact Ex-Im Bank online at www.exim.gov, or call (202) 565-EXIM.

To help support small-business exporters, the bank has developed several small-business programs:

▶ *Working Capital Guarantee.* This program guarantees 90 percent of the principal and interest on working capital loans made by commercial banks to credit-worthy small-business people who will use the money to purchase or produce American merchandise or services for export. You apply for a Preliminary Commitment, a sort of letter of credit from the Ex-Im Bank, then take it to your own bank as an enticement for that bank to give you the best terms. The guarantee, which usually comes due in six months, can be for a single transaction or a revolving credit line.

▶ *Export Credit Insurance.* The program provides various policies to guard against a foreign buyer neglecting to pay you.

▶ *Direct Loans.* The Ex-Im Bank will lend money to importers wishing to purchase American-made goods, thus indirectly helping your cause. These are competitive, fixed-rate, term financing options for international buyers. The loans are for up to 12 years (18 years for renewable energy projects).

▶ *Guarantees.* Ex-Im Bank helps foreign buyers and indirectly helps you as an exporter by covering the importer of U.S. goods or services against the political and commercial risks of nonpayment.

▶ What Does "Made in America" Mean?

According to the FTC, the phrase "Made in America" must only be displayed on automobiles, textiles, wool, and fur products. The laws do not stipulate that other products must be labeled.

However, many U.S. manufacturers want to let it be known that they make their own products. This means they must comply with the FTC's "Made in the USA" policy, which means that "all or virtually all" of the product was made within the U.S. This also includes products advertised. For more information, go to www.FTC.gov and search the topic "Complying with the Made in America Standard."

► Your Business Plan

If you are looking for any type of funding, from family, banks, friends, venture capitalists, or anyone else, you should write a formal business plan. Every business plan should include the following seven sections:

1. *Executive Summary*. This provides an overview of the business in a few paragraphs. Although it appears first, it should be written last, since you will have then thought through the various sections of the plan.

2. *Company Description*. This high-level view of your company should explain what your company is about. You should include your legal structure here.

3. *Products and Services*. Provide a brief overview of what you will be selling or buying and any services you'll offer.

4. *Sales and Marketing*. This is how you'll make sales and how you'll spread the word about your business.

5. *Operations*. This is the place to explain how the business will work. Briefly detail the nuts and bolts of the business.

6. *Management Team*. This may be you alone or a few people who are helping you get started. Either way, include some pertinent information about why you (or you and your team) are the right people to invest in.

7. *Competition and the Marketplace*. Who else is out there? What do they do? What will make you stand out against your competitors?

At the end you should include key financial information, including some forecasts for the next three to five years. Be conservative in your projections. Avoid hype, and provide just the facts.

To guide you through the business plan creation process, you can choose from a variety of software programs and websites . Take advantage of these tools to ensure you include all the necessary information and that it's properly formatted. LivePlan (www.liveplan.com) and Business Plan Pro (www.businessplanpro.com) are two popular options. You can also download free business plan templates by visiting SCORE's website: www.score.org/news/best-business-plan-software.

Last but not least, before you share your business plan with potential investors, don't forget to proofread it.

Invest in Your Own Business

The first investor in your business should be you. Why should anyone invest in your business if you won't invest in it yourself? Putting your own money into the business will entice others to take the plunge.

However, you need money available beyond your living expenses, emergency fund, and home mortgage. Therefore, plan ahead and save enough to start a business without putting yourself at financial risk. Look at assets you can sell, a second job you can take on, or seek money from additional sources.

Be creative, but don't fall into debt—it's a bad way to start a business. Most entrepreneurs use a very exclusive source to finance their startup expenses—family and friends. You may choose to go this route yourself. You'll have a lot less paperwork to fill out, and you can let your financiers share in the excitement as your business takes off.

Remember, you'll still need to figure the repayment of borrowed funds into your costs, and you should treat your repayment agreement as seriously as you would any bank loan. If you offer a stake in your company as an incentive, keep the percentage low, and make it clear that while you may entertain suggestions, you have the final say as owner. Always maintain at least a 51 percent ownership in your company.

To be on the safe side, draw up agreements so you don't destroy relationships with your family and friends. Spell out how they can expect to be repaid. Also, read the language on financial brochures (or get a lawyer to help) so you include a disclaimer that essentially spells out the risks of investing.

Don't Finance Your Biz Using Credit Cards!

Another route many entrepreneurs take to obtain financing involves an entity as close as your back pocket—the credit card. Before you choose this option, look at your available credit balance and at the annual percentage rate you will be charged. Calculate interest payments in advance so you understand the cost associated with using a credit card.

Keep in mind that you can easily build up credit card debt, so this is a risky approach unless you're good at paying your credit card bills quickly. Relying on credit cards to fund your startup business is very rarely a good idea. Avoid this option, if possible.

Employees, Insurance, and Business-Related Topics

Depending on how much growth you envision for your business, you may never need employees. However, at some point, your business might grow to where you simply can't do everything yourself. This is when you'll need to consider taking on assistants or employees.

Employees are one of those elements within a business that bring with them as many potential cons as pros. When you hire help, suddenly there's payroll to be met, workers' compensation insurance, and state and federal employee taxes to be paid, and work to be delegated. You'll also have to manage other people and deal with their unique personalities, wants, and needs.

Some people are born employers and managers. They find it easy to teach someone else the ropes, then hand over the reins while serving as a manager. Others never feel comfortable telling someone else what to do or how to do it. When an employer cannot give up some control or manage properly, it can easily lead to a disconnect between the owner and the employees, which will ultimately impact every aspect of the business, including the bottom line.

One of the many perks of the import/export business is that you can accomplish a great deal *without* hiring anyone. You can easily start as a one-person operation, and singlehandedly manage all the tasks related to your business. As your company flourishes, you may one day find that you need to magically find more work hours in the day. This is an indication you're probably ready for some assistance (i.e., part-time or full-time employees).

Instead of doing every chore and managing every responsibility yourself, you can let others handle those responsibilities so you can spend more of your time working on tasks that will help your company expand and grow.

Fun with Filing

A tremendous amount of the work in international trade involves correspondence, invoicing, and preparing documents. As your company grows, you may discover that you can't handle all the paperwork (even if it's done electronically) and at the same time market your services to clients, arrange deals with representatives and distributors, and promote your clients' products.

When you reach the point where your paperwork and other daily grind tasks are cutting drastically into your marketing and customer service time, you'll probably need to hire an administrative assistant. This valuable member of your team can work on a part-time or full-time basis, depending on your needs, the work that needs to be done, and your personal work habits. Your new assistant might work alongside you or could be hired to work remotely.

You will want an organized, detail-oriented person who can think independently. Seek someone who has a cheerful phone personality and manners, top-notch written and verbal communication skills, and a knowledge of the computer applications your company uses. Of course, any previous experience working in the import/export field will be beneficial.

No matter what position you're trying to fill, the first employees you hire should be as versatile as possible. In small businesses, people wear many hats. Look for someone willing to do whatever is needed, even if an occasional task is outside of their job description or requires working extra hours.

If you can do it, hire your first few employees on a temporary basis. This strategy saves you from having to let an employee go if they don't work out, or if you don't need help on a continual basis. You can always expand temporary (one-to-six-months long) positions into permanent ones, based on your company's needs and how things work out with each new hire.

Family members can make ideal first hires. Not only are they usually willing to go above and beyond, but they typically have a loyalty to you and your company. Of course, family members have to be able to do the job that's required. You have to impress upon

► Create Detailed Job Descriptions

Before you start seeking the perfect employees, invest the time to create a detailed job description for each position you're looking to fill. This should be a written document that outlines everything that's expected of the employee.

According to the job search website Indeed, a job description summarizes the essential responsibilities, activities, qualifications, and skills for a role. Also known as a "JD," this document describes the type of work to be performed. It should include important company details, including company mission, culture, and any benefits you provide to employees. It may also specify to whom the position reports and salary range. An effective job description will provide enough detail for candidates to determine if they're qualified for the position.

In addition, a well-written job description should include a job title, a job summary, and a detailed list of duties and responsibilities. It should also spell out what qualifications and skills are required, and what your expectations are for the employee.

For help creating job descriptions, there are a range of free tools available online. For example, check out Indeed (www.indeed.com/hire/how-to-write-a-job-description), Workable (https://resources.workable.com/tutorial/how-to-write-a-good-job-description), and Glassdoor (www.glassdoor.com/employers/blog/5-tips-on-writing-great-job-descriptions).

them that you're running a "real business," and they need to put down their smartphones, stop texting their friends, and take their job seriously.

Your administrative assistant (or whatever you choose to call the first person you hire) will hopefully free up some of your time so you can go out and market your business and service your accounts.

As you continue to grow, sooner or later you'll likely discover that you can't do everything yourself. You'll need to hire another team member, such as an account supervisor, to help recruit and service accounts. Look for people who nicely compliment your skillset and experience, and who bring something extra to your company and what it will be able to offer moving forward.

Enthusiasm Is a Key Ingredient for Success

Ideally, your new account supervisors will have a working knowledge of international trade, but this is not as important as enthusiasm. For starters, you'll assign them an account to service. Then, as they learn how your company operates and what services you offer, they can potentially recruit their own accounts.

Depending on the size of the account, a person with extensive experience in international trade should be able to handle three to five accounts per year. If the accounts are small and don't need a lot of support, the employee may be able to handle more.

Because nobody works for free and salespeople are best motivated by incentives, you'll want to provide your account supervisor(s) with either a draw vs. commission or salary plus commission on the accounts they handle.

In a draw-vs.-commission arrangement, you provide your employees with a draw, a set monthly income so they can be assured of money coming in to pay their own bills and cover living expenses. Any commissions they earn are offset against the draw, so they don't receive money from their earned commissions until they've gone over the amount of their monthly draw. (If the draw is $500, for instance, and they earn $800 in commissions, they are paid $300 in commissions with the balance of $500 going to repay the draw.)

In a salary-plus-commission arrangement, you pay your employees a set monthly income, but in this case, any commissions they earn are *added* to the monthly

> **tip**
>
> You can protect yourself against former employees stealing your accounts by having every account supervisor sign a noncompete agreement. Consult your attorney for the finer points, but you can usually limit the competition from a former employee by both geographic area and time period.

▶ Provide Top-Notch Customer Service

One way to ensure your company's prosperity is to always provide top-notch customer service and demonstrate a friendly, professional attitude to everyone you encounter. When a customer calls or emails, whoever responds to the customer should be able to deal with that person's needs based on a full understanding of who they are and what they require.

Beyond just using a powerful contact management application to keep track of people's names, addresses, and phone numbers, consider using customer relationship management (CRM) software, and make it available to all employees who will be dealing with customers.

CRM software is like a contact management application on steroids. It maintains a database of all interactions with each customer, and keeps track of all details about them. With a few clicks, you can find out everything you or an employee needs to know about a customer.

There are many desktop and cloud-based CRM options that can grow with your company. Salesforce is one of the best-known, but there are plenty of others, like SugarCRM, NetSuite CRM, Zoho, Capterra, and Microsoft Dynamics CRM. To discover what's available, enter the search term "CRM" in your favorite internet browser.

payment instead of being subtracted from it. If their monthly salary is $500 and they earn $800 in commissions, they get the whole $1,300.

Draw vs. commission is usually the best way to motivate your account supervisors to perform at peak efficiency. Of course, if you have a particularly valuable team member, you might pay them on a salary-plus-commission basis. This will help ensure that they stay with you instead of going off on their own and potentially taking your accounts with them to a competitor.

How to Find the Best Employees

How do you find the right team members? Here are some practical suggestions for finding employees:

▶ Try headhunting from companies with products that are related to yours.

aha!

Even though English is the international language for business, you'll have a major advantage if at least one of your team members speaks the languages and understands the cultures of the countries you're doing business in. This strategy can help avoid misunderstandings or breaches of etiquette, not to mention make your communications more effective.

▶ Recruit from freight forwarding or customs broker firms.

▶ Place an ad online. There are many fee-based online services, such as ZipRecruiter.com, Monster.com, and Indeed.com, that offer employers powerful tools for quickly finding the right employees.

▶ Post an ad on the websites of various international trade associations. (See the Appendix for a list.)

▶ Post an ad on your own website.

▶ Recruit at local colleges that offer courses in international trade. You can post an ad on the department's bulletin board or talk to professors, or even the dean, about recommending graduating students.

warning

When you schedule work on various accounts, keep in mind not only American holidays but holidays in your international trading partners' country. There's no point, for example, in trying to schedule a phone meeting during the Chinese New Year, when all commerce screeches to a halt for a minimum of a week.

Hiring an Employee

Hiring an employee is one of those take-a-deep-breath-or-hyperventilate steps. You're taking on an extension of yourself, someone who hopefully will become not just another pair of hands but a backup brain, a friend, ally, and member of your business family. How do you choose someone to fill all those shoes?

Your administrative assistant should not just be a desk jockey. You want them to become an integral part of your team. You'll need to rely on them to field all the problems that might arise while you're out traveling the world. You'll want someone who possesses the following skills and abilities:

▶ *Analytical skills.* They think through a problem and arrive at a solution.

▶ *Verbal communication.* Their communication skills are excellent in person and on the phone, and they have a strong vocabulary.

▶ *Written communication.* They possess effective writing skills, with good grammar, spelling, and punctuation.

▶ *Visual detail skills.* They can enter correct information on an invoice or lading document without transposing or scrambling it.

▶ *Feedback acceptance.* They can accept feedback and follow directions, without getting insulted or defensive.

▶ *Complementary personality.* Their work habits mesh with your own.

Put Prospective Employees to the Test

When it comes to interviewing a potential employee or evaluating their skill set before hiring them, consider the following strategies:

▶ Provide a typical scenario in which the terms of a letter of credit cannot be completed for a fairly simple reason. You might use a case in which a certificate of origin has not been received from the exporter. Ask your prospects to solve the problem.

▶ Present a scenario of an importer who's worried because the merchandise your company exported has not arrived. Ask candidates to imagine that you are out of the country. How would they handle the situation? (You can even role play, with yourself as the worried importer.)

▶ Ask candidates familiar with import/export to fill out a few documents.

▶ Test prospects on more mechanical tasks, like producing a letter, sending appropriate and well-structured emails, or entering checks into an accounting program.

After you have evaluated your tests, read resumes, and checked references, use your own people skills. How do you feel intuitively about your candidate(s)?

Set Salaries Based on Qualification Requirements

Employees need to be paid using real money, in addition to benefits and a heartfelt "thank you." The amount you pay your employees will depend on many factors, including the job description, your region, the local cost of living, and the employee's experience level. An extremely experienced assistant might make 40 to 60 percent more than an inexperienced one.

Although you are required by law to provide employees with workers' compensation and time off to vote or attend to other civic duties, offering any other benefits are up to you.

Optional benefits include:

▶ Retirement, medical, dental, vision, and/or life insurance plans

▶ Paid vacations, holidays, or sick leave

▶ The ability to occasionally work from home

▶ Free lunches and/or coffee and snacks at work

▶ Reimbursement for commuting expenses

To attract good (i.e., dedicated, hardworking, and loyal) employees, many companies provide some or all these benefits. If you provide employees with benefits that are important to them, they'll be likelier to feel committed to your company.

Maintain Open Communication with Your Employees

Another way to ensure greater employee commitment (not to mention higher morale) is to make a real effort to connect with your employees. As with any relationship, this takes work. Try the following:

- ▶ *Encourage communication.* Useful suggestions and feedback, rather than just criticism, are most effective. Give your employees the chance to provide feedback about the company, preferably anonymously.
- ▶ *Reward creativity.* Employees who provide original, innovative suggestions should be rewarded. The size of the reward is often irrelevant. People simply like to be recognized and appreciated.
- ▶ *Avoid micromanagement.* Don't breathe down your employees' necks. You hired them, so let them work! Just make sure they're provided with a clearly defined job description so your employees know what they're supposed to do, and they understand your expectations.
- ▶ *Acknowledge your mistakes.* If a problem arises because of your own error, admit it. Everyone probably knows it anyway, but honesty is appreciated, especially when it comes from those in power. If employees make mistakes, don't chastise them; train them, help them, and let them learn from their mistakes.
- ▶ *See your employees as people.* Employees can tell when an employer appreciates them as people. Interest, if it's genuine and nonintrusive, is usually seen as a plus.

Training Considerations

Despite your best efforts, you may lose some employees just as you've gotten them trained. Wahib Wahba has found this to be the case more than once. "You train them for six to eight months, they work for two or three years, and then they move on and you have to repeat the whole thing," he said.

Some of this is unavoidable, given the highly mobile society in which we run our businesses. But you can keep it to a minimum by carefully choosing your employees and by implementing policies and a management style that rewards longevity.

Multiple Types of Insurance Are Required

You'll need insurance for many aspects of your business, from employees to cargo. Once you hire employees, you'll need to care for them. Workers' compensation insurance laws vary among states, so check with your insurance agent for details in your area.

Workers' comp covers you for any illness or injury your employees might incur on the job. If your employees work in your home office and someone is injured there, your homeowners' insurance will typically refuse to pay on the grounds that it's a workers' comp case. Check with your insurance agent and make an informed decision about the types of insurance your business requires.

Insurance from the Ex-Im Bank

Thanks to the Export-Import Bank of the United States, you can purchase several types of export credit risk insurance designed for the newbie exporter and the SME (small- to medium-sized enterprise). These policies protect you in case your foreign buyer decides not to pay you for either commercial or political reasons. The Ex-Im Bank hopes policies such as these will encourage both you and your financial institution to take on higher-risk foreign markets. Your menu options at Ex-Im are the following:

▶ *Small-business policy.* This multi-buyer policy requires that you insure all your export credit sales with Ex-Im. It's designed to free you from the "first-loss" deductible of most commercial policies. To take advantage, your export credit sales volume must have been less than $5 million in the last three years before application, your company must qualify as a small business under the SBA's definition, and you must have been in business at least one year with a positive net worth. How do you find out if you qualify? Call the SBA's Office of Size Standards at (800) 827-5722, or check the website at www.sba.gov/size.

▶ *Umbrella policy.* This policy boasts the same coverage and eligibility as the small-business policy above, but it allows you (as an EMC or ETC) to act as an administrator or intermediary between Ex-Im and your clients.

▶ *Short-term single-buyer policy.* This one, which covers a single or repetitive sale, is for the exporter who doesn't want to insure everything with Ex-Im. A special reduced premium is offered to small businesses.

Cargo Insurance

You already know the importance of cargo insurance. The cost of this crucial insurance usually runs about 1 percent of the insured value, although this varies with the type of goods and method of shipping.

So, what do you get for your money? Peace of mind, for one thing, as with all insurance. In the event of a cargo misadventure, your insurance coverage should include enough to repay you for not only lost or damaged products, but for your extra time and trouble related to those lost profits.

You'll want to purchase all-risk insurance, which covers your cargo against everything except man's inhumanity to man—war, strikes, riots, and civil commotion—and inherent vice in the cargo. What is vice? It refers to any sort of plague or pestilence that might attack your cargo, such as boll weevils in those gorgeous cotton blankets, for example, or E. coli on your Texas steaks.

You might also want to consider general average insurance. This protects you in the event of someone else's cargo loss. Say the ship carrying your containers runs afoul of stormy weather. The captain decides to jettison a portion of the cargo to save the rest, and he dumps somebody else's stuff into the briny deep. Fine, you say. Not quite. According to maritime law, even though your merchandise has made it to port safe and sound, you can't take possession until you've paid for your share of the loss.

> **tip**
>
> Insure an additional 10 percent of the CIF value of your cargo. If your merchandise is worth $5,000, for example, and your ocean freight charge is $400, then you'll want to buy about $6,000 worth of insurance.
>
> $5,000 + $400 = $5,400
>
> $5,400 + $540 (10 percent) = $5,940
>
> (Rounded up to $6,000)

The Blanket Policy

Say the other party in your transaction has purchased insurance—for example, the exporter who's shipping to you CIF (Cost, Insurance, and Freight)—but you've got a funny feeling that his coverage is not too reliable. You can purchase a contingent policy, which is about half the price of regular insurance and will serve as backup insurance in the event of a catastrophe.

As a newbie trader, your best bet will be to purchase insurance through your freight forwarder, who has a blanket policy, or directly from the air carrier. As you grow, you may wish to purchase a blanket policy of your own, which will cover you for everything you ship over the course of a year.

Take Proactive Measures to Protect Your Goods

Out on the high seas, your cargo may be subjected to rough and stormy weather. On the docks, it can be equally buffeted about by tough longshoremen. What can you do to help ensure your cargo doesn't become a marine insurance claim?

1. *Pack with dock loading and unloading procedures in mind.* Your cargo may be slung around (or skewered) by anything from a forklift to a sling or net, and then,

▶ Export Graffiti

The importer usually specifies export marks that should appear on the cargo for easy identification by receivers. These marks include the following:

- ▶ Shipper's mark
- ▶ Country of origin
- ▶ Weight marking in pounds and kilograms
- ▶ Number of packages and size of cases in inches and centimeters
- ▶ Handling marks using international pictorial symbols (if appropriate)
- ▶ Cautionary markings in English and the language of the country of destination (if appropriate)
- ▶ Special labels for hazardous materials
- ▶ Destination and order number
- ▶ Port of entry

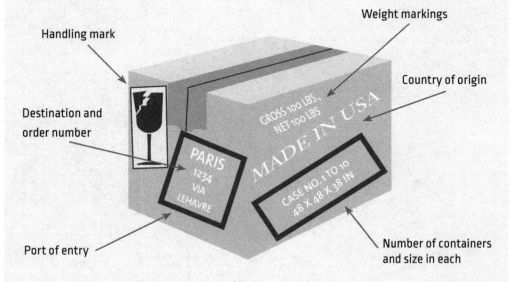

if it survives that, left outdoors to rot. Often, cargo is "stored" on port decks or on airplane cargo tarmacs without any covering. If you're unfamiliar with overseas port operations and don't have the right packaging, you can lose cargo.

2. *Pack to expect Mother Nature's worst.* Container loads can shift during heavy seas and storms. Someone else's cargo can smash into yours—or vice versa. A sea voyage can be murder on merchandise. Think heat and humidity, salt air (which is incredibly corrosive), rain, and sea spray. When any or all of this gets into your containers, you can end up with rust, blistering, mold, mildew, and moisture damage.

3. *Pack to expect human nature's worst.* Theft can be a problem, especially when containers are left on the docks for a long time.

With all these potential disasters in mind, pack smart. Use adequate packaging materials; make sure your merchandise is cushioned against blows. Waterproof everything possible. Have package exteriors shrink-wrapped. Use waterproof lining on interiors. Coat exposed metal parts on machinery, for example, with grease or some other rust arrester. Use heavy strapping and seals. Discourage theft by eliminating trademarks or content descriptions on container exteriors.

Tools
of the Trade

Your office will house your most vital equipment—your computer and printer. With the help of these tools, your operations will likely run smoothly, speedily, and much more efficiently.

Similarly, even if no clients see it, the location of your office and its setup can have a significant impact on the success of your business. With that mind, this chapter focuses on equipment and office decisions.

Savvy Shopping

Properly outfitting your office is an important task. The decisions you make should be based on your personal work habits and requirements. This chapter includes a checklist (see Figure 10–1, page 167) to help you determine what you'll need.

After you've read this part of the chapter, go through the checklist and evaluate what you already have. You might not need to go out and buy everything new. For example, do you have sufficient memory in your computer? Do you have the software you need? How about that printer? Will it be up to the job?

A Computer Is Your Most Important Tool

Your computer will be the centerpiece of your office setup. It will likely be used for coordinating your invoicing, accounting, word processing, scheduling, email, and contact management. With the help of the internet, you'll also use your computer for travel arrangements, market research, and general research on businesses worldwide. It will be your most important startup purchase. If you already own a computer, you'll want to make sure it's capable of handling the tasks you'll need it for.

Your import/export business computer should be running the latest version of the Windows or MacOS operating system, be connected to the internet, and have the most current versions of the software you'll need to run your business installed and ready to use.

Among your computer decisions will be whether to buy a laptop or a desktop computer, or both (which is recommended). In a business in which you will be traveling a lot, you'll need a laptop computer (also called a notebook computer). However, you might be able to get by using a tablet. If you expect to work often in your home office or in a business office, a desktop computer can provide a larger screen (or even multiple screens).

Computer technology has evolved a lot in recent years, and prices have dropped considerably. First decide if you want to go with a Windows PC or Apple MacOS-based computer.

If you're planning to have a desktop computer and a notebook computer, they should both run the same operating system. For example, go with an Apple iMac desktop computer and a MacBook Air or MacBook Pro notebook computer. Then, once you've decided to go the Apple route, consider an Apple iPhone smartphone and Apple iPad Pro tablet. This way, all your data, documents, and files will automatically sync and be easily accessible.

The Trader's Office Checklist

Use this handy list as a shopping guide for equipping your office. It's been designed with the one-person home office in mind. If you have partners, employees, or a high budget, you may want to make additions or modifications.

After you have done your shopping, fill in the purchase price next to each item, add up the total, and you will have a head start on the Startup Costs Worksheet in Figure 4–1, page 48!

Computer

❑ Desktop computer $_____

❑ Notebook computer or Chromebook (Windows or MacOS)   _____

❑ Tablet (such as an iPad Pro)   _____

❑ Uninterruptible power supply/surge protector   _____

❑ Website (design & hosting)   _____

❑ Printer/copier/scanner/fax   _____

❑ Internet service (modem, wireless router)   _____

Software

❑ Office suite (word processor, etc.)   _____

❑ Customer relationship manager (CRM)   _____

❑ Accounting/bookkeeping   _____

❑ PDF file creator & editor   _____

❑ Email manager   _____

Phone Equipment

❑ Smartphone (with cellular service)   _____

❑ Landline phones (two or three lines with voice mail)   _____

❑ Voice-over-IP calling service (e.g., Skype)   _____

Additional Essentials

❑ Office supplies (see mini-list on page 171)   _____

❑ Comfortable desk chair   _____

❑ Desk   _____

❑ Filing cabinets   _____

❑ Bookcases   _____

Total Expenditures $_____

FIGURE 10–1: **The Trader's Office Checklist**

Meanwhile, if you consider yourself to be more of a Windows PC person, make sure your desktop and laptop computer run the same version of the Windows operating system. Your tablet should also be Windows or Android-based, as should your smartphone.

While you don't need to buy the latest, most expensive, state-of-the-art equipment, you need to make sure your computer will have the processing power, memory, and internal (hard drive) storage space that you'll need to handle your work. Visit any Apple Store, Microsoft Store, or consumer technology superstore to discuss your computer hardware needs and options, especially if you're not tech-savvy.

Whatever equipment you wind up with, make sure it comes with technical support. For example, for an additional fee, you can purchase a two-year AppleCare+ support package for any Apple equipment.

A Reliable Printer Is a Must

You'll be using your printer a lot, so a good printer is a must. You can expect to pay $300 to $800 for a color inkjet printer and $500 to $1,500 for a color laser printer. In a business setting, a laser printer generates higher quality results and typically prints more pages per minute than an inkjet printer.

Before buying a printer, look for a fast print speed and make sure to check the price of ink (or toner) cartridges. Also keep in mind that you probably do not need a color printer unless color is important in your products. Black-and-white printers are faster and cheaper, and do not need new cartridges as often as their color counterparts.

Define Your Software Needs

A dazzling array of software is available to help you perform every business task: Design and print your own checks; manage mailing lists, forms, and labels; develop professional quality marketing materials; and be your own accountant.

New computers come already loaded with much of the software you will need for basic office operations. However, you'll also need some type of office suite, such as Microsoft Office 365, Google G Suite, Apple iWork, or OpenOffice, all of which include a word processor and spreadsheet applications, for example.

You may also want an accounting program, such as QuickBooks (www.quickbooks.com) or one of many variations. Also, go to Capeterra for accounting software reviews at www.capterra.com/accounting-software.

Don't forget about CRM software and other specialized applications that will help you get your work done faster and more efficiently, such as applications designed to help you create, fill out, and submit forms electronically.

There are also freebie downloadable software programs available online. Browse through a selection of free, open-source software by visiting: www.openoffice.org. You can also do a Google search for free business software. Use the search phrase, "Open Source Business Software," or "Open Source Accounting Software," for example.

There's also vertical market software for the import/export industry. Visco, for example, makes software specifically for importers. You can find information about it at: http://viscosoftware.com.

▶ First Impressions

Your business needs a professional image that tells potential clients and customers you're a savvy trader. This falls under what's called "branding" your business.

Your company's branding should be consistent across your printed materials (e.g., letterhead, business cards, invoices, brochures), and your online activities (e.g., your company's website, email, social media presence).

As with deciding on a business name, be sure that the image or branding you're beaming to the minds of buyers and clients is the one you want. Leave the over-the-top, trendy, or oh-so-cutesy branding to other types of businesses.

Your most important goal is to convey the impression of international trade efficiency and expertise. This is what you're selling. Have a friend or family member with business experience look over your designs and overall brand before you commit to a print run of 2,500 brochures, business cards, and sheets of letterhead.

Watch for typos and amateur-looking design elements. Look at what other companies do to present their image and brand, then determine what might make your brand stand out—without going overboard. You want consistency so your brand, including your company's logo, remains the same on everything from printed marketing and sales materials to the appearance of your website.

Finally, you should create a powerful and believable mission statement that is short, yet straightforward. You will be placing your mission statement in many areas, from your website to your marketing materials, where potential buyers and clients will see it, so it should clearly state what your business is all about. For example, "Our mission is to export goods safely, quickly, professionally, and within the laws of both sending and receiving countries."

You'll Need More than Voicemail

To operate a productive business, you need more than a basic voice-mail service to answer your calls and record messages when you're not available and a time-sensitive matter arises. There are a wide range of online-based call-management services that you'll likely find useful. Prices start as low as $20 per month.

Once you define your needs and how you'll handle urgent, time-sensitive calls (potentially from people overseas in other time zones), check out what's offered by companies like: RingCentral (www.ringcentral.com), eVoice (www.evoice.com), Grasshopper (www.grasshopper.com), and CallHippo (https://callhippo.com).

Reliable Power Is a Must

You should invest in an uninterruptible power supply (UPS) for your computer system, especially if you live in an area where lightning or power surges happen frequently. If you're a computer newbie, you may not realize that even a flicker of power loss can shut down your computer, causing it to forget all the data you've carefully entered during your current work session, or even fry your computer's hard drive entirely.

With a UPS, you won't lose power to your system when the power fails or flickers. Instead, the unit flashes red and sounds a warning, giving you ample time to safely shut down your computer. You can expect to pay $125 and up for one of these devices.

A Photocopier Is a Useful Business Tool

You should never send a piece of paper out of your office unless you've kept a copy. So a photocopier can be very useful. However, to save on significant paper use and avoid the need for numerous filing cabinets, most document storage can be done electronically and stored within your computer or in the cloud. Then, you can always print hard copies of documents as you need them.

tip

Back up your data every day—not once in a while. You can use a flash drive, external hard drive, or a cloud-based service, all of which will give you peace of mind if something goes terribly wrong. There are countless stories of businesses losing valuable data—don't take a chance, back up!

For a low-cost and secure cloud-based service, check out Microsoft OneDrive (www.onedrive.com), Google Drive (www.google.com/drive), or Dropbox (www.dropbox.com). These services can also be set up to automatically sync your important data, documents, and files between all your computers and mobile devices.

Some forms, like the Shippers Export Declaration and other government-driven documents that you can't always generate from a computer, demand a copier-made duplicate.

Copiers come in a very wide price range, from $150 to $2,500 (or more). Keep in mind, you can also get a combined printer/copier/scanner/fax machine, or three out of those four, packed into one desktop unit for less than $500.

Don't Forget Office Supplies

Although they're easy to forget, small items like pens, paper clips, tape, and sticky notes are useful. Keep your office well stocked with these supplies. An office supplies shopping list is included within Figure 10–2.

Office Supplies Shopping Mini-List

Printer/copier/fax paper $_____

Business cards   _____

Letterhead stationery   _____

Envelopes (all sizes)   _____

File folders   _____

Notepads and notebooks   _____

Return address self-stamper or labels   _____

Printer toner/ink cartridges   _____

Computer backup equipment (flash drives, external hard drive)   _____

Miscellaneous office supplies (pencils, pencil sharpener, paper clips, etc.) _____

Total Expenditures $_____

FIGURE 10–2: **Office Supplies Shopping Mini-List**

Stay Comfortable in Your Office

Office furniture is another necessity. It's important that your work environment be comfortable and ergonomic. At the very least, you need a functional desk to work from and a comfortable office chair to sit in. File cabinets and bookcases will also help you stay organized.

Your office chair is a very personal item. Look for something that is comfortable and mobile (has wheels), and good for your back. An office chair is one thing you should invest in so you're not sitting in a dining room chair or a folding chair that doesn't have the support you need to protect yourself from back and neck pain as a result of hours of sitting. And either make sure the chair is the right height for you or is adjustable. Office chairs range from $200 to $2,000, so shop around. Prices for other office furniture, like desks, file cabinets, and bookcases, will vary greatly, so shop based on your needs, budget, and personal taste.

Trading Spaces

Whether you're a trader on the move, always flying from one exotic locale to another, or an armchair traveler who conducts most of your business from home, you'll need a business office.

One of the perks of running an import/export business is that it lends itself to the home-based entrepreneur. Your office doesn't require a high-traffic or high-visibility location and it doesn't need to be in a trendy part of town. Although you may have an occasional client stop in, you won't need a mahogany-paneled office with a lobby and conference room. The only real space requirement is an area large enough for your desk, chair, filing cabinets, and perhaps a bookshelf.

The Home Office

If you choose to be homebased, locate your office work space anywhere in the house that's convenient. Ideally, however, you should have a dedicated office, a room that's reserved just for the business. You could locate this room in a den, the garage, within a finished basement, or in a spare bedroom, for example.

Focus on a space that is:

▶ Roomy enough so you don't feel claustrophobic
▶ Has good lighting
▶ Has good ventilation

> ▶ Has heat or A/C
> ▶ Is relatively quiet

If a dedicated office is not an option, you can always station yourself in a corner of the kitchen or at the dining room table. If you have a boisterous family, however, an area within your bedroom is likely to be much more conducive to quiet and clear thinking.

Working from Home Has Its Tax Advantages

Another advantage to the home office is the ability to write it off as a home business expense. The IRS allows you to deduct money from your income taxes if you're using a portion of your home as your income-producing work space. You can deduct a percentage of expenses that are equivalent to the percentage of space your home office occupies.

If, for example, you're using one room in an eight-room house, you can deduct one-eighth of your rent or mortgage plus one-eighth of your utility bills. There is, of course, an "if" involved here. You can use this deduction only if you're using this space solely as your office. If you've turned your spare bedroom into your office and you don't use it for anything but conducting your business, then it qualifies.

However, if your office is tucked into a corner of the kitchen and you're still feeding people from the kitchen, you can only take a tax deduction on the portion of the room you use for business.

Growing Pains

As your business grows, you may decide that it's time to move up to outside or commercial office space. Because the import/export business doesn't rely on client traffic or a prestigious address, any area that appeals to you and your pocketbook is up for grabs.

Consider going the office/warehouse route within an industrial park. If product storage is a consideration, perhaps keep your home office and rent space from a local self-storage facility.

If storage is not a concern, but you want an office away from home, look for commercial space in other areas but not in the retail arena. You don't want to rent retail space when you're running a service business.

What's the Alternative?

If commercial office space isn't your bag, consider a more unconventional approach. Rent a house or apartment (provided you check the zoning laws first). If you already live in an apartment, you may choose to rent another unit in the same building to use as your office.

▶ The Psychological Component of Working from Home

In addition to the logical implications of working from home and using valuable living space for work-related furniture, for example, there's also a psychological component to being self-employed and working (alone) from home. Many people simply are not cut out for it.

If you're accustomed to working in an office environment and being surrounded by coworkers, things are going to feel very different when you begin working alone from home. For one, you will lose the opportunity for continuous socialization.

Furthermore, you need to ensure you have what it takes to stay motivated, focused, and on schedule. When you're at home, it's very easy to get sidetracked by your pets and children, tasks you need to do around the house (meal preparation, cleaning, and laundry), or watching TV. If you're someone who gets easily distracted, lonely, or who won't enjoy the isolation of working on your own—all day, every day—a homebased business is probably not right for you.

The same is true if you have trouble focusing on and completing tasks, maintaining a schedule, and meeting deadlines if someone is not breathing down your neck demanding results. Before going all in and launching a homebased business, make sure you'll be able to deal with the psychological and logistical aspects of being entirely on your own (at least until you're able to hire an assistant or at least one employee).

Should you discover that a homebased business is not a good fit, this doesn't mean you should abandon plans for launching your import/export business. It simply means you need to figure out a work-space alternative, such as a shared office space, where you're more likely to thrive. Carefully consider your personal work habits and emotional needs as you make decisions about where you'll work.

Or you can take a space over a downtown storefront. How about over a coffeehouse or maybe a doughnut or bagel shop? What better incentive to get to work in the morning?

Coworking spaces are also becoming more prevalent, especially in larger metropolitan areas, and many are geared toward a specific cohort of professionals, from tech pros and artisans to those interested in incubator space. These spaces typically offer a variety of membership options, including secured, designated office suites; bullpen-style desks; community-style memberships that allow you to grab a spot to sit; and access to wifi, printing and copying, and coffee/snack offerings. Coworking spaces also come with the benefit of built-in networking opportunities so you can make new contacts while tapping away on your laptop.

Focus on Efficiency When Setting Up Your Office

If your office is in a commercial space, you'll need the same setup with plenty of room for your files, desk, chair, and visitors' furniture, as well as a desk and chair for any employee(s) you may hire. Your computer should occupy a place of honor away from dirt, drafts, heat, and blinding sunlight. Ditto for your printer and fax machine.

In a commercial office, you'll also want that American office altarpiece, the coffee maker, and if you can provide a plate of cookies, doughnuts, or healthy snacks when you know guests are arriving, you'll go a long way toward building business relationships.

No matter where you decide to locate your office, with a little effort you can maximize the productivity of the time you spend in it, which, of course, will help to strengthen your business.

Advertising, Marketing, and Distribution

A s an international trader, your mission is sales—in three different but overlapping arenas:

1. Knowing what your customers want and need so you can market to their needs and sell accordingly

2. Selling yourself and your company to clients as an import/export manager for their products

3. Selling the products themselves to representatives and distributors

Success in any one of these arenas will ultimately contribute to your success in the others. Once you've established a favorable sales record with one client's goods, you'll have a track record with which to entice other clients. However, don't fall into the trap of assuming that one size fits all. Each satisfied customer will contribute to your own self-confidence, which will lend that air of confidence to your negotiations with new prospects.

So, which comes first, selling the product or yourself? The answer is: neither. Knowing the wants and needs of your customers (as well as potential customers and clients) comes first. You could have a great product or be a great salesman, but if your customers don't want or need what you're selling, you're out of luck.

Next, you'll need to sell your company and yourself, because until you have a client's trust, you're not going to get very far. Marketing your import/export management company involves two main steps:

1. Convincing a prospective client that they have a product worth exporting to customers who want what they're selling
2. Persuading a potential client that you're operating a company that they can trust to do the job

Hunting for Exports

A surprisingly small percentage of domestic producers export their wares. Your marketing goal is to convince the huge remainder that they can increase profits by exporting—with your guidance—to specific target countries. You can accomplish this through targeted emails (not spam), making connections through in-person or online networking, via social media, or by attending trade shows. Cold calling (telemarketing) is also an option, but it's time consuming, and getting people to answer their phone these days is very difficult.

Before you initiate contact with any manufacturer, you'll need to do some basic market research:

▶ What products are hot sellers in the domestic marketplace? Focus your attention on products that you know well or that are (or could be) bestsellers in their market niches.
▶ Are these products hot sellers in your target countries (or could they be)?
▶ If not, are there situations or markets that would put these products in great demand if the products were available?
▶ Who manufactures these products?

▶ What is the selling price of each product and of competing products or brands, domestically and in your target countries?

Taking the Lead

These days, international traders rarely use print ads to attract customers. Instead, they take advantage of the trade lead sources (previously explored in Chapter 7 and elsewhere within the book). If you live in a trade-rich area, like Miami, you might advertise in online directories and business magazines (and online publications) where hopeful manufacturers or vendors can look you up.

If you decide to go with a phone directory ad, you need to jump into the 21st century. Ask anyone under the age of 21 what a Yellow Pages is, and they'll give you a blank stare. Nobody uses a printed phone directory anymore. It's more essential that you obtain a business listing in relevant online directories.

No matter where your ads appear, make sure they stand out from the crowd with clever copy that tells what you do. Your ads should showcase what products or regions you specialize in and why you excel above and beyond your competition.

Reaching Out

Look for manufacturers of the viable products you have researched. Next, contact that company and ask for the name of the person you need to speak with. If the company is small, you will probably want its president or owner. If it's a larger company, direct your inquiry to the vice president in charge of sales or to the sales manager.

In your email or during an introductory phone call, make sure to address the following points:

▶ Start Networking on LinkedIn

LinkedIn (www.linkedin.com) was designed from the ground up to cater to the needs of small-business owners and entrepreneurs. The core service is free to use, and it provides a powerful, yet easy-to-use professional networking tool and information resource.

A Premium subscription is also available, which unlocks additional tools for communicating with business leaders from around the globe. Start by creating a free LinkedIn account and profile for yourself and your import/export business. LinkedIn has more than 660 million members representing more than 200 countries and hundreds of industries.

▶ Introduce yourself and your company.

▶ Briefly outline the potential of the overseas market(s) you represent.

▶ Outline the product's potential within that market.

▶ If possible, explain why and how your company, out of all others, will be able to position their product best. For example, if you have experience with similar products, say so.

▶ If you already have contacts with foreign distributors, explain that you have foreign reps for overseas sales.

▶ Let customers know you care about them, their wants, and their needs.

▶ Ask for an in-person meeting (or video call) to further discuss the possibilities.

Check out the sample letters in Figures 11–1 and 11–2, on pages 181 and 182. One is for the newbie with no experience with the product, and one for the newbie with a background in the field.

Set up a plan to send your emails or letters to multiple companies at the same time. After the initial solicitation, wait a week or so. If you haven't heard from your target manufacturer, send an email follow-up. Suggest some available times to talk on the phone or meet in person. Figure 11–3 on page 183 can help with closing the deal.

Desperately Seeking Imports

Now that you understand how to find export products to send abroad, let's consider imports. How do you find goods to bring into the U.S. to sell? You have several options:

▶ Travel abroad on an import search mission.

▶ Wait for foreign manufacturers to contact you.

▶ Attend trade shows.

▶ Contact foreign embassies' trade development offices.

▶ Contact the U.S. Commercial Service's International Trade Administration (ITA).

▶ Track down leads on the internet and by reading print and online trade publications.

The Travel Log

Traveling abroad is a great way to discover new business opportunities. However, it's not always practical in terms of time, money, or other commitments you may have.

While traveling abroad, you can learn about and view foreign products in a realistic setting and discover what sells. If you're interested in general merchandise, traveling in

Sample Direct Sales Letter #1: Newbie with No Experience

Gum Tree Trading Company

123 Eucalyptus Lane
Sea Terrace, CA 92000, USA

July 5, 20XX

Mr. Murray Mulch, President
Mulch Products Inc.
456 Tea Tree Street
Sea Terrace, CA 92000

Dear Mr. Mulch:

How would you like to exponentially increase your company's sales and expand your market with a minimum of time, trouble, and expense?

As owner of Gum Tree Trading Company, I am currently researching the profitable sales of mulch in the European market. As you may know, organic garden products are very popular in Europe, with sales continuously on the rise. [Insert specific sales figures, if possible.]

I am familiar with your company's mulches, and after preliminary research, I believe they have tremendous export potential in this area.

To complete my research, I would like to receive pricing information, any brochures and marketing information that you can offer, and a few sample bags of mulch, which I will send on to my foreign representatives.

If we find that we can sell your products profitably in Europe, we will handle all export details, including shipping, distribution, and securing payments. This is potentially a wonderful opportunity to increase your company's sales with little cost or risk.

Can we set up a time to discuss how we might work together in the near future? I look forward to speaking with you and exploring your business needs.

Sincerely,

Andrea April

Andrea April
Gum Tree Trading Company

AA/ta

www.GumTreeTrading.com • (000) 000-1234 • (000) 000-4567 (fax) • email: GumTree@Holiday.com

FIGURE 11–1: **Sample Direct Sales Letter #1: Newbie with No Experience**

Sample Direct Sales Letter #2: Newbie with Experience

Gum Tree Trading Company

123 Eucalyptus Lane
Sea Terrace, CA 92000, USA

July 5, 20XX

Mr. Murray Mulch, President
Mulch Products Inc.
456 Tea Tree Street
Sea Terrace, CA 92000

Dear Mr. Mulch:

How would you like to exponentially increase your company's sales and expand your distribution with minimal time, trouble, and expense on your part?

As owner of Gum Tree Trading Company, I am currently researching the profitable sales of mulch in the European market. As you may know, organic garden products are very popular in Europe, with sales continuously on the rise. I am familiar with your company's mulches, and after preliminary research, I believe they have tremendous export potential.

To complete my research, I would like to receive pricing information, any brochures and marketing information that you can offer, and a few sample bags of mulch, which I will send to my foreign representatives.

If we determine that we can sell your products profitably in Europe, we will handle all export details, including shipping, distribution, and securing payments. With more than ten years of experience in international garden product sales, I am confident that my company can successfully sell your mulches within the European marketplace.

This is a terrific opportunity to increase your sales with little cost or risk to your firm. Can we set up a time to talk in the near future? I look forward to speaking with you and exploring your business needs.

Very best,

Andrea April

Andrea April
Gum Tree Trading Company

AA/ta

www.GumTreeTrading.com • (000) 000-1234 • (000) 000-4567 (fax) • email: GumTree@Holiday.com

FIGURE 11–2: **Sample Direct Sales Letter #2: Newbie with Experience**

Selling Checklist

When you contact a manufacturer for the first time, you probably won't know if you'll be able to handle their merchandise profitably. You'll have to find out their import or export price, and then perform additional market research to determine the sales potential for the product within the countries where you do business. How do you accomplish this?

❑ Take one of the products you've already researched, one you know well and believe in or one that's a bestseller in its market niche.

❑ Contact the manufacturer and ask how they would feel about taking their product abroad.

❑ See what their thoughts are before steamrolling them with your international distribution plans for their business.

❑ If they're interested, explain that you would like to sell their product abroad. Tell them you'll need to conduct more market research so you can find out all you can about the product, including cost, the trade channels they engage in, whether their company can provide any advertising assistance, what size orders they can fill, and how long it will take to fill orders.

❑ Perform a pricing analysis. How much can you sell the product for in a targeted country? What type of commission can you add? How much are competitors getting for the product? Can you keep the price competitive? Don't forget to figure your shipping costs, tariffs, and other operating expenses.

❑ Build your relationship with the company owner by letting them know what you will do next and asking what suggestions they have.

❑ Talk with some of their existing distributors or sales reps.

❑ Once you're satisfied that there's a viable market for the product, formulate an initial marketing plan.

❑ Sit down with the owner or VP of sales to discuss what they need from you and what you can do for them. Remember, business is all about building relationships, some of which can last for years.

❑ Based on initial agreements, draw up a formal contract. (Seek the help of your lawyer for this step.)

FIGURE 11–3: **Selling Checklist**

search of goods can be the best way to garner immediate results. As in domestic exporting, there are many manufacturers out there who have never considered selling their products in the U.S., even though the market may be extremely profitable. The most effective way to find these companies is through field research and in-person meetings.

tip

Visit the International Trade Administration's website (www.trade.gov) for contacts in your field. These people are ready to help you export.

Don't limit yourself by looking only at what products you want to import. Consider what kinds of strategies you'll use to make your profits. Are you more interested in importing products with brand-name identities, or can you lean toward low price and high volume?

If you're going the low-price/high-volume route, you'll want to focus on countries that are low cost-goods producers, like India and Mexico. Because these countries usually have

► Dear Manufacturer

Keep these tips in mind if you choose to write a letter:

► Try writing as if you're speaking to a friend. You want your letter to sound professional, of course, but stiff and stodgy doesn't create interest. Keep it peppy!

► Do some research so you can include a few details about the potential client's product and why it could sell well abroad. This lends credibility by demonstrating that you've done your homework. You know and understand the field at home and in your target market.

► Have you spelled the potential client's name and the company name correctly? Errors will instantly show that you are an amateur.

► Do you have everything else spelled correctly, and is your grammar and punctuation perfect? If you're not a whiz at these things, use your word processor's spelling and grammar checker, but also consider using a tool like Grammarly (www.grammarly.com). Have someone else proofread your letter. (Electronic spelling and grammar checkers don't catch every error.)

► Remember to stick to the point. Your letter should be short but informative.

► Ask the prospect what their goals are, and make it clear that you're flexible and will be able to help them reach their business goals.

emerging economies, your importing mission may be a little more complicated and require a little more patience.

The potential profits in these types of ventures are often much greater for the newbie importer than going the brand-name route, which often brings with it a lot of competition.

Just Call Me

Traveling in search of products to import is fun and potentially lucrative, but experienced importers also rely on manufacturers contacting them. This method has two important bonuses: You don't have to go anywhere to search for merchandise, and you don't have to persuade anybody to export their merchandise. If they are contacting you, you know they are interested.

Of course, if you're new to international trade, this latter option is probably not going to do you much good because no one knows you're out there to contact. But as your company grows, and as you make contacts all over the world, you'll find that other companies will come to you.

Not all your calls for help will come from manufacturers with a product to export. You'll also potentially receive calls from importers seeking a particular U.S. product—sometimes merchandise with which you have no familiarity. Where do you go to fulfill their requests? One terrific source is the Thomas for Industry, which is a database of products and companies that boasts more than 700,000 manufacturers and distributors from many countries with over 10,000 product categories. Access the register for free at www.thomasnet.com.

> **aha!**
>
> Trade shows, held for every industry from bridal planning to building supplies, are a good way to scope out products and do some professional networking. You'll get a rep's-eye view of what's hot and what's new in the market.

Exploit Trade Show Opportunities

Trade shows are a terrific way to meet foreign manufacturers, distributors, and representatives. Everybody attending a trade show is there for the purpose of conducting business and making contacts. So get out there and mingle!

Foreign trade shows or fairs, set up by foreign governments to showcase their own manufacturers, are held to tempt you, the potential importer. You'll have to travel abroad to attend some shows. Others come to various locales in the U.S. Call the embassy or consulate of the country you're interested in to find out when and if they have trade shows scheduled. You could also visit www.eventseye.com to look for upcoming trade shows. Search this website by country, industry, name, date, organizer, or keywords.

Many countries and geographic regions sponsor trade offices where you can find specific information on manufacturers of everything from toothpicks to truck tires to fur coats. Call or email the consulate, or Google "trade development office in (name of location, country or city)."

Once you've made contact, ask for a list of suppliers eager to do business with American importers. These people are on the job just to match you up with a supplier back home.

The U.S. Commercial Service's International Trade Administration can also help you locate various trade groups and development agencies that will help you find specific kinds of manufacturers or suppliers.

tip

Like a good bounty hunter, you'll want to explore every avenue. Don't forget the many online trade lead sites. For starters, check out The Federation of International Trade Associations (http://fita.org/tradehub.html) and TradeKey (www.tradekey.com).

Selling Yourself

You've located foreign manufacturers or suppliers whose products have U.S. sales potential. Now you have to sell those companies on the idea of entering the American marketplace and convince them that you're the person to usher them in.

Handle this challenge pretty much the same way you'd pitch domestic manufacturers—by sending a letter or email. However, today most traders rely on email. The Trade Lead Response Letter in Figure 11–4, on page 187, will help you with your pitch. In your letter, outline the various opportunities available in the U.S. for their product, and highlight that you'll handle all import logistics with little cost to the manufacturer.

Also, check out the sample letter in Figure 11–5, on page 188. Notice this letter is very similar to the domestic one, with two exceptions:

1. We've addressed the owner of the company as Monsieur (abbreviated M.) instead of "Mr." Even though the letter is in English, this little touch shows that you know something about the French language and you've taken the care and courtesy to address M. Picard in his own tongue.
2. We've checked to make sure we've eliminated any slang that may be confusing to non-native speakers.

Sample Trade Lead Response Letter

Treasure Bay Traders
789 Seekers Cove
Sea Terrace, CA 92000, USA

July 5, 20XX

Mr. Nigel Owens
Managing Director
Sterling Frames Ltd.
62 Gosham Street
Chipping Huntbridge, Sussex, England

Dear Mr. Owens:

We are responding to your trade lead, which we viewed with great enthusiasm via the International Trade Administration. We are very interested in importing fine English interior design products, such as your sterling silver frames. Our research shows a great demand for this type of product in the American market, and although we are a newer trading company, we are positioning ourselves as a leader in European interior design imports.

Please send us your current catalog and best export prices, along with any samples you feel would help us promote your products. We would then like to discuss any questions or concerns you may have. Let us know a date in the coming weeks that would work for you to talk by phone.

Very best,

Eric Williams

Eric Williams
Treasure Bay Traders

EW/ta

www.TreasureBayTraders.com • (000) 000-1234 • (000) 000-4567 (fax) • email: TreasureBay@Holiday.com

FIGURE 11–4: **Sample Trade Lead Response Letter**

Sample Foreign Sales Letter

Gum Tree Trading Company

123 Eucalyptus Lane
Sea Terrace, CA 92000, USA

July 5, 20XX

M. John Pierre Picard
Picard & Fils et Cie
456 Rue des Matins
75007 Paris, France

Dear M. Picard:

How would you like to exponentially increase your company's sales and expand your market at almost no cost?

As owner of Gum Tree Trading Company, I am researching the profitable sales of European mirrors in the U.S. As you may know, these interior design products are very popular in America. I am familiar with your company's high-quality mirrors, and after preliminary research, believe they have tremendous export potential.

I would like to discuss the opportunity to sell your products overseas and answer any questions or concerns you may have. In the meantime, I would appreciate it if you would send me pricing information, appropriate brochures and marketing information, and a few sample mirrors.

If we determine that we can sell your products profitably in the U.S., we will handle all export details, including shipping, distribution, and securing payments.

This is potentially a terrific opportunity to increase your sales with little cost or risk to your firm. I look forward to hearing from you soon to discuss this exciting program in further detail.

Very best,

Andrea April

Andrea April
Gum Tree Trading Company
AA/ta

www.GumTreeTrading.com • (000) 000-1234 • (000) 000-4567 (fax) • email: GumTree@Holiday.com

---

FIGURE 11–5: **Sample Foreign Sales Letter**

After establishing initial contact, follow up in a few days with another email. Think of the follow-up as a firm but gentle nudge, or an opportunity to strengthen your position and demonstrate real interest in importing the merchandise.

tip

Consider using Google Translate or a similar service to translate your emails or printed correspondence into your recipient's native language.

Check out the sample follow-up letter in Figure 11–6 on page 190. Remember that part of your task is to convince the potential client that your company is the best one for the job, so you have to supply reasons for this. You also want to strike up a conversation with them. The trade industry is largely predicated on relationships, and if you are the pushy American, you may not make a lot of connections. Always be cordial and take an interest in your (potential) customer or client.

When speaking with non-native English speakers, talk a little slower and as clearly as possible. Some people tend to mumble or slur speech, which will make it difficult for foreign ears to comprehend what you're saying.

The Marketing Plan

Whether you're planning to export or import, be prepared to present your prospective client with a detailed marketing plan. If the manufacturer is close to home, you'll naturally present it in person. If they're overseas, you may still have to arrange a personal visit to close the deal. If you feel strongly enough about the product's U.S. potential, the trip will be worth the time and expense. Otherwise, consider setting up a video call.

To prepare your marketing plan, start with research. Find out what products or trends are popular in their land or what products of theirs will be hits in your land. You don't want to waste time having them send you (or you send them) products and/or literature for which there is no market potential. It's only once you see a possible fit that you'll need information, such as pricing, product brochures or literature, and product samples. If your prospect balks at supplying these materials, tell them you'll need them to develop a sales presentation, outlining the market strategy you plan to pursue.

Once you have the materials in your office, sit down and figure out every possible expense you'll incur so that you can arrive at your sales price. If you've already been in contact with distributors or representatives, find out if this price will sell in their market. If you don't have any reps yet, you'll need to locate one and determine if they can work with your calculated pricing. Assuming the answer is yes, you've got a viable product.

Sample Foreign Sales Follow-Up Letter

Gum Tree Trading Company

123 Eucalyptus Lane
Sea Terrace, CA 92000, USA

July 5, 20XX

M. John Pierre Picard
Picard & Fils et Cie
456 Rue des Matins
75007 Paris, France

Dear M. Picard:

I am writing to follow up on the email I sent last week. My company is very interested in representing your fine mirrors in the U.S. We would purchase directly from you and handle all export details ourselves.

We are experienced in interior design product sales in the U.S. and in Europe. Please let us know when you will be available to set up a phone call to discuss this business opportunity.

Sincerely,

Andrea April

Andrea April
Gum Tree Trading Company

AA/ta

www.GumTreeTrading.com • (000) 000-1234 • (000) 000-4567 (fax) • email: GumTree@Holiday.com

FIGURE 11–6: **Sample Foreign Sales Follow-Up Letter**

Write out your marketing plan, which should include:

▶ *Target Market*. Which country or countries will you or your representatives sell in? Why are these markets viable? Include positive market research information, and be sure to assemble it in a clear, concise, easy-to-digest format. This is where your computer and spreadsheet software will shine. Create colorful charts, graphs, and tables interspersed with facts, figures, and text.

tip

To make sure you're not calling clients in the middle of the night, check out time zones for hundreds of international cities at www.worldtimeserver.com, or use the world clock feature on your smartphone.

▶ *Sales*. Explain at what price you'll sell the product. Give your annual sales forecast, your fee structure, and the profits the manufacturer can expect.

▶ *Marketing*. Briefly touch on any special marketing or promotions for the product; for example, foreign or domestic trade shows or any local advertising your reps will do. Make it clear how you will get the product in front of people who are most likely to be interested.

▶ **Money Talks**

If the merchandise you're interested in isn't branded (i.e., it doesn't carry a brand name, trademark, copyright, or is otherwise restricted in some way), perhaps your best profit potential lies in acting as an import merchant.

You'll purchase the goods outright, then sell them to your own distributors. Provided you have the necessary capital and marketing power, your contact with the foreign supplier will be geared more toward negotiation. Ask that all relevant information, such as price, terms of quote, and financial requirements, be in written form.

If you're serious about buying, most foreign suppliers will be eager to talk. Make sure the price quoted will give you enough room to make an acceptable profit. When you're ready to buy, be prepared to present a letter of credit. Virtually every overseas supplier will want one, especially if you're a first-time customer.

We Now Present

Your presentation package must look professional. Use the appropriate computer software and your own creativity to develop the following elements:

- ► Your marketing plan
- ► Your company brochure with a current client list (when you have one)
- ► A personal resume or bio highlighting any background relevant to the product or to sales or international trade

Take a Meeting

Arrive at a personal presentation looking as sharp and professional as your marketing plan. Even if you live in a casual area where shorts and T-shirts are the norm, put on a suit. Be prompt. Tardiness is a sure way to jeopardize your chances for success. It demonstrates that you don't have a lot of respect for your prospective client and that you're not very efficient.

Once you're face-to-face with a prospect, present your pitch. Consider using a PowerPoint presentation or printed charts and graphics to help emphasize important points and showcase your professionalism. Be sure to cover:

- ► How cost-effective exporting the product can be
- ► The potential returns the manufacturer will realize
- ► Any costs involved to export the product, that is, any special labeling or marking and export packing
- ► Your fee structure

Be sure to emphasize the following points:

- ► Exporting opens additional markets to the manufacturer at little cost to your perspective client.
- ► You'll handle all logistics, including shipping, the securing of payments, and documentation.
- ► All your prospect has to do is fulfill the orders you'll bring in and prepare them for shipment.

warning

Your exact distribution and marketing plans are your trade secret. Don't initially give your prospect anything but a general outline, until contracts are signed. If you provide too much information too soon, they could pursue the opportunity themselves and cut you out of the deal.

Representative or Distributor?

As a new trader, if you pitch yourself as a sales representative who's working on commission, you probably won't be able to close a deal on the first or even second call. Without a track record, you'll have to be both persuasive and tenacious.

As an alternative, you may want to offer yourself as a distributor. The good news here is that it's easier to convince the manufacturer to go with you. They don't have to lay out money for commissions or anything else except a few samples. The bad news is that buying the product yourself will add a sizable amount to your startup costs. If you strongly believe in the product, however, and you have the funds (or can get a loan for them), this is one way to quickly position yourself in the trade channel.

Shake on It

After your brilliant sales presentation, your prospect will hopefully be anxious to shake on the deal and get exporting. Close the deal by having them sign a sole representative contract, which you'll have your attorney draw up. This contract should cover the various guidelines of the agreement, including:

- ▶ Responsibility for promoting the product
- ▶ Territory
- ▶ Method and times of commission payments
- ▶ Handling methods required for letters of credit
- ▶ Any necessary product modification
- ▶ Annual sales forecasts (be realistic and conservative in your forecasts)

Join Facebook Groups Related to International Trade

Participate in online import/export groups. Whether you post frequently on social media platforms or talk (and listen) to people in groups or associations with import/export websites, always present yourself professionally.

Social media platforms, like Facebook and Twitter, allow you to speak to a world of people, some of whom may be legit while others may be questionable characters. Rather than seeking other importer/exporters, which is preaching to the choir, search for folks with whom you can discuss your product(s). Don't forget to take advantage of LinkedIn and other professional networking services as well.

First, spend some time on the online platform to see how it operates. For example, Facebook is mostly social interactions, but you can use it for business. Just be subtle and do not "sell." Provide information, and prove that you are the expert. Make people come to you.

Twitter is about brief ongoing messages and following people with similar interests. Again, don't sell; get them interested in you. There are many social media sites. Each has its own culture, privacy policy, and rules, so look around, join, then watch and learn before posting your comments.

It's not necessary for you and your company to be active on every social network. A smarter strategy is to pick the two or three platforms that are most popular with your market, then establish your presence on them. As a small-business operator, LinkedIn should certainly be on your list. Use it as a sales, marketing, networking, hiring, and research tool.

There are points to be gained by simply getting involved. Remember you are always representing your company, so act accordingly:

- ▶ *Project the positive.* You are the public face of your trading company, so act like it. If you feel the need to post something negative, think on it first, then do so in the most professional manner possible.
- ▶ *Become an expert exporter.* Offer quotes for news articles, post useful information on social media, and position yourself as an expert in your field. Answer questions and make your presence known. Again, this is something you can do very well on LinkedIn.
- ▶ *Check that grammar.* You don't need to be Shakespeare to have good, solid, basic grammar skills. Consider using a service like Grammarly (www.grammarly.com) to help automatically fix your errors.
- ▶ *Be someone who wants to help others.*
- ▶ *Teach.* Consider providing a free online course or webinar to a group or association. Ask them for their emails to send them more information. People are appreciative when you give them something for free that they perceive to be valuable.

Your Company's Website Should Look Professional

Website creation and maintenance is cheaper and easier than ever. For the price of a Netflix membership, you can create and manage an online presence that will be available to possible clients all over the world. You don't need to know a lot about web design, programming, or maintenance to make it happen.

Most website design sites offer a "what you see is what you get" (WYSIWYG) approach to design. Using templates created by the hosting company, simply enter text and post photos or images to your site, then make changes as often as you like.

You choose the colors, graphics, and fonts that best express your company and what it stands for. If you want a simple site, with a few pages that showcase who you are, what your company does, and how to reach you, this is the fastest, easiest, and most polished looking approach for the absolute beginner.

▶ Be a Content Creator

Creating your own online newsletter, blog, or podcast is a simple and effective online marketing tool. Each edition should contain information your target audience will perceive as valuable and informative, not a blatant commercial. Remember, people won't read what looks like obvious advertising.

A Google search will help you find easy-to-learn newsletter/blog creation programs. Your blog could focus on any number of possible topics, either related to the items you import or export, world news (as it relates to your business), or timely information about your industry.

Podcasting is quickly becoming a popular way for businesses in all industries to informally communicate with their (potential) customers/clients using audio-based, radio-style content that's distributed free via the internet. Be sure to check out the book *Start Your Own Podcasting Business* (by Jason R. Rich and published by Entrepreneur Books) for information on how to create a podcast for your business and learn ways to use it as a powerful and low-cost lead generation, sales, and marketing tool.

Check out website hosting companies, like Network Solutions (www.networksolutions.com), GoDaddy (www.godaddy.com), Hostwinds (www.hostwinds.com), SnapNames (www.snapnames.com), Verio (www.verio.com), WordPress (www.wordpress.org), and Wix.com.

If you want to go above and beyond what these turnkey solutions offer, you can spend a bit more time and money to hire a professional website designer and have a company website designed for you from scratch. For most startup business ventures, however, this expense is not necessary. Instead, use of one the template-based website design services to create and host your company's website.

Consider supplementing your website by establishing a free Facebook page for your business. To do this, visit www.facebook.com/business.

Advertising and Marketing

There are two primary ways to get your message out there. One is by marketing. This means getting your name out to people by writing blogs and guest blogs for industry publications, as well as issuing press releases to get journalists and reporters to work you into their stories. You should send press releases featuring interesting news relating to your product(s) or industry to editors, writers, bloggers, podcasters, and anyone in the media who can do a story about your business. Don't forget to offer a unique angle. Keep your press releases short, properly formatted, and to the point.

Press releases are free to create (minus your personal labor cost) and send out to a media organization via email. Consider taking time once or twice a month to compile a press release about big news in your industry or current trends on which you can comment as an export/import expert. Perhaps there's something news-oriented related to the international trade war. A press release must follow a pre-defined format. Using your favorite search engine, enter the phrase "how to write a press release" for more information.

Next, create an address and email list from attending trade shows, conferences, and conventions, and from networking. Buying lists can be costly and dangerous because you do not know how the list was compiled and how many addresses are no longer valid. Plus, if you get email addresses from people who did not give permission to have their email address given out (or sold), you will then be spamming them.

Once you start building your list, use an email-management program and fire off nicely formatted marketing emails. These activities can help you position yourself as an expert, reach a broader audience, and potentially attract new business.

Essentially, marketing means finding ways to get information about your business publicized, without paying the higher costs of advertising. This can also include using promotional pieces with your company name on it, handing out business cards at chamber of commerce meetings, or even sponsoring local events.

If you have some money in your budget for advertising, you'll need to start with a plan. Begin by doing some research for places in which you can buy selective ad space, such as a trade magazine or website that your customers are likely to visit.

For many small businesses, search engine marketing on Google, Yahoo!, Facebook, Instagram, Twitter, LinkedIn, and other online services is a low-cost and highly targeted opportunity. To learn more, use the phrase "search engine marketing" or "keyword advertising" in your favorite search engine. You could also visit an online service's home page and click on the advertise link.

To learn about highly targeted and low-cost online advertising opportunities with Google, visit https://ads.google.com. To discover advertising opportunities on Facebook, visit www.facebook.com/business/ads. Advertising can be costly so make sure you are properly reaching your potential target market.

Getting the Product Out

You've successfully landed a client with what you believe is a perfect product to sell. You've also determined which countries you're going to sell it in. Now comes the next phase of the project. You need to get your product into the marketplace and generate sales. After all, you're not going to earn a cent if the product just sits unsold in a warehouse.

Import sales is essentially a hands-on job. It requires meeting with retailers and wholesalers. Export sales, however, are more difficult to organize. After all, you're dealing in foreign territory. This is why exporters often rely on foreign sales representatives or distributors. How you decide to set up your distribution network depends on what you're selling and how closely you want to be involved with sales.

The good news is you don't have to hire anybody. Lots of exporters run the whole show themselves. However, if you do decide to go with a rep, remember that these people will represent your client and their product to everyone in the trade channel down to the final consumer. Since you are the manufacturer's representative, your rep's performance will be a direct reflection on not only the client and their product, but on you and your company as well.

Assuming you're going to hire sales help, which specific conduits in the trade channel will be most effective for you? The three most common options for the export management company are:

► Selling direct to foreign markets (you hire your own people to work in the country as sales representatives)
► Hiring a commission representative or representative company
► Working with an established distributor

The best trade channel options for the importer are:

► Manufacturer's representatives
► Distributors
► Retailers

Let's review the various conduits and their responsibilities:

► *Representative.* This is a person who can work alone or as part of a company with various reps on board. They make sales calls for you to wholesale or retail buyers. When they've solicited a sale, they pass it on to you. In most cases, you then send the merchandise directly to the buyer. A typical representative's commission is 5 percent of the cost of the goods, but this varies slightly from one part of the world to another, and from product to product.
► *Distributor.* This is a company that buys your goods and resells them to a retailer or other representatives for further distribution through the channel until the product reaches the consumer. A distributor who determines their own sales price for your product may wait until sales have accumulated before buying the merchandise, or

they may purchase the merchandise up front and warehouse it, thus acting as a wholesaler. You won't have as much control as you would with a representative, but you will not have as many worries because the distributor handles all advertising, promotions, returns, and customer service. A distributor acting as a wholesaler, buying your imported merchandise and warehousing it before accumulating sales, is sometimes called an *import house*.

▶ *Manufacturer's representative.* This is a salesperson who specializes in a specific product or line of complementary products; for example, home electronics. They often provide additional product assistance, such as warehousing and technical service. They can work alone or as part of an agency or "stable" of reps, in which case each rep divides their selling time among the various products promoted by their agency. This allows you to field a regional or national sales force without expending any capital. The downside, however, is that because these people carry a variety of product lines, yours may end up at the bottom.

▶ *Retailer.* The ultimate distributor who sells to the consumer.

▶ *Direct sales.* Direct sales can work for products with a limited market in which each sale is substantial. If you're selling jet engine nozzles, for example, you can easily send out your own reps to pitch jet engine manufacturers. There aren't many out there. When you make a sale, you'll probably be assured of repeat business. There aren't many nozzle suppliers either. But for most products, the markets are so large and complex this method is just not feasible.

Pursuing the Perfect Rep

Finding the perfect sales rep is just as important as finding that perfect manufacturer and product. Because some reps are better than others at pitching different types of products, the trick lies in choosing one who best complements your merchandise and, preferably, already has experience and contacts.

If you plan to sell in more than one corner of the world, you may need to locate several representatives. If your target countries are all in close proximity, however, you'll do better to find a distribution company or rep that can handle them all.

So, where do you find the perfect reps? If you're talking exports, go back to Chapter 7 and take another look at the services offered by the ITA's Commercial Service, including the Agent/Distributor Service.

Other foreign rep sources include:

▶ Freight forwarders and customs brokers
▶ Trade associations in the countries you are targeting

▶ Seek Exclusivity

During your negotiations with each manufacturer, ask for *exclusive distribution rights*—at least for the area(s) in which you will be selling. Many companies initially look for three-year exclusive rights, with the stipulation that they can renew each year thereafter.

If you're selling products for a manufacturer that doesn't have any U.S. sales yet, you may think this is not a problem, but it can be. Once you do your job and the product is selling well, another importer may come along, approach your manufacturer, and undercut your prices. Insist on an exclusive contract from the start, before you have competition to worry about.

If a manufacturer is afraid to give you a three-year exclusive, negotiate. You can sign an agreement, for example, stipulating that if you sell a pre-determined amount of product within a specified time, you'll then retain exclusive rights for a specific number of years. Whatever deal you ultimately sign, make sure your interests are well protected moving forward.

▶ Foreign consulates, embassies, and trade offices
▶ American chambers of commerce abroad
▶ International business-to-business directories (which you can find on the internet)
▶ International trade publications
▶ LinkedIn

Sources for domestic distributors and representatives include:

▶ Domestic trade associations, publications, and journals that cover your product's industry (including online publications)
▶ Referrals from your international banker
▶ Manufacturer's Agents National Association (see the Appendix for contact information)
▶ Online business directories or even your local phone directory
▶ U.S. and state trade centers
▶ LinkedIn

Choose the Best People to Work With

After you've compiled a list of reputable distributors or representatives, choose the best one for your company and products. Interview your prospects with as much care as you'd take to interview prospective employees.

A good place to start is with a sort of interview in a kit: a three-part packet consisting of a one-page fact sheet, product literature, and a questionnaire. You should prepare a packet for each client and have enough printed so that you can pop them in the mail or pass them out as the need arises. Have an electronic (PDF file) of the paperwork available to email as well.

tip

To help you recruit and hire more effectively, use talent management programs, such as ClearCompany (http://info.clearcompany.com) or VidCruiter (www.vidcruiter.com), which allows you to conduct video-based interviews via the internet.

The fact sheet should outline your client's commission structure, agreement policies, and company information so that each prospective rep has a snapshot of who they'll be dealing with and what they can expect as compensation. The questionnaire, which you'll ask prospects to fill out and return to you, is designed to elicit as much pertinent information as you'll need. Check out the sample in Figure 11–7, on page 201.

Once you receive a prospect's questionnaire, make sure you check references. Find out if other companies that deal with this rep are satisfied with the relationship. Determine what size territory (and geographic locations) the rep is most capable of covering.

If a prospect doesn't return the questionnaire, call or email him with a friendly nudge. If you still don't receive a response, cross them off your list. A person who doesn't take the time to respond to a potential associate may have already found work with a competitor or is someone who potentially does not follow through on their obligations.

Ideally, should now meet with your prospect in person. You can find out if you really click, and you can size up the way they handle themselves in a one-on-one situation rather than on paper. If you're in two different countries, however, and your budget simply won't allow for an in-person meeting, be sure to conduct a video call, or at the very least, a phone interview.

Sign on the Dotted Line

Once you've decided which reps you want on your team, sign contracts with them. You need a written agreement or contract to clarify their responsibilities and duties, as well as yours. Be sure to consult an attorney familiar with international law, especially as a newbie, because you might overlook details that could turn into costly problems in the future.

The specific details of each agreement will vary from one situation to another, but they should all include the basics:

Product Representative Questionnaire

Name: _____

Company name: _____

Address: _____

_____

Phone number: _____

Email address _____

1. What import products do you handle? _____

   _____

   _____

2. What export products do you handle? _____

   _____

   _____

3. Where do you make the majority of your sales? _____

   _____

   _____

4. How do you prefer to work (as distributor, sales rep, manufacturer's rep)?

   _____

5. What territories do you cover? _____

   _____

6. What commission would you feel comfortable with? _____

   _____

7. Do you work on your own, or do you have a company? If so, how many branches and salespeople do you have? _____

   _____

   _____

FIGURE 11–7: **Product Representative Questionnaire**

Product Representative Questionnaire

8. Please list pertinent bank references, including address, phone number, and contact person: _____

   _____

   _____

9. Please list at least three recent client references, including address, phone number or email address, and contact person: (Use reverse for more, if necessary.)

   a. _____

   _____

   b. _____

   _____

   c. _____

   _____

10. Provide details about your professional history (if you work on your own) or your company's history.

    Number of employees: _____

    Years in business: _____

    Annual sales: _____

    Assets: _____

    Liabilities: _____

    Net worth: _____

11. Please list any other information you feel would be helpful to us in considering you to represent our client: _____

    _____

    _____

    _____

FIGURE 11–7: **Product Representative Questionnaire,** continued

▶ *Responsibilities of the distributor or representative and your responsibilities.* Make sure these are clearly delineated and spelled out.

▶ *Term of the contract*

▶ *Compensation details*

▶ *Any bonus or incentive programs*

▶ *Territory.* Does the distributor or rep have exclusive or nonexclusive rights to a territory? This is an important consideration. Most reps prefer exclusive rights to market your product in a specific territory. Furthermore, granting the rep exclusive rights is a good way to give them a starting perk to help build a solid relationship.

▶ *Pricing.* This is often the most significant variable determining sales success. Price your product carefully, neither too high nor too low. Remember that your representative will earn a specific percentage, while a distributor will buy at the prevailing wholesale market price.

▶ *Warranty and returns.* Who's responsible for returns or repairs? What is the policy? This can be a critical section of your agreement depending, of course, on what you're selling. Consider whether you'll need product liability insurance, and if so, obtain it right away.

▶ *Does the rep have the right to use trademarks, patents, and copyrights in advertising and marketing (online and in the real world)?* Make sure the product doesn't require or infringe on any intellectual property rights.

▶ *Marketing and advertising.* Spell out who's responsible for this. Remember that you or the manufacturer may have to defray some of these costs. Consider a clause stipulating that you must sign off on all paid advertising and marketing activities, since they are essentially representing your business.

▶ *Record-keeping.* Both parties should keep sales and other pertinent records, and reserve the right to examine each other's documents.

▶ *Language.* What language in the agreement is legally binding?

▶ *Contract termination.* Give yourself an out. If the rep fails to meet certain requirements, such as a minimum number of sales within a specified period, make sure you can terminate the contract and hire someone else.

▶ *Arbitration.* Make sure your agreement contains a clause outlining what happens if you and your rep disagree on the interpretation of the terms of the contract. Most contracts stipulate arbitration by the International Chamber of Commerce.

Advertising and Marketing Considerations

Although your main concern is finding buyers to distribute the product abroad or domestically, don't drop your responsibilities related to promoting the product.

Ultimately, your success depends on how well the product sells to consumers. Some products may not require advertising. Others that face stiff competition in the marketplace may benefit from online or real-world advertising and marketing campaigns.

Advertising can be a major expense. The distributors you deal with and their distributors or reps along the trade channel may not have much in the way of advertising budgets. Again, look for ways to display (and market) your products to the people of a specific region.

Your reps will also probably be dealing with several product lines in addition to yours, which means they may not be spending the ad dollars they have exclusively on your merchandise. In such a scenario, you may want to initiate a cooperative advertising program with the manufacturer.

Co-op advertising will reduce your distributors' advertising expenses and promote your client's product. It's a cost-efficient and effective way for both the manufacturer and retailer or distributor to reach their target markets.

Maintain Some Marketing and Advertising Control

You may need to give your manufacturer some major guidance in their advertising or marketing efforts. An ad blitz that takes one country by storm may fall flat or even backfire in another country. The annals of international trade are filled with horror stories of novice (and even major league) companies that lost millions of dollars because they didn't understand the cultures of the countries in which they were trying to do business.

Make sure you, your manufacturer, and anyone doing advertising or marketing take these kinds of issues into consideration:

- ▶ *Language.* Don't try to translate things literally. Some slang and colloquialisms have no direct translation; others transmute into something ridiculous, rude, or both. Use a translation website, such as Google Translate (https://translate.google.com) or ReversoTranslate (www.reverso.net), or a translation app on your smartphone, such as iTranslate, or Google Translate.
- ▶ *Cultural taboos.* In many countries, particularly Islamic ones, states of dress or undress that we may think look alluring in advertising will come across as lewd, lascivious, and possibly even illegal.

▶ *Colors and gestures.* Colors mean different things to different cultures. For example, white is the color of mourning in China, and in some tropical countries, green implies danger. Gestures also vary by culture. The thumbs-up sign is rude in Australia, and in Argentina, the OK sign has lewd connotations.

▶ *Educational levels.* In emerging countries where literacy levels are low, print ads are not going to get you very far. Likewise, in regions where people don't have internet access, relying on online advertising will be a waste of money.

Look for the Label

By law, almost every product imported into the U.S. requires a "made in wherever" label, but beyond that it's up to you how fancy or informative you want your label to be. French mirrors, for instance, may not need supplemental verbiage, while organic mulch will probably benefit from a bag that extols its environmental virtues.

You'll have to decide how important labeling is based on each product and the country it's being sold in, although it can always be a benefit. For example, labels let the consumer know how to use and care for the product.

aha!

Clever, consumer-friendly tags add to the buyer's perception of a product's value. Artisans who sell at crafts shows and gift boutiques, for instance, have found that a piece that carries a tag describing the artist and the craft will sell for a higher price than one without a tag.

▶ Proper Labeling Is Essential

Don't forget that your manufacturer will have to do some specific marking and labeling to meet government and shipping regulations, ensure proper handling, and help receivers identify shipments.

Also remember that certain products that fall under regulatory guidelines must be clearly marked as such. For example, if you're importing latex gloves that have not been approved for medical use, you can't use the description "exam gloves" in any way. If you do, the Food and Drug Administration will hold your shipment until you change each inner box and outer carton to read "industrial use" or "general purpose."

A customs broker will be able to guide you through these sorts of regulations, but it's your responsibility to do some of your own research and forward the information to your supplier(s).

You'll want to impress upon your clients that labels are a terrific way to build goodwill and additional brand recognition among both dealers and consumers.

However, let them know that they may need to translate and reprint their labels into the target language. They may also need to convert sizes and measurements to the metric system so local consumers will understand them.

Public Relations Patter

Once you land your first clients, continue to promote yourself to them and to new prospects through public relations, marketing, advertising, and promotions. Use materials garnered from your brochure, your copious market research, and your own import/export experiences to submit articles to pertinent print and online industry association journals, or give talks for local business associations. Word-of-mouth is a powerful advertising tool. Each person who reads your article or hears you speak is a potential client or networking resource.

Also, be sure to join applicable industry organizations and get involved in their events and activities.

How about appearing on radio talk shows or podcasts that discuss business or international trade? Call or email the radio station to get the name of the producer, then call them and ask about being a guest on their program. Listeners can then call in and ask questions about international trade.

To get booked as a guest on podcasts (which is often easier than getting booked on radio shows), check out a few podcast directories to find shows that cover topics about which you can speak with authority. Then contact the appropriate podcasters directly. There are podcasts that cover just about every topic imaginable, and many have huge loyal audiences.

Three popular podcast directories include: PodSearch (https://podsearch.com), PodBean (www.podbean.com/all), and Buzzsprout (www.buzzsprout.com/learn/podcast-directory).

Market by Educating Your Customers

One of the most efficient and effective ways to promote any business is through content marketing, defined by the Content Marketing Institute as "a marketing technique of creating and distributing relevant and valuable content to attract, acquire, and engage a clearly defined target audience—with the objective of driving profitable customer action."

Some people refer to content marketing as education marketing. The idea is to provide information that has value to your audience through your online content. You can share and promote that content through a variety of ways, including through the creative use of social media (via a Facebook page, LinkedIn account, or Twitter feed, for example.)

You can also use the internet to publish your own blog, podcast, or webinar. However, if you're going to do it, you need to do it right. Read other blogs, listen to other podcasts, and attend other webinars and get a feel for how they work. Also look up the top bloggers and podcasters in your field or find out which are the most popular webinars.

Social media marketing should be an important component of your overall marketing strategy. Every business should have its own Facebook page, Twitter feed, and LinkedIn account. Figure out how your company could benefit from using social media, then do what's best for your company and what matches your overall strategy. Keep in mind, using social media is typically free, but it can be very time consuming.

These steps will help you get started:

1. *Set clear goals for your social marketing efforts.* Be specific and keep those goals in mind with everything you do.
2. *Dedicate human resources to social marketing.* You need someone on your team (and it could be you) who understands social marketing, is comfortable with the platforms you'll be using, and has the time to manage your social marketing program.
3. *Be prepared to produce sufficient and ongoing fresh content.* Content is the fuel for your social marketing vehicle; without it, your efforts will stall.
4. *Prepare your website for social media attention.* Be sure your website is ready for the increased traffic social marketing could generate.
5. *Remember that it's a conversation.* Don't simply talk at your audience; engage them. One goal of social media is to create a virtual community around your company and its products/services.
6. *Create a social media policy for your employees.* Employees need to know what they can—and can't—say about the company when they are online.
7. *Be realistic in your expectations.* Don't anticipate monumental results for a minimal investment. Realistically, building a large and dedicated social media following takes years and a lot of manpower.

Service That Customer

In international trade, your customer service procedures fall into three categories: representatives, retailers, and end users. Like everything else in import/export, these categories overlap.

By servicing one, you'll be helping the others. The best way to do this is through dealer assistance programs. You'll want to steer your clients to your directory of products, which should be online, since bulky, heavy catalogs are not popular anymore.

An online catalog is something they can look at before your rep shows up. This way they can get a good idea of what they want, and your rep will have a more concise visit. You could always leave a printed catalog and brochures with the customer, as well as direct them to your website for more information.

Next supply your reps with a variety of printed and online-based informational materials. One set is designed to help the rep land the account. This set should include:

- ▶ Price lists
- ▶ Sales letters
- ▶ Point-of-purchase marketing materials, such as in-store posters or sample merchandise giveaways

The next set of materials is designed to help the retailer sell to the end user. These materials can include:

- ▶ Product management tools
- ▶ Display materials and ideas
- ▶ Stock control plans
- ▶ Sales promotion kits

Aside from these kinds of materials, your customer service program should emulate that of any domestic program. Your reps need to know that if they or someone further down the trade channel has a problem with the product, the manufacturer will take care of it.

Your reps need to be reachable (by phone or email) as close to 24/7 as possible. There should always be backups whom they can contact if your rep is out of reach or with another customer.

If you're acting as a distributor and you've purchased the product outright, you'll either have to handle after-market problems and servicing yourself or write servicing into your contract with the manufacturer.

Making sure your clients are satisfied with their service is a huge step toward ensuring the financial health of your business. Your customers are the core of your business. Therefore, you should always provide knowledgeable and polite customer service. Clients should be able to reach your customer service people by phone or email and get the help they need promptly.

Effectively Controlling Your Finances

Whether you are a chronic number cruncher or one of the finance-phobic, you'll want to give your company periodic financial checkups.

When you're running a small, fledgling operation, you'll want to conduct periodic safety checks to make sure your business is financially healthy. If there's a problem, find out before it becomes critical.

For example, if you discover that your commission fees barely cover your travel expenses, you can change gears and raise your commission rate before signing another client at the same rate. You can also take measures, like cutting back on travel.

Financial checkups don't have to be negative. They can potentially demonstrate how well you're doing. If you've been saving for a new printer or a market research trip, or if you're hoping to take on an employee, you can judge how close you are to achieving that goal by analyzing and understanding your company's finances.

More significantly, you will always know how much cash you have available, which is a must in business. Cash flow can make or break your business, especially when you need access to cash quickly, such as when sudden fees pop up that you may not have anticipated or accounted for. Likewise, if you have employees, you'll need to always make sure you can cover payroll. People do not like it if they don't get their paycheck on time, and your reputation of not paying promptly will spread quickly.

There are numerous ways to ensure you have enough money available when you need it. Vigilance is the name of the cash flow game. Watch what you spend, look hard for ways to save money, and make sure clients pay you on time.

If you take on a distributor function, keep a close eye on inventory. Don't overbuy. Research thoroughly. Be conservative and don't buy more than you need, and always put money away for the business.

Make sure you have available cash first, then pay yourself. Many new business owners work without taking a salary until they have enough money to keep the business up and running. Realistically, sometimes this takes a year or two. Don't go into business without having some money in reserve. If you think you may eventually need to borrow money, take steps ahead of time. Opening that line of credit before you need it can save you from high interest rates.

Number Crunch Your Way to Financial Success

An *income statement*, also called a *profit-and-loss statement*, charts the revenues and operating costs of your business over a period of time, usually a month. Check out the income statements (see Figures 12–1 and 12–2, on pages 211 and 212) for two hypothetical import/export services, Fair Trade Imports and Trade Winds Exports. Fair Trade handles $810,000 worth of business annually, while Trade Winds breezes along with $2,193,600 of annual business.

Fair Trade Imports Income Statement

Income Statement
For the month of April 20XX

Monthly Income		
Gross sales	$67,500.00	
Cost of sales	59,150.00	
Gross Monthly Income		**$8,350.00**
Monthly Expenses		
Rent	$ 0.00	
Phone/utilities	168.00	
Postage/delivery	33.00	
Licenses/taxes	339.00	
Employees	0.00	
Benefits/taxes	0.00	
Advertising/promotions	410.00	
Legal services	148.00	
Accounting services	220.00	
Office supplies	115.00	
Transportation/travel	550.00	
Insurance	157.00	
Subscriptions/dues	26.00	
Miscellaneous	170.00	
Total Monthly Expenses		**$2,336.00**
Net Monthly Profit		**$6,014.00**

Note: Cost of sales refers to the cost of the product as well as all documentation required to complete all trade transactions.

FIGURE 12–1: **Fair Trade Imports Income Statement**

Trade Winds Exports Income Statement

Income Statement

For the month of April 20XX

Monthly Income		
Gross sales	$212,400.00	
Cost of sales	182,380.00	
Gross Monthly Income		**$30,020.00**
Monthly Expenses		
Rent	$1,850.00	
Phone/utilities	320.00	
Postage/delivery	80.00	
Licenses/taxes	805.00	
Employees	2,213.00	
Benefits/taxes	378.00	
Advertising/promotions	1,160.00	
Legal services	246.00	
Accounting services	425.00	
Office supplies	166.00	
Transportation/travel	1,480.00	
Insurance	376.00	
Subscriptions/dues	45.00	
Miscellaneous	360.00	
Total Monthly Expenses		**$9,904.00**
Net Monthly Profit		**$20,116.00**

Note: Cost of sales refers to the cost of the product as well as all documentation required to complete all trade transactions.

FIGURE 12–2: **Trade Winds Exports Income Statement**

Fair Trade, a one-man band, is owner-operated and has its home base in the guest bedroom. Trade Winds has one full-time employee, an administrative assistant, and makes its base in a 900-square-foot downtown office. Neither owner draws a salary yet; they both rely on a percentage of the net profit for their income.

Both companies operate on a commission basis, with the owners taking their compensation from pretax net profits.

You'll want to tailor your income statement to your business. To calculate what's listed within the income statement correctly, you'll need to prorate items that are paid annually, such as business licenses, tax-time accounting fees, or Export.gov subscriptions, and pop those figures into your monthly statement. For example, if you pay an annual Export.gov fee of $200, divide this figure by 12, and add the resulting $14.58 to your subscriptions expense. Use the worksheet, Figure 12–3, on page 214 to chart your own income statement.

To make managing your company's finances much easier and to be able to create colorful charts and graphs in seconds that showcase your company's financial stability (or lack thereof), use a popular bookkeeping/accounting software application, such as QuickBooks (www.quickbooks.com).

The Cost of Credit

One issue that can vitally affect your finances is the extension of credit to your customers. Virtually any business beyond the level of street vending is forced to make credit-term decisions early on.

As an international trader, you'll find yourself faced with these same decisions. As you start out, however, a large part of the problem will be lifted from your shoulders by virtue of the letter of credit. Because the L/C is an intrinsic part of the import/export world, your customers will take it for granted. This is how they pay you through the international bank.

As your company grows and you and your customers get to know each other, you may be asked for credit terms. Sometimes it's difficult not to extend credit. Your customer may want to purchase exactly what you want to sell in an amount that's too sweet to resist. However, they also want 60 days' credit before they pay. How you respond is up to you. In Belgium, Jan Herremans accepts only L/Cs and cash for payment. "Due to many bad experiences, I take cash or irrevocable letter of credit only," she explained.

In Germany, Michael Richter accepts several different payment forms. "If the customer is buying merchandise, we agree for starters on a secure payment by L/C or bank draft," explained Michael. "Later we take payment as per an agreement or contract to be made. With bigger businesses, we may take financing in various percentages."

Income Statement Worksheet

Income Statement

For the month of _____

Monthly Income		
Gross sales		
Cost of sales		
Gross Monthly Income		$
Monthly Expenses		
Rent		
Phone/utilities		
Postage/delivery		
Licenses/taxes		
Employees		
Freelance and independent contractor fees for services rendered		
Benefits/taxes		
Advertising/promotions		
Legal services		
Accounting services		
Office supplies		
Transportation/travel		
Insurance		
Subscriptions/dues		
Internet services		
Vehicle/transportation expenses		
Professional/industry association membership fees and dues		
Miscellaneous		
Total Monthly Expenses		$
Net Monthly Profit		$

Note: Cost of sales refers to the cost of the product as well as all documentation required to complete all trade transactions.

FIGURE 12–3: **Income Statement Worksheet**

If you choose to extend credit, remember that any time you do, you're allowing your customer to use *your* money interest-free. This can be a good way to extend goodwill and build customer loyalty, but it can also be a good way to lose your shirt, while setting a bad precedent.

warning

According to U.S. Customs and Border Protection, many new importers are surprised by bills for duty tariffs, merchandise processing fees, and broker service charges. Don't be one of them! Again, make sure you do your homework.

Make sure your cash flow can cover the credit period before you approve. Likewise, be as sure as you can that your customer can come up with the funds owed when they're due.

This can be achieved by one of these options:

▶ Ask your banker to investigate.

▶ Order a financial report about your client from a service like Dun & Bradstreet, which has more than 100 million business records on file.

▶ Request a World Traders Data Report from your local U.S. Department of Commerce district office or visit this website: www.wto.org/english/res_e/reser_e/wtr_e.htm.

Many businesses extend credit only to proven customers. It's a gamble, because you may lose a sale here and there, but you won't be ripped off by companies that may disappear. It's not easy to chase down payment from another part of the world.

There Will Be Tough Financial Times

During economic downturns, keeping an international trading business in good fiscal shape can become challenging. Fortunately, most recessions are not global. So, chances are, some countries will be unaffected, or at least substantially less affected by a downturn.

Typically a global recession will not have an adverse effect on all sectors of international trade. In both fair and foul economic times, traders need to be able to switch gears, if necessary, and look for new or alternate opportunities.

Sometimes this means shifting to another product, and other times it means shifting focus to a different territory. You need to do your due diligence and determine which will work to your benefit. You will often find that greater diversity is valuable, especially if you foresee rocky economic waters on the horizon. Start focusing on various products and territories so you can formulate alternate plans if one part of the world or one product is not working out for you.

► Taking Inventory

Perhaps you've found some excellent merchandise and have decided to serve as a distributor for it. You've since taken title to the product—purchased it yourself—and are working with reps to sell it around the country. Now that you have inventory, it needs to be stored somewhere and accounted for.

Remember that your capital is tied up with your inventory. If you don't move it quickly, you're liable to run into a cash flow problem. So, try to line up buyers *before* you purchase goods.

If you don't, start an inventory system to ensure that you have enough stock on hand to supply your buyers, but not so much that you're paying through the nose for storage space. Keep careful track of how quickly items are moving, determine how long it will take to replace them, then order new shipments accordingly.

Do this at regular intervals so you can develop a better feel for how quickly items are selling and how long shipments take to arrive. This is one of the biggest challenges for small-business operators because making smart and accurate inventory decisions requires careful calculations and a little bit of fortune-telling to determine what the future might have in store.

For example, under President Donald Trump's administration, the trade war with China made it much more difficult to do business in the U.S., especially for smaller international trade companies.

Consider Your Bank as a Resource

From your first import/export venture, you should get used to thinking of your bank as a resource. After all, you're going to be working with your bankers a lot as you fulfill letters of credit. Your international banker should also be able to help you do the following:

- ► Locate new overseas markets.
- ► Develop data on the business climate in the country to which you're planning exports.
- ► Secure introductions to banking and trade contacts abroad.
- ► Secure letters of introduction and letters of credit when you're traveling abroad.
- ► Find credit information on potential overseas buyers.
- ► Establish your good credit when someone checks up on you.
- ► Stay current on export regulations.

- ▶ Exchange currencies.
- ▶ Secure financing for exports.
- ▶ Collect foreign invoices, drafts, letters of credit, and other foreign receivables.
- ▶ Transfer funds to other countries.
- ▶ Lend credit assistance to your foreign buyers.

Bankers are extremely important in the import/export industry. Add finding a compatible banker to your startup list of projects, then start interviewing, either by phone or preferably in person.

Interviewing bankers gives you the opportunity to establish a relationship. The closer your relationship with the bank manager or other banking executive(s), the better your chances of getting approved for loans or receiving special favors/treatment when you need them.

The fact that you're a newbie with a small startup account is not a drawback. You're offering the bank the prospect of future business. It doesn't hurt to cite examples from your projected income statements and market research. Remember, be realistic in your projections. Bankers will know when you exaggerate. Choose a banker who believes in you and that you can run the business.

Take Advantage of OPIC

The Overseas Private Investment Corporation, also known as OPIC, is a self-funded U.S. government agency that provides project financing, investment insurance, and a variety of investor services.

OPIC services are available for new and expanding business enterprises in more than 160 countries worldwide. OPIC encourages American overseas private investments to generate domestic exports and create jobs. For more information, visit www.opic.gov.

International Currency

As an international trader, you'll often deal in other currencies besides the U.S. dollar, so you'll need to develop an awareness and appreciation of world currencies. See Figure 12–4, page 218, for a list of currencies and their

tip ⓘ

To make currency conversion a breeze wherever and whenever you need it, install a currency converter app on your smartphone. If you're an iPhone user, visit the App Store (Android users go to the Google Play Store), and search for "currency converter" to see a listing of currency conversion apps Want to also easily check real-time foreign exchange rates? Visit http://x-rates.com or www.xe.com.

Countries' Currencies

Country	Name of Currency	Code
Australia	Australian dollar	AUD
Belgium	European euro	EUR
Brazil	Brazilian real	BRL
Cambodia	Cambodian reil	KHL
Canada	Canadian dollar	CAD
China	Chinese renminbi (ren)	CNY
Egypt	Egyptian pound	EGP
France	European euro	EUR
Germany	European euro	EUR
Hungary	Hungarian forint	HUF
India	Indian rupee	INR
Indonesia	Indonesian rupiah	IDR
Israel	New Israeli shequl	ISL
Japan	Japanese yen	JPY
Mexico	Mexican peso	MXN
Netherlands	European euro	EUR
Panama	Balboa	PAB
Philippines	Philippine peso	PHP
Poland	Polish zloty	PLN
Russia	Russian ruble	RUB
Saudi Arabia	Saudi Arabian riyal	SAR
South Africa	South African rand	ZAR
South Korea	South Korean won	KRW
Spain	European euro	EUR
Taiwan	New Taiwan dollar	TWD
Turkey	Turkish new lira	TRY
United Kingdom	British pound sterling	GBP
United States	U.S. dollar	USD
Venezuela	Venezuelan bolívar	VEF

FIGURE 12–4: **Countries' Currencies**

abbreviations. Anyone who has traveled outside the U.S. finds out almost immediately that one U.S. dollar isn't always worth a dollar when spending it abroad. Its value changes from country to country and from day to day, according to the U.S. and other national economies.

tip

If you'll be doing a lot of ongoing business in a particular country, it might make financial sense to maintain a bank account in that country and keep a balance of money in the local currency that you'll use to conduct your business. Over time, you'll save money on currency exchanges, but there are some tax and legal ramifications you'll need to iron out.

Whenever you discuss prices with your clients, customers, or anyone else in your trade channel, you'll need to think about the currency exchange rate. Because this rate constantly fluctuates, and you may have to alter your prices to reflect the current rate, this adds another calculation element to the import/export game. Don't forget to consider any currency conversion fees your bank may charge.

Let's say, for instance, that you are working with Egyptian goods and the U.S. dollar goes down in relation to the Egyptian pound. If you're importing from Egypt, you will groan because you'll now have to pay more in dollars to purchase the merchandise.

However, if you are exporting to Egypt, this same news will put a smile on your face. As an international trader, it behooves you to always keep your eye on currency exchange rates. When the currency rate swings one way, you might want to import. When it swings the other, think about exporting.

Meanwhile, you might make it a general rule to import goods from emerging economy countries whose currencies are always weak in relation to the U.S. dollar (so you can buy more for less), and export goods to countries with economies that are generally stronger than ours.

Ways to Exchange Currencies

Sometimes you'll be responsible for exchanging foreign currencies into U.S. dollars, which is generally done two ways:

1. *The Spot Transaction.* This involves the sale of U.S. dollars and the purchase of foreign currency (or the reverse) for immediate delivery, or on-the-spot delivery. For instance, if you sell merchandise to a company in Japan, you'll quote your price in either U.S. dollars or yen. Now the exchange rate may change before the deal is complete, but you've already set your price. This is where your tactical ability comes in. If you quote the price in dollars, the Japanese company assumes

the risk of a change in rates because it will have to pay the dollar value no matter what, and this change may or may not be to its benefit. If you quote the price in yen, you're the one assuming the risk. On the date of payment, you have the bank change the yen to dollars (or buy dollars with the yen). If the yen is weaker, you lose a percentage of your profits. If the yen is stronger, you gain profits.

tip

Often when you're exchanging money, the larger the amount, the better the rate. Sometimes, certain credit cards offer highly competitive exchange rates, but this varies by the card and the card issuer.

2. *The Forward Transaction.* If you don't want to sit around worrying about whether the exchange rate will go up or down, purchase the foreign currency at the time you make the deal. If you quote your price in yen, you immediately purchase the yen from the bank at the rate that coincides with your price quote. This way both parties are free from risk. However, if the foreign currency increases in value, you'll have lost an extra percentage point of potential profit.

Taxes and Other Considerations

When you earn money from your trading business, the U.S. government (the IRS) will be queuing up for a piece of the action. If your budget allows, work with an accountant (CPA). You probably won't need them for your daily or monthly concerns, but it's well worth the expense to have someone in the know available when April 15 comes around or to answer those finance-related questions that come up now and again.

If you are exporting, be aware that tax breaks for exporters are sometimes available. You or your accountant should investigate whether there are any current advantageous tax laws in effect.

Your tax deductions should be about the same as those for any other small or home-based business. The IRS has added all sorts of permutations, including that the total amount of the deduction is limited by the gross income you derive from the business activity, minus all your other business expenses apart from those related to the home office. Basically, the IRS doesn't want you to come up with so many home office deductions that you end up paying no tax at all. This is why working with an accountant (CPA) can be highly beneficial. These financial experts can often help you save money when it comes to paying taxes.

Foreign Taxes

Many countries have taxes that will affect the import and export prices of goods headed into and out of the country. Make sure you have taken foreign tax laws into account. It may also mean reaching out to an accountant in another country for some help.

Let Me Entertain You

In terms of your taxes, you can also deduct some entertainment expenses, such as wining and dining clients during a sales pitch, or hosting potential reps at a coffeehouse. Hold onto your receipts and keep a detailed log of these expenses. (If you're entertaining at home, have your clients or prospects sign a guest book.)

You must have a business-related purpose for entertaining, such as a sales presentation. General goodwill toward your fellow professionals doesn't count in the eyes of the IRS, so be sure your log contains the reason for the partying. Also, some forms of partying and entertainment are not acceptable by the IRS for deductions, so consult your accountant before raking up huge bills.

> **aha!**
>
> Index Mundi (www.indexmundi.com) provides statistics and other information, including everything from demographics to the economy, on a country-by-country basis. The source for most of the information is the CIA World Factbook (https://www.cia.gov/library/publications/resources/the-world-factbook/index.html).

Brilliant Deduction

What else can you deduct? Business-related phone calls, the cost of business equipment and supplies, subscriptions to professional and trade journals, business-related travel, and transportation expenses.

When it comes to work-related driving, it's wise to keep a log of your business miles. It's no fun to have to backtrack at tax time and guesstimate how many miles you drove that year. There are smartphone apps that can help you automatically calculate mileage for work-related travels.

Planes, Trains, and Automobiles

When you travel for business purposes, you're able to deduct airfares, train tickets, rental car mileage (and rental fees), ground transportation expenses (taxis, Uber rides, etc.), and related expenses. You can also deduct hotels and meals.

Because the IRS allows deductions for any business trip you take to expand your awareness and expertise in your field of business, it makes sense to take advantage of any conferences or seminars that you can attend while traveling. Also try to set up business-related meetings. Since tax laws and IRS deductions change often, check with the IRS's website (www.irs.gov), or consult your accountant to make sure you understand what is allowed.

Beware of Global Dangers

The world is, unfortunately, not as safe as it once was, and traveling abroad can put you in harm's way. Learn about where you are going beforehand. Research details about the economy, the safety, and the areas you do and do not want to visit.

Make sure you know exactly where you are going. Map everything out ahead of time, and if you have cellular data connectivity while you're abroad, take advantage of the maps app that's built into your smartphone.

Many traders are traveling less frequently due to the high cost of traveling, security issues, and the fact that they can do a lot more of their jobs from their internet-connected

▶ Innocents Abroad

While technology can cut down on some of your travel needs, you will still, most likely, find yourself on the road a lot. Traveling can be half the fun of international trade. But make sure you're not an innocent abroad. Plan your itinerary carefully to make your trip as personally and professionally productive as possible.

To make every moment count, combine several business activities, such as:

▶ Finding new clients, reps, and/or suppliers

▶ Seeking new products or product categories to specialize in

▶ Reinforcing your relationships with current clients and reps

▶ Evaluating your competition

▶ Updating your market research

Set up meetings before you leave home so you're assured that the people you want to see will be available. As always, do your homework. Will you be arriving in a country during a holiday or festival period when offices will be closed? Be sure to research local customs.

computers. It's hard to cut out traveling entirely, but you may be able to minimize some of it.

Anytime you're traveling abroad, be sure to acquire travel insurance from a well-respected company, such as Travel Guard (www.travelguard.com) or Travelex (www.travelex.com). The per-trip expense of travel insurance will typically cost about 10 percent of the overall trip's cost, but if something goes wrong or you have a medical emergency, the travel insurance will prove extremely useful.

If you do a lot of overseas travel, consider purchasing a customized, annual travel insurance plan. Keep in mind, purchasing travel insurance from your current health insurance provider will cover health-related emergencies that occur overseas, but these plans typically do not cover your luggage or personal property, or any problems with travel providers (airlines, hotels, tour companies, cruise lines, etc.).

Passport Considerations

If you don't yet already have a valid U.S. passport, apply for one now. Processing can take four to six weeks (sometimes longer). Once you have a password, make sure you keep it current. Some countries will deny you entry if you have six months or less left until your passport expires.

As you're planning trips abroad, determine if you need to apply for a travel visa or work permit in advance. This can sometimes be a time-consuming and costly endeavor, especially if you wait until the last minute. The CIBTvisas website (https://cibtvisas.com) can help you determine when and if a visa for a specific country will be need.

To save time re-entering the U.S. after a trip abroad, consider signing up for the Customs and Border Protection's Global Entry program. Approved program members simply pass through automatic kiosks at the airport to get expedited entry into the U.S. It takes several months for an application to be approved, but once you're admitted into the Global Entry program (the fee is $100), it lasts for five years. For more information, visit www.cbp.gov/travel/trusted-traveler-programs/global-entry.

Fair Winds or Foul Seas

M ost people succeed in the import/export business by following the tried-and-true business methods of persistence and hard work, with a healthy dose of optimism sprinkled in. All the raw talent in the world doesn't change the fact that becoming an international trader involves a lot of work. It can certainly be rewarding and sometimes exhilarating, but it's almost always hard work.

Industry expert Wendy Larson noted that building strong ties is crucial to success in the trade industry. "There is no substitute for face-to-face relationships," she said. She also stressed the importance of familiarity, both business-wise and culturally, with the part of the world in which you're trading.

Becoming an international trader is not the same as becoming an overnight success. It takes lots of market research, loads of planning, hours of financial calculations, sore knuckles from knocking on virtual doors, the abundant application of creativity to land that first client, and more of the same to land the ones that follow. Be persistent and do what's necessary to stay motivated!

Develop a Passion for Your Work

Whether or not you're earning money, the success of your business is contingent on being passionate for what you do. Because it's a lot of work and responsibility, you may discover that you'd be just as happy, or more so, working for someone else. That's OK, as long you determine this early on, before losing a lot of money.

▶ The Right Reputation

How are U.S. products viewed abroad? How do they stack up against similar goods produced in other countries? Questions like these are important to those traders looking to export American products.

Sam Nelson, trading in North Carolina, has many clients who consider American medical equipment to be high quality. "They say it's expensive, but the quality is good," he noted. "Chinese equipment is cheaper, but not made as well."

Lloyd Davidson agreed. "The U.S. overall has a good reputation for its product quality. Foreign companies like to deal with us." Products the U.S. is particularly noted for include aircraft, medical and scientific equipment, and agricultural products.

If you export, you'll want to be known as a trader who reliably supplies high-quality goods. Choosing your export products carefully, with a constant eye toward quality as well as price, will serve your business well. Your business is one of many U.S. companies contributing to the future reputation of this country's products. A continued positive reputation for U.S. goods will help your company continue to grow.

What seems to be the common denominator for all international traders is they all have a winning attitude, as well as a passion and dedication to their work. If you go into this business with the right stuff—a willingness to work hard and learn everything you can, the confidence to promote yourself and your business, and the drive to succeed—chances are you will!

More Advice from International Trading Experts

The need to find and work with mentors and experienced international trade experts who have skills and knowledge that you lack cannot be emphasized enough. As you set out to establish your own trusted network, take advantage of the advice offered by the experts interviewed within this chapter.

Ethan Frisch
Cofounder, Burlap & Barrel Single Origin Spices
www.burlapandbarrel.com

Ethan Frisch is an experienced international trader and cofounder of Burlap & Barrel, which he describes as the only single-origin spice company in the U.S. His company works with small spice producers and spice farms in 13 countries, many of which have never exported their products before. Burlap & Barrel handles all the logistics involved with setting up each company to export for the first time. His company buys and exports their spices and imports them into the U.S.

Before launching this company, Ethan had extensive experience working as a chef at several high-end restaurants, as well as experience in international development. After leaving his career as a chef to attend grad school, Ethan moved to Afghanistan to become an aid worker for several years. He then went on to handle logistics for Doctors Without Borders in the Middle East (on the Syrian/Jordanian border), then returned to the U.S. in 2016 to launch Burlap & Barrel.

"I had never done any importing or exporting like this before," explained Ethan. "I learned what I needed to on the job. In the U.S., we work with very high-end restaurants, so the spices we supply need to be the absolute highest quality possible. In some cases, restaurants request specific spices and we then seek out a source for them. In other cases, we seek out small spice farmers and look for products that we believe will be a good complement to our current product lineup. Our goal is to find unusual, high-quality spices that other companies are not importing. For us, finding good, reliable sources in countries around the world is a difficult challenge. We source spices from countries like Guatemala, Tanzania, and Vietnam. We often go into a country with few or no leads, set out to meet people, develop good relationships with them, set them up to export, and then import their spice products into the U.S."

Since you work with so many small spice growers from all over the world, how do you ensure that each will provide the consistent quality you require?

Ethan: Knock on wood, we have not had any issues so far. I think our partners recognize this is a great financial opportunity for them, and they're willing to take whatever extra steps are required to make the relationship work. We are a public benefit corporation, which follows a hybrid for-profit/nonprofit model. A big part of our mandate is to connect small, independent spice farmers with profitable export opportunities. One way we do this is by paying them between five and 20 times the commodity price for their crop. We spend a lot of time visiting with farmers in person to find the perfect long-term partners.

What skills or knowledge did you need to acquire once you decided to launch Burlap & Barrel?

Ethan: I had traveled extensively around the world and lived in more than a half dozen countries prior to launching this company. I knew nothing about exporting products, especially something as challenging as a food item that's also an agricultural product, from the country of origin and then importing them into the United States. I needed to learn all about international trade logistics. I spent a lot of time speaking with customs brokers and reading books about importing and exporting.

For our first bunch of shipments into the U.S., I went to the airport myself and had long discussions with the Customs and Border Patrol agents. I took the education aspect very seriously, studied hard, and learned what I needed to know. That said, there is still a huge amount that I don't know. With every shipment I learn something new, and I expand my knowledge every time something does not go as planned with a shipment. Import and export requires an endless learning process.

You work with customs brokers. How did you find a knowledgeable and trustworthy customs broker to work with when you were first starting?

Ethan: A customs broker is a necessary part of any import process. I started by getting a recommendation for a custom broker who specializes in importing spices and who had extensive experience with this. He had a very positive reputation within the industry as someone who was knowledgeable and reliable. I also worked with customs brokers who were associated with our freight forwarders. Basically, I have relied on recommendations and referrals.

Early on, I seriously thought about taking the customs broker exam myself, and did all the required studying for the exam. This helped me understand the foundation of the process so I knew more about what to look for when hiring a customs broker. I now understand many of the processes they use to get their job done, so that's very helpful.

How do you choose which countries or regions you'll import spices from?

Ethan: We work with farms in 13 different countries right now. The initial relationships were ones that I had developed from previously working with NGOs and nonprofits. Our first suppliers were from Afghanistan, where I lived for a few years. Another country we began working in shortly thereafter was Tanzania. I have a close friend who lives there who manages a direct trade coffee project. She put me in touch with a spice co-op that was interested in doing their own exporting. I basically began in counties where I already had connections and contacts. Using established connections was also how we linked up with spice farmers in Guatemala, Egypt, and Turkey, for example.

The other countries we now work in have come about as a result of needing to source specific spices or utilizing contacts who provided introductions that we needed. In every case, I travel to that country and meet in person with the farmers we hope to do business with. Most recently, we have had small, independent farmers in various countries reach out to us through Instagram and through our website. This is how we developed a relationship with one of our growers in India, for example. We just accepted our first shipment from a spice farmer in Indonesia who made contact with us through email. He was interested in exporting his products to the U.S. for the first time. I already had a trip planned to Indonesia, so I went to visit him and cultivated that relationship in person.

Is it easier to work with some countries as opposed to others when importing spices?

Ethan: Yes, very much so. The FDA has lists of approved products from different countries. When our spices don't fit on that list, our importing activities can become a bit more challenging. For example, the spices we import from Nicaragua are rarely ever imported into the U.S., so on the FDA side, this initially caused some delays to acquire the appropriate clearance and approval.

Because we're working with very small producers, who are not experienced exporters, we need to help those partners navigate through their local regulations. Believe it or not, the bigger and more established export countries have posed a greater challenge for us to work in, because they tend to be more bureaucratic. There is often a system of licensing, and we need to work through a licensed exporter, since small farmers are unable to export on their own.

For someone launching their import/export business, do you recommend that they seek out emerging markets to do business in?

Ethan: It totally depends on the products you're looking to import or export. A huge driver for our business is that we're able to source and import rare spices that other spice importers do not or cannot offer. This often requires us working with farmers from emerging markets. Working with first-time exporters, as well as the FDA, sometimes provides additional challenges, but for us, it's worth it. The advice I offer is to figure out exactly what product you want to work with, and then determine the best places to source that product from. There are almost always then ways to figure out the import/export side of it.

Since you launched Burlap & Barrel, how has international trade changed or evolved?

Ethan: There's a piece of legislation, called the Food Safety Modernization Act, which has had a huge impact on our business recently. It has changed the way spices, and food across the board, are imported into the United States. This legislation has thrown the whole food industry into a little bit of an uproar. The downside is that it's become a lot more challenging to figure out how to import food products into the United States. On the upside, this legislation has put us on a more level playing field compared to our larger competitors. This legislation requires importers to have a more traceable supply chain. Food exporters from other countries, as well as importers, now need to be registered with the FDA. I believe this is an important piece of legislation, but it's also added more complexity to the food import process.

Over the next five to ten years, what changes or challenges do you see emerging regarding international trade?

Ethan: The changes that I am seeing or anticipating are ones that I am looking forward to. There is a growing interest among consumers in terms of where their food is coming from and how it's being produced.

In the past few years, I have seen improvements in shipping methods, lower carbon emissions systems, better tracking systems, faster turnaround times, and the ability of freight forwarders to pick up products from very remote locations. Communications technology and transportation around the world has also improved greatly in recent years. These are all trends that I see continuing, and that will make the importer and exporter's job that much easier.

You mentioned government bureaucracy and the associated red tape can be a challenge to deal with. What are some of the other challenges that an importer/exporter has to contend with on a regular basis?

Ethan: Managing timelines is a huge challenge. Both on the import and export side, timelines can be slow and unpredictable. There are very specific processes that items need to go through in order to be imported or exported. Sometimes those processes are quick. Other times they are not. There's not a lot of visibility into why something might be delayed or for how long. There are also a lot of surprise fees that come up that need to be accounted for.

Understand that the various processes involved with importing and exporting are going to take a certain amount of time, and even if you do everything correctly, you can't always have control over your timelines. Being impatient or pushy will never serve you well. You need to learn how to be patient and work within the bureaucracy, not fight against it. A successful importer or exporter must pay attention to all the details and be a detail-oriented person. You also need to develop an understanding of how the overall process works.

Going hand in hand with being patient, the most successful importers and exporters are also extremely friendly.

How does your company account for the unexpected fees and expenses, yet remain profitable?

Ethan: One of the things we do is that we always start off with small shipments. In these cases, the fees are sometimes much more expensive than the product itself. As quantities go up, the impact of the unexpected fees goes down, so it's more manageable. Basically, from experience, you build knowledge about what some of the surprise fees will be, and you build them into your price calculations from the start. We never quote prices to our customers until we physically have product in hand, because unexpected fees can dramatically increase what we need to charge. Having a close relationship with our customs brokers and freight forwarders also helps us accurately predict what our fees and expenses will be. A lot has to do with learning from experience.

Is there a piece of information you know now that you wish you understood from day one?

Ethan: Yes. Customs and importing is a hugely complicated field that people spend many years trying to become experts in, yet very few people, if anyone, knows everything about it. Everyone needs to figure out the ins and outs of importing and exporting as they go. Some people have more experience than others, but there's always a lot of learning involved.

How much travel is involved in your job now that Burlap & Barrel is in full operation and successful?

Ethan: Running this business requires a tremendous amount of travel. It's probably the most exciting aspect of my job. My last trip, for example, took me to Spain, Turkey, Afghanistan, and Tanzania. For the past three years, I have embarked on at least four big, multi-destination trips per year. I spend a lot of time meeting and working with our partner farmers. It's very exciting when I am able to create a brand-new supply chain that never existed before. We are creating new opportunities for small spice farmers located all over the world.

In addition to meeting with suppliers in person, I rely a lot on modern communication technology to discover and establish new business partnerships around the world. In recent years, smartphones have become much more affordable and available to farmers working in some of the more remote locations around the world. Whatever communication platform our partners use is what we rely on. This is often WhatsApp and Facebook Messenger. In some cases, we also use email or traditional phone calls. I personally use Google Translate a lot when I communicate with people from other countries.

Today, we have access to so much information. Importing without utilizing the information available to us, via the internet, for example, puts you at a disadvantage. We are working in one of the oldest industries in the world. Importing and exporting has been done for thousands of years. We are very aware of the shoulders we're standing on. My goal is to keep doing it, but to do it better.

Is there any other advice you'd offer to someone getting started in international trade?

Ethan: My main tip is to just get started. You're never going to have all the answers or learn everything you'll ultimately need to know. The best thing you can do is start doing it. You're going to learn so much more by actually doing the job than thinking about or preparing to do the job. Start small. Mitigate risk in all the ways you can, and then get started!

Umberto Luchini
President, Wolf Spirit Distillery
https://www.wolfspiritdistillery.com/

Umberto Luchini is another example of a highly successful entrepreneur who spent the majority of his life living and working in a variety of countries, which allowed him to grow up learning about many different cultures. He was born and raised in Italy. At the age of 18, he moved to the UK to pursue his education and learn English. "My father encouraged me to travel abroad for my education and learn to live in other countries," said Umberto. "After graduating, I never returned to Italy. I worked for eight years in Formula 1 racing, managing sponsors for a team. This job allowed me to travel for 10 months per year to all the Grand Prix races around the world. This is where I really developed my passion for meeting people and learning about different countries and cultures."

Umberto's next job was with the Olympic Committee in Switzerland. His responsibilities involved planning and coordinating the 2000 Olympics in Sydney, Australia. From there, he left sports marketing and re-entered the corporate world. He landed a job with Campari America, the parent company for Skyy Vodka. The company was looking for Italians who were willing to relocate to America. He answered the call, and in 2005, he moved to California and has lived there since.

In January 2017, Umberto decided to leave Campari and launch his own company, Wolf Spirit Distillery, to pursue his own American dream. "I wanted to create my own story. It was time for me to abandon the safety net that having a corporate job provided," said Umberto. "I was more excited for the opportunity that starting my own business provided than I was afraid of the significant financial risk. As an entrepreneur, you need to have a core belief that what you are doing is going to succeed. This creates a positive energy that is contagious. This positive attitude will impact the people around you. Of course, you still need a solid business plan and a strong understanding of the finances. As an entrepreneur, the hard skills you need can always be acquired. It's the soft skills and the ability to gather the right team of motivated people around you that many entrepreneurs lack."

As much ambition, excitement, and positive energy that you have, Umberto stresses that nothing replaces the need for hard work. "The goal is to engage in this hard work, but because of your passion, it should not feel like hard work. What you're doing should be fun, challenging, and rewarding at the same time. This is what will help you succeed," he added.

Right away, Umberto created two separate vodka brands. One of the vodka brands is produced in Eugene, Oregon, and is distributed to 23 U.S. states. His plan is to begin exporting this vodka to select European markets and Canada in 2020. The second vodka brand is produced in Finland and imported to the U.S. It's also sold in 10 other countries.

Between his decades of international travels and work experiences, Umberto has established a vast network of professional relationships all over the world, which he credits for allowing him to succeed as an entrepreneur in international trade. "We're living in a globally connected world which offers a greater opportunity for imports and exports than ever before," stated Umberto.

As an importer and exporter, what do you see as the biggest challenges your company faces?

Umberto: There is a lot of concern about new tariffs and expanded trade rules being established by the U.S. as well as other countries. It's not a matter of which country is right or wrong. Their actions are creating uncertainty in the import/export business, and one thing businesses require is certainty. If there are known tariffs or regulations, we can easily deal with them. It's not knowing what to expect in the months ahead that continues to create a series of challenges, especially when it comes to financial projections and price setting. Despite this uncertainty, we are doing our best to continue with business as usual. When changes occur, we're as prepared as we can be to react. As a smaller company, we are able to react faster than larger competitors that have well-established ways of doing things.

Right now, economies are generally strong in the countries we do business in. However, uncertainty leads to negative perceptions, and those perceptions have the ability to help define future reality. That's my concern.

What are some of the biggest changes in import and export that you see happening over the next few years?

Umberto: International trade is going to become more important to countries all over the world, and individual people are going to be traveling much more than ever before. As a result, brands that offer an inherent value will become more popular, because consumers will be exposed to those same brands wherever they go in the world.

How do you go about building a brand and a demand for your products in foreign markets?

Umberto: It all comes down to building relationships with the right partners abroad. The way you select these partners is to build a network of trusted people who are business professionals. As a businessperson, you need to develop a positive reputation as someone with a great attitude, and who is honest and does business ethically. Business is all about one-to-one relationships. Having trusted partners and networks in the countries where you're exporting to is more important than advertising your products and brand.

Online platforms, like LinkedIn, allow people to discover and communicate with potential business partners all over the world. One of the ways I decide which countries to export to is to determine where our largest pool of potential customers live. By selling the product in our home country, we already know who our target customer is. It's just a matter of identifying that market in other countries. Next, I research whether those countries have distribution capabilities in place that we can utilize.

An entrepreneur looking to export products should always look for efficient opportunities when it comes to shipping and distributing products abroad. If you have a product that's popular in North America, for example, chances are you'll discover similar markets for that product in Canada and in many countries in Europe and possibly Australia, due to similarities in those cultures. As a business operator, you need to develop an understanding of the cultures where you plan to do business. Start by looking for export countries that are geographically convenient and culturally compatible with your product.

The next thing you need to look at is tariffs and pricing. When we ship a vodka product from the U.S. to Finland, for example, that single bottle of vodka needs to be priced three times higher in Finland than in the U.S. in order to cover our costs. You need to determine if consumers in the countries you'll be exporting to are willing to pay what you'll need to charge in order to earn a profit. As you're forced to increase your pricing, you need to rely much more on the strength of the brand you create.

If you're a U.S.-based export company, is it better to work with U.S. trade partners or seek emerging markets when choosing where to distribute your products?

Umberto: I would personally start with U.S. trade partners. However, the U.S. is such a global powerhouse, you'll likely discover that companies all over the world will be willing to work with you, based on what you're selling, of course.

You mentioned the importance of building a strong international network of people you trust. How do you go about this, beyond finding referrals or business listings on LinkedIn, for example?

Umberto: The internet is a powerful networking tool. There are also useful international trade associations that have global reach and can help you with your professional networking. Nothing replaces the need to meet and work with people in-person, however. Attend trade shows and trade fairs, as well as association meetings, for example. Once I make a potential connection online, I will always make a point to fly to that person and meet them in person before I do business with them.

I am a firm believer in jumping on an airplane and setting up a one-to-one meeting with that person. I want to look straight into the eyes of someone I will be doing business with and shake their hand. This sends a strong message to the other partner and allows me to feel more comfortable in the choices I make. Being able to do this requires a strong commitment to your business and a willingness to spend a lot of time away from your home and office in order to personally cultivate relationships.

What are some of the personality traits and special skills someone needs to succeed as an importer or exporter in today's business world?

Umberto: You need to be easygoing. When you travel, expect flight delays and hotels to fall short of your comfort expectations. This is all part of the job, and you need to accept it, without getting upset or frustrated.

Be open-minded! As a business leader, you need to understand that situations will arise where you're required to change your mind about something. Be open to learn and change your mind, especially when you're working with other cultures and in foreign markets. Humility, not arrogance, will be a huge asset. In the beginning, when your business is a startup, chances are your business partners do not need you anywhere near as much as you need them. Always be humble and respectful.

What are some of the biggest mistakes you made yourself, or you've seen others make when starting as an international trader?

Umberto: The number-one mistake was thinking that I knew and understood a lot more than I actually did about international trade. I relied too much on what I thought I could do myself, as opposed to bringing on board experts who could help me. Try to surround yourself with talented people who are experts in the things that you are not good at or not as excited about. If you try to do everything yourself, this is a shortcut to disaster. Invest time and money in surrounding yourself with the people who will be able to bring your business to the next level.

You may think that Steve Jobs was the driving force behind the success of Apple or Bill Gates was the sole reason why Microsoft became successful, but behind these two visionary businesspeople were many talented people helping and supporting them along the way.

Nobody can create a large and successful business by themselves. I lost almost a full year and a lot of money when I launched Wolf Spirit Distillery, because I believed I could do everything myself.

How important is it to work with a customs broker or freight forwarder?

Umberto: Working with a skilled, knowledgeable, and experienced customs broker and/or freight forwarder is essential, depending on the type of work you're doing. Especially in the beginning, having these trusted partners will be extremely cost effective.

Is there any additional advice you're willing to share?

Umberto: Yes. Become a world traveler. Don't just sit at your desk and rely exclusively on the internet to conduct your business. Don't rely on what other people say about specific countries, cultures, or economies. Go there and see for yourself.

When I needed to learn about the Mexican market, for example, I went to Mexico and spent six weeks driving around the country to discover the culture and business opportunities firsthand. Traveling is not always comfortable or easy, but you need to break out of your comfort zone and be open to acquiring new knowledge and having new experiences in order to learn about different cultures.

Schuyler "Rocky" Reidel
Managing Attorney, Reidel Law Firm
www.reidellawfirm.com

Throughout this book, you've read about the importance of working with a skilled and knowledgeable attorney, as well as an equally skilled, knowledgeable, and experienced customs broker.

Schuyler Reidel is unique in that he's both an attorney and licensed customs broker based in Texas. He works with clients from all over the world, including Europe and the Middle East, helping them handle import/export compliance, project startup and management, and dealing with product seizures and licensing requirements.

"I grew up near the ports in Texas," Schuyler said. While in law school, I determined that I wanted to pursue business law. I quickly discovered, however, that there are very few attorneys who specialize in international trade who are also licensed customs brokers. After opening my own legal practice, I studied and took the exam to become a customs broker, which was a more challenging endeavor than I had anticipated.

"These days, most of my clients come from face-to-face marketing and word-of-mouth. I do not need to do any traditional advertising. I attend trade shows and give talks about international trade. Texas is home to large shipping ports, but also hosts several prominent trade shows related to mining and the petrol chemical industries, for example."

Now that Schuyler's firm is well-established and his clients are based all over the world, he finds himself traveling extensively. "Because of the trade war, for me, business relating to China has virtually dried up, but I spend a lot of time traveling to the Middle East, Russia, and Europe. In 2019, for example, I spent about two months overseas," said Schuyler. "I identified a need that small to medium-size businesses had for a lawyer and customs broker with an international trade specialty, and I set out to fill that need."

When you begin working in a new country, how important is it to spend time learning about the local culture?

Schuyler: Based on my experience, this varies based on where you'll be doing business and how tolerant they are of Western business practices. In general, you should do research to determine what you can do to make the best possible impression and make a better deal. I will always do research to learn about a country's business culture before traveling to a new country. The U.S. Commercial Service [www.trade.gov/cs] is one of the best resources for entrepreneurs looking to learn about and do business with partners in foreign countries.

Depending on what country I will be working in, I will sometimes retain a translator to help ensure accurate communication. For me, this has been a necessity in China, for example. The further you get away from Western business culture, the more help you're going to need. It's important to understand the nuances of what's happening in an important business conversation or negotiation.

If you have a trusted friend in the country you plan to do business with, that person can also teach you about local customs and business practices. When I travel, I have discovered that friendships develop very naturally and very quickly.

Does being an American help you or hurt you when it comes to working with people from other countries and conducting international trade?

Schuyler: Typically, being an American will help you, because many foreign businesspeople recognize the United States as being a potentially huge market for them to break into. People from other countries also have a natural curiosity about Americans, the American culture, and American politics.

Being an importer or exporter means dealing with government bureaucracy and red tape. Your job is to help your clients cut through the red tape. How do you stay current on all the latest laws, tariffs, and regulations?

Schuyler: Trade associations are an important resource for me. I also need to do a lot of research on various government websites to stay current. Especially these days, with trade being unstable in regard to the rules, laws, and compliance requirements, I need to go back to square one for each new project and figure out what knowledge I will need to make it successful. Things change very quickly.

How can a startup find the perfect lawyer and/or customs broker to work with?

Schuyler: There are lots of approaches. First determine if your overseas business partners already have an established relationship with a customs broker. In this case, the customs broker will likely already be familiar with the product or industry. Another option is to seek referrals from a trade association. Always do your due diligence. Research the customs broker's experience and reputation before hiring them.

Ask a potential customs broker if they've worked with your category of product before and if they have any insight about the type of requirements that are going to be involved. Ask how they'll go about putting the supply chain together and how they're going to get your product from location A to location B.

Some ports are more efficient at processing imports and exports than others. Depending on what your customs broker decides for your supply chain, if your products go through a port that's not efficient or does not have an expertise in your type of product, you'll likely experience long and potentially costly delays, especially if there are compliance issues involved. An experienced customs broker can help avoid this.

Should a startup opt to work with U.S. trade partners or be open to working with emerging markets early on?

Schuyler: A lot depends on the types of products or industry you're dealing with. If you're working with products that are highly regulated, it's probably easier to work with established and trusted U.S. trade partners. If you're working with emerging markets, you'll likely encounter more paperwork and more challenges to ensure that you are compliant. A lot of what you'll encounter is product specific, so it's important to consider where you're sourcing your materials from.

In your opinion, how has importing and exporting changed over the past few years? Has it gotten better or worse for U.S.-based international trading companies?

Schuyler: Whether it's gotten better or worse, it's very hard to say. There's a very wide spectrum. It's impossible to make a general statement. Even with the trade war with China, I still see companies doing very well working with China, for example. I have also seen many companies feel pressure as a result of the trade war. In general, international trade is less stable then it has been in the past. There are a lot of changes taking place, especially from a legal and geopolitical perspective. I think that for the years to come, we can expect to experience similar instability and continued changes, even if the trade war ends tomorrow.

There's going to be a period when the dust needs to settle. This is happening on a global scale. Importers and exporters are looking for new opportunities and new countries to do business in. Instead of sourcing a product from China, for example, an importer may now look to a country, like Vietnam or Indonesia, for better quality products or better pricing.

Regardless of what happens with the 2020 presidential election in the United States, I don't know how much can be rolled back in terms of the impact of the international trade war that's been taking place in 2018 and 2019. The United States will likely continue to rely on Chinese products, and China will continue to rely on American products moving forward. Once the trade war ends, however, I do not anticipate that all the previous business will return to China, since America and other countries have already discovered viable alternatives.

I predict that moving forward, we'll see a growing importance in multinational trade hubs, like Dubai, Singapore, and Panama City. Panama. These will become more important regional hubs where people from various countries gather to do international trade business, as opposed to going directly to the country of origin, for example.

If a prospective startup client came to you today seeking advice about whether to launch an import/export business, what would you tell them?

Schuyler: The American market is huge, even beyond consumer products. This country has a tremendous demand for imported products, and there's plenty of potential for exporting as well. There are always going to be aspects of import/export that are vital to the U.S. economy. What I suggest is that startups quickly find their unique niche and become experts related to that niche, whether it's a specific product, product category, and/or a geographic region. Dig in deep. Figure out what's going on in that industry and who the key trade partners are for your product category. Find an area or industry that's underserved and strive to fill a need. If you pursue this approach, you'll likely discover a lot of lucrative opportunities.

What are some of the biggest challenges an import/export business faces today?

Schuyler: Establishing a supply chain with reliable and trustworthy partners is a major challenge but one that can easily be overcome with due diligence. Do your homework and stay up-to-date on the continuous changes taking place. Also, become an expert in your product, industry, and/or the geographic regions you choose to serve. This will help you anticipate and ultimately overcome whatever challenges you encounter.

From my perspective, the biggest mistake I see companies make is not knowing or understanding the importing or exporting compliance issues that relate to their products. For example, just because you see a product listed and being sold on Amazon.com, this does not mean it's legal. At some point, if you do something illegal or that's not in compliance, you will get caught, and it will be costly.

Clients often bring me in to fix compliance-related problems after they occur. You're much better off working with an attorney in advance. Obtain a detailed import/export compliance report for your product before you attempt to do any importing or exporting. Creating this report might cost you a few thousand dollars upfront, but it will help you prepare and allow you to avoid potentially much more costly mistakes in the future.

Based on your experience, is there a specific skill set or personality type that's required to succeed as an international trader?

Schuyler: You need to be friendly and open to different cultures. It also helps to be curious so you want to learn more about potential opportunities. You also need to be inquisitive so you know when to ask questions and what questions to ask to ensure you're pursuing viable opportunities. You also cannot be risk adverse in the import/export business. People who are risk-takers, but only willing to make educated and well-researched decisions related to taking on risk, will be at an advantage.

Surround yourself with experienced and trustworthy experts, especially as you're starting. Try to find experienced mentors who can offer you guidance and honest feedback along the way. Your mother may be very supportive, but she's probably not the best person to give you business advice about a potential international trade deal.

International Trade Resources

They say you can never be rich enough or thin enough. While that's arguable, we firmly believe you can never have enough resources. Therefore, we're giving you a wealth of sources to check into, check out, and harness for your own personal information blitz.

These sources are tidbits—ideas to get you started on your research. They are by no means the only sources out there, and they should not be taken as the ultimate answer. We have done our research, but businesses tend to move, change, fold, and expand. As we have repeatedly stressed, do your homework. Get out there and start investigating!

Associations

The American Association of Exporters & Importers, 1717 K St. NW, #1120, Washington, DC 20006, (202) 857-7843, www.aaei.org

The Federation of International Trade Associations, 172 5th Ave., #118, Brooklyn, NY 11217, http://fita.org

International Chamber of Commerce, 33-43 Avenue du President Wilson, 75116 Paris, France, 33 (0)1-49-53-28-28, http://iccwbo.org

International Federation of Customs Brokers Associations, 55 Murray St., #320, Ottawa, ONT K1N 5M3, CAN, http://ifcba.org

International Organization for Standardization, Chemin de Blandonnet 8, CP 401–1214 Vernier, Geneva, Switzerland, +41 22 749 01 11, www.iso.org

Long Island Import Export Association, 2652 Dorothy St., Bellmore, NY 11710, (516) 783-1369, www.liiea.org

Organization of Women in International Trade, 1100 Vermont Ave. NW, #715, Washington, DC 20005, http://owit.org

The Small Business Exporters Association of the United States, 1156 15th St. NW, #1100, Washington, DC 20005, (202) 552-2903, www.sbea.org

Southern U.S. Trade Association (SUSTA), 701 Poydras St., #3725, New Orleans, LA 70139, (504) 568-5986, www.susta.org

Western United States Agricultural Trade Association, 4601 NE 77th Avenue, #240, Vancouver, WA 98662, (360) 693-3373, www.wusata.org

World Trade Centers Association, 120 Broadway #3350, New York, NY 10271, www.wtca.org

Customs Brokers and Freight Forwarders

AirSea International, 1320 West Blancke St., Linden, NJ 07036, (732) 607-0600, www.airseaint.com

Serra International, 75 Montgomery St., #300, Jersey City, NJ 07302, (201) 860-9600, http://serraintl.com

Credit Reports

Dun & Bradstreet, (866) 970-3568, www.dnb.com

Helpful Government Agencies–Import/Export

Bureau of Industry and Security, Outreach and Educational Services, 14th St. & Pennsylvania Ave. NW, U.S. Department of Commerce, Washington, DC 20230, (202) 482-4811, https://www.bis.doc.gov/index.php/about-bis/organization/program-offices; check BIS's website for Western regional addresses and phone numbers.

Export Assistance Centers around the country can be found on the Export.gov website at: www.trade.gov/export-solutions.

Export-Import Bank of the United States (Ex-Im Bank), 811 Vermont Ave., NW, Washington, DC 20571, (800) 565-3946, www.exim.gov

The Export Legal Assistance Network, 1919 Pennsylvania Ave. NW, #500, Washington DC 2006, https://2016.export.gov/exportbasics/eg_main_017480.asp

Foreign Agricultural Service, U.S. Department of Agriculture, 1400 Independence Ave. SW, Washington, DC 20250, www.fas.usda.gov

International Trade Administration, 1401 Constitution Ave. NW, Washington, DC 20230, (800) USA-TRADE, http://trade.gov

Let Us Connect You to Europe, http://2016.export.gov/europe

Overseas Private Investment Corporation (OPIC), 1100 New York Ave. NW, Washington, DC 20527, (202) 336- 8400, www.opic.gov

U.S. Census Bureau, Foreign Trade Division, https://www.census.gov/foreign-trade/index.html

U.S. Census Bureau, International Trade Division, U.S. Department of Commerce, U.S. Bureau of the Census, 4700 Silver Hill Rd., Suitland, MD 20746, Room 2179, Building 3, Washington, DC 20233-6700, (800) 549-0595 (option 4), www.census.gov

U.S. Commercial Service, International Trade Administration, U.S. Department of Commerce, 1401 Constitution Ave. NW, Washington, DC 20230, 800-USA-TRADE (872-8723), http://trade.gov/cs or http://buyusa.gov

U.S. Customs and Border Protection, 1300 Pennsylvania Ave. NW, Washington, DC 20229, (877) 227-5511, www.cbp.gov

U.S. Department of Commerce, 1401 Constitution Ave. NW, Washington, DC 20230, (202) 482-2000, www.commerce.gov

Helpful Related Government Agencies

Agricultural Marketing Service, 1400 Independence Ave. SW, #3071-S, Washington, DC 20250-0201, (202) 720-5115, www.ams.usda.gov

Animal and Plant Health Inspection Service (APHIS-USDA), United States Department of Agriculture Animal and Plant Health Inspection Service, 4700 River Rd., Riverdale, MD 20737, (844) 820-2234, www.aphis.usda.gov/aphis/home

Bureau of Alcohol, Tobacco, Firearms, and Explosives, Import/Export, Office of Public and Governmental Affairs, 99 New York Ave. NE, Washington, DC 20226, www.atf.gov

Center for Biologics Evaluation and Research, 10903 New Hampshire Ave., Silver Spring, MD 20993-0002, (888) INFO-FDA, https://www.fda.gov/about-fda/fda-organization/center-biologics-evaluation-and-research-cber

Center for Food Safety and Applied Nutrition, Food and Drug Administration, 5100 Paint Branch Pkwy., College Park, MD 20740, (888) 723-3366, https://www.fda.gov/about-fda/fda-organization/center-food-safety-and-applied-nutrition-cfsan

Centers for Disease Control and Prevention, 1600 Clifton Rd., Atlanta, GA 30333, (800) CDC-INFO (232-4636), www.cdc.gov

Drug Enforcement Administration, 8701 Morrissette Dr., Springfield, VA 22152, (202) 307-1000, www.dea.gov

Environmental Protection Agency, Ariel Rios Building, 1200 Pennsylvania Ave. NW, Washington, DC 20460, (202) 272-0167, www3.epa.gov

Federal Communications Commission, 445 12th St. SW, Washington, DC 20536, (888)225-5322 (CALL FCC), www.fcc.gov

Federal Trade Commission, 600 Pennsylvania Ave. NW, Washington, DC 20530, (202) 326-2222, www.ftc.gov

Food Safety and Inspection Service, U.S. Department of Agriculture, 1400 Independence Ave. SW, Washington, DC 20250. For phone number, search regional offices in your area, www.fsis.usda.gov

International Mail Calculator, https://ircalc.usps.com

ISO 9000 Information, www.iso.org/iso-9001-quality-management.html

National Institute of Standards and Technology, 100 Bureau Dr., Gaithersburg, MD 20899, (844) USA-GOV1, www.nist.gov

Office of Engineering and Technology, 445 12th St. SW, Washington, DC 20554, (202) 418-2470, www.fcc.gov/engineering-%26-technology

Office of Regulatory Affairs, 10903 New Hampshire Ave., Silver Spring, MD 20993, (888) INFO-FDA, www.fda.gov/ora

Pipeline and Hazardous Materials Safety Administration, U.S. Department of Transportation, East Building, Second Fl., 1200 New Jersey Ave. SE, Washington, DC 20590, (202) 366-4000, https://www.phmsa.dot.gov/

U.S. Consumer Product Safety Commission, Office of Compliance, 4330 East-West Hwy., Bethesda, MD 20814, (301) 504-7923, www.cpsc.gov

U.S. Department of Agriculture, 1400 Independence Ave. SW, Washington, DC 20250, (202) 720-2791, www.usda.gov

U.S. Department of Energy, 1000 Independence Ave. SW, Washington, DC 20585, (202) 586-5000, www.energy.gov

U.S. Department of Health and Human Services, Secretary's Office, 200 Independence Ave. SW, Washington, DC 20201, (877) 696-6775, www.hhs.gov

U.S. Department of Justice, 950 Pennsylvania Ave. NW, Washington, DC 20530, (202) 514-2000, www.justice.gov

U.S. Department of Transportation, 1200 New Jersey Ave. SE, Washington, DC 20590, (202) 366-4000, www.transportation.gov

U.S. Department of the Treasury, 1500 Pennsylvania Ave. NW, Washington, DC 20220, (202) 622-2000, www.treasury.gov

U.S. Fish and Wildlife Service, 1849 C St. NW, Washington, DC 20240, (800) 344-WILD, www.fws.gov

U.S. Food & Drug Administration, 10903 New Hampshire Ave., Silver Springs, MD 20993, (888) 463-6332, www.fda.gov

U.S. Nuclear Regulatory Commission, 11545 Rockville Pike, Rockville, MD 20852-2738, (301) 415-7000, www.nrc.gov

U.S. Postal Service, (800) ASK-USPS, www.usps.com

U.S. Small Business Administration, International Trade, 409 Third St. SW, Eighth Floor, Washington, DC 20416, (202) 205-8800. For loans: (800) 827-5722, www.sba.gov

International Trade Directories

Panjiva (online directory), 20 West 22nd St., #706, New York, NY 10010 (888) 902-3511 (Inside U.S.), (646) 205-0594 (Outside U.S.), https://panjiva.com

Magazines and Publications

Export USA, offered through the Department of Commerce, www.think.global/exusa

The Journal of Commerce, The JOC Group, 2 Penn Plaza East, Newark, NJ 07105, (973) 776-8660, www.joc.com

Market Research

Foreign currency exchange rates: https://x-rates.com or www.xe.com

The U.S. Commercial Service, www.export.gov

The World Bank, http://data.worldbank.org

The World Trade Organization, https://www.wto.org/

Thomas for Industry, Thomas Publishing Co., 5 Penn Plaza, New York, NY 10001, (212) 695-0500, www.thomasnet.com

Marketing Associations

American Marketing Association, www.ama.org

eMarketing Association, http://emarketingassociation.com

Miscellaneous International Business Websites

Embassy.org, www.embassy.org

Executiveplanet.com, www.executiveplanet.com

FedEx, (800) GOFEDEX, www.fedex.com

The Internationalist, http://internationalist.com

LinkedIn, www.linkedin.com

Skype, www.skype.com

Seminars and Workshops

The American Association of Exporters & Importers, 1717 K St., NW, #1120, Washington, DC 20006, (202) 857-8009, http://events.aaei.org

The Federation of International Trade Associations, 11654 Plaza America Dr., #120, Reston, VA 20190, (703) 621-1900, http://fita.org/seminars

Successful International Trade Businesses

Global Partners Inc., Wahib Wahba, 303 Second St., Suite D, Annapolis, MD 21403, (410) 626-1515, www.globalpartnersusa.com

Intyre, Jan Herremans, Veldstraat 21a, B-9220 Hamme, Belgium, 011-32-52-481136, https://intyre.com

LND Export Management, Lloyd N. Davidson, 749 SW Watson Pl., Port St. Lucie, FL 34953-6340, (561) 336-0139, email: lnd@lndexportmanagement.com

Marketing-und-vertriebsberatung international, Michael Richter, MBA, Hauptstrasse 27-88422 Seekirch, Germany, 011-49-(0)7582-933371, www.marketing-und-vertrieb-international.com

Nelisco Inc., Sam Nelson, 10911 Raven Ridge Road, Suite #103 Raleigh, NC 27614, (919) 217-3948, http://nelisco.com

Trade Leads and Education

International Trade Administration, http://trade.gov

TradeNet, https://tradenet.com

Note: The Federation of International Trade Associations has a trading hub webpage with links to most international trade lead sites. Check it out at: http://fita.org/tradehub.html.

Glossary

Abatement: reduction or discount given as a result of damage to a shipment or overcharge in bill payment.

Absolute quota: limit on the amount of a product that can be brought into a country during a specified time period.

Adjustment: changes in information submitted to U.S. Customs.

Ad valorem: according to value.

Advising bank: the seller's, or exporter's, bank in a letter of credit transaction.

Acceptance draft: see *Sight draft*.

Advanced emerging market: A nation with good export potential due to its relatively strong combination of income and infrastructure.

AES: see *Automated Export System*.

African Growth and Opportunity Act (AGOA): U.S. legislation offering special tariff rates and other advantages as incentives to

African countries to open their markets. The legislation significantly enhances market access to the U.S. for qualifying Sub-Saharan African (SSA) countries.

Agent: salesperson who pitches a product to wholesale or retail buyers but does not take title to the product.

Air waybill: bill of lading from an air carrier.

All-risks clause: insurance provision for extra coverage (but despite the name, it doesn't cover everything).

Anti-Dumping Act: U.S. legislation designed to counteract the practice of dumping.

APHIS: acronym for Animal and Plant Health Inspection Service, a division of the Department of Agriculture.

Applicant: the buyer or importer in a letter of credit transaction; also called an opener.

Assist: a tool, mold, engineering drawing, artwork, or other item that assists in the assembly and sale of the product.

ATA carnet: an international customs document allowing duty-free entry for goods, such as product samples; also called a carnet. They are typically good for one year but can be extended.

Automated Export System: electronic process used to file export information directly to customs.

Available at sight: letter of credit term meaning the funds will be paid as soon as the conditions of the L/C are met.

Backhaul: return of transport vehicle from the destination to the point of origin, with cargo picked up at destination or elsewhere, usually resulting in a favorable freight rate, since the vehicle is not returning empty.

Balance of trade: balance between imports and exports.

BEM: big emerging market; in other words, an emerging nation with great export potential.

Beneficiary: the exporter or seller in a letter of credit transaction.

Bill of exchange: see *Draft*.

Bill of lading: a receipt from the ship, air, or trucking line showing that it has the merchandise.

BIS: see *Bureau of Industry and Security*.

BISNIS: International Trade Administration's acronym for its Business Information Service for the Newly Independent States.

Bonded warehouse: warehouse or other storage area within customs territory where imported goods can be stored without paying a duty.

Branded product: A product that carries a brand name.

BRIC countries: Brazil, Russia, India, and China, which are considered newly advanced economic developing nations.

Bureau of Industry and Security (BIS): U.S. government agency that administers exports.

Carnet: see *ATA carnet*.

Carriage and insurance paid to (CIP): same as cost, insurance, and freight, except that the exporter pays for delivery to the importer's door and retains title up to that point.

Carriage paid to (CPT): Delivery of goods to a mutually agreed upon location.

Carrier: transportation line that hauls cargo.

Cash against documents: see *Collection draft*.

Cash in advance: payment term meaning the importer pays for the goods before they are shipped.

Certificate of manufacture: document verifying that the merchandise has been manufactured and fulfills the general product requirements.

Certificate of origin: form verifying the product was manufactured in the country of origin.

CFR: see *Cost and freight*.

CIF: see *Cost, insurance, and freight*.

CIP: see *Carriage and insurance paid to*.

Clean bill of lading: one in which no damages, discrepancies, or problems with the goods have been noted.

Clean draft: draft to which no documents are attached.

Clean on board bill of lading: see *Clean bill of lading*.

Collection documents: shipping documents or records.

Collection draft: agreement in which buyer takes title to the shipment once it reaches its destination and pays for it there.

Commercial invoice: finished version of the pro forma invoice.

Commercial service: see *US & FCS*.

Commission agent: an intermediary commissioned by a foreign firm searching for domestic products to purchase.

Commission representative: foreign independent sales representative.

Commodity control list: a listing of potential export items subject to BIS export controls.

Conference line: association of ocean freight carriers with common shipping rates and conditions; also called ocean freight conference.

Confirm: letter of credit term meaning the bank guarantees payment as long as the conditions of the L/C are met.

Consular invoice: document demanded by a country, along with a fee, before it will allow entry of merchandise.

Consularization of documents: practice of paying a fee at import to have entry documents stamped as legal; also called legalization of documents.

Consumption entry: customs entry for goods intended for immediate resale.

Contingent policy: an insurance policy that backs up the regular policy in the event of a catastrophe.

Cost and freight (CFR): shipping term meaning the exporter has the goods transported to the port or airport and loaded onto the carrier and pays the shipping charges to the destination.

Cost, insurance, and freight (CIF): shipping term meaning the exporter pays all costs, including insurance and freight, to the product's destination.

Country-controlled buying agent: foreign government agency or quasi-governmental firm charged with locating and purchasing products.

CPT: see *Carriage paid to*.

Customs broker: individual or company licensed by the Department of the Treasury who acts as the importer's agent for the product's entry into a country; also called customhouse broker.

DAT: see *Delivered at terminal.*

Date of expiry: the date the letter of credit expires.

DAP: see *Delivered at place.*

DDP: see *Delivered duty paid.*

Dealer assistance program: a program in which the importer or exporter provides sales representatives with product information aids and materials.

Delivered at place (DAP): Designated place of arrival by buyer.

Delivered at terminal (DAT): Designated terminal or location within.

Delivered duty paid (DDP): shipping term meaning the exporter takes on all costs, including customs duties, to have the goods delivered to the importer's door.

Dimensional weight: a value of the cargo that considers its weight and volume.

Discrepancy: letter of credit term meaning a problem in fulfilling the L/C's conditions.

Distributor: a company that buys an imported product, then sells it to a retailer or other agent; also called a wholesale distributor.

Dock receipt: document verifying that the merchandise has arrived at the dock.

Documentary credit: see *Letter of credit.*

Draft: banking term meaning the buyer's order to pay the seller.

Drawback refund: a refund on duties paid on imported merchandise that is processed or assembled for re-export.

Dumping: the practice of flooding a market with an imported product that's far cheaper than a comparable domestic one.

Duty: import tax.

EAR: acronym for Export Administration Regulations.

EBB: Economic Bulletin Board, a trade service of the U.S. Department of Commerce.

ECCN: see *Export control classification number.*

ECU: see *European currency unit.*

ELAN: the Export Legal Assistance Network, developed by the Federal Bar Association and the SBA.

EMC: see *Export management company.*

Entry for consumption: see *Consumption entry.*

EU: see *European Union.*

Euro: see *European currency unit.*

European currency unit: a standard monetary unit for the nations of the European Union; also called an ECU or a euro.

European Union (EU): a single nontrade barrier marketplace originally formed by 27 Western European nations.

Evidence of right to make entry: a bill of lading or air waybill submitted to the portside customs office.

Ex Dock: shipping term meaning the importer takes title to the product at the export dock.

Ex Ship: shipping term meaning the importer takes title to the product at the ship before it departs.

Ex Works (EXW): shipping term meaning the importer takes title to the product at the exporter's or manufacturer's "works," or factory.

Ex-Im Bank: the Export-Import Bank of the United States.

Export control classification number: number given by the Bureau of Industry and Security to all U.S. exports and that must be listed by the exporter.

Export management company (EMC): a business that handles export operations for a domestic company.

Export trading company: a business that exports goods and services or provides export-related services.

FAS: see *Free alongside ship.*

FCA: see *Free carrier.*

FOB: see *Free on board vessel.*

Foreign distributor: a foreign merchant, similar to a wholesale distributor in the U.S., who buys for his or her own account, then distributes the product.

Foreign trade zone (FTZ): a warehouse or other storage facility in which imported goods can be stored or processed without having to pay duties.

Formal customs entry: one in which the merchandise is valued at more than $2,500.

Forward transaction: term used when foreign currency is purchased at the time an export price is quoted.

Foul bill of lading: one in which a problem with the goods has been discovered.

Free alongside ship (FAS): shipping term meaning the exporter will have the goods loaded onto the ship or air carrier, where the importer then takes title.

Free carrier (FCA): shipping term meaning the exporter loads the goods onto the truck or other carrier at his works, where the importer takes title.

Free on board vessel (FOB): shipping term meaning the exporter loads the goods onto the ship or vessel, where the importer takes title.

Freight forwarder: individual or company that acts as the exporter's agent for product export.

FTA: see *United States-Israel Free Trade Area.*

FTZ: see *Foreign trade zone.*

Full set: shipping term referring to the three original bills of lading traditionally issued and signed by the captain.

GATT: see *General Agreement on Tariffs and Trade.*

GDP: see *Gross Domestic Product.*

General Agreement on Tariffs and Trade (GATT): international agreement designed to reduce trade barriers between countries.

General average insurance: covers the holder against general cargo loss on board ship as opposed to covering only the holder's merchandise.

General order (G.O.): goods considered abandoned by customs and put into a bonded warehouse.

Gross Domestic Product: total value of all goods and services produced within a country in a year.

Harmonize: to develop a single or matching system of tariffs.

Harmonized Tariff Schedule of the United States: listing of all U.S. tariffs.

Immediate transport entry: customs entry for goods to be shipped to another location for customs clearance.

Import/export merchant: a businessperson who purchases goods directly from a domestic or foreign manufacturer, then packs, ships, and resells the goods.

Import quota: a limit on the quantity of a particular product that can be brought into a country over a specified period of time.

Importer security filing: electronic filing required of importers and shipping lines to provide customs with information about the contents of shipping containers well before the goods arrive in the U.S.

Incoterms: International Chamber of Commerce terms that are a worldwide standardization of shipping terminology.

Independent line: shipping line not allied with an ocean freight conference.

Informal customs entry: one in which the imported goods are valued at $2,500 or less.

Inherent vice: damage that could arise due to the nature of the goods being shipped.

Inspection certificate: document certifying the quality, quantity, or conformity of the product.

Insurance certificate: document confirming that marine insurance has been provided and indicating type of coverage.

Intellectual property: a product that has been patented, trademarked, or copyrighted and is protected by law.

In-transit entry: official customs entry designating import goods moving from the port of unloading to the port of destination.

Irrevocable letter of credit: a letter of credit that cannot be rescinded by the buyer, or importer.

ISF 10+2: see *Importer security filing.*

ISO: International Organization for Standardization; organization composed of representatives from many nations that decide worldwide industrial and commercial standardization.

ISO 9000: international quality management certification.

ISO 14000: international environmental management certification.

Issuing bank: see *Opening bank.*

ITA: International Trade Administration; a division of the U.S. Department of Commerce.

Joint venture: a partnership between two or more companies.

KORUS: see *Republic of South Korea and U.S. Free Trade Agreement.*

Lading: freight or cargo.

L/C: see *Letter of credit.*

Legalization of documents: see *Consularization of documents.*

Letter of credit (L/C): document issued by a bank per instructions from an importer authorizing the exporter to draw payment after fulfilling terms set out in the document; also called a documentary credit.

Liquidate: to complete a customs entry.

Mail entry: official customs entry designating import items sent via another country's mail system.

Manufacturer's representative: an independent salesperson who operates out of an agency that handles an assortment of complementary products.

Median age: age at which half of the population is younger and half older.

Most favored nation: see *Normal trade relations.*

NAFTA: see *North American Free Trade Agreement.*

Negotiable bill of lading: same as "To order of shipper," meaning the bill is not consigned specifically to the importer.

Normal trade relations: trading partner status with the U.S. allowing standard duties on goods (formerly known as most favored nation).

North American Free Trade Agreement (NAFTA): agreement among Canada, Mexico, and the U.S. created to phase out all trade barriers.

NTDB: National Trade Data Bank; a world trade database available through the U.S. Commercial Service.

Ocean freight conference: see *Conference line.*

OEM: original equipment manufacturer.

On board bill of lading: document that confirms the cargo has been placed on board the vessel.

On consignment: payment term meaning the importer pays for the goods after he's sold them.

On deck bill of lading: document used when the goods must be transported on deck, as with livestock.

Open account: payment term meaning the importer sends payment to the exporter or seller when he receives the goods.

Opener: see *Applicant*.

Opening bank: the customer's, or importer's, bank in a letter of credit transaction; also called an issuing bank or an originating bank.

OPIC: the Overseas Private Investment Corporation, a U.S. government financing agency.

Order bill of lading: negotiable bill that must be endorsed by the shipper before it's handed over to the bank.

Order notify bill of lading: similar to an order bill of lading except that the importer and sometimes the customs broker must be notified when the ship reaches port.

Originating bank: see *Opening bank*.

Packing list: document detailing the number of items in shipment, how they are packed, serial numbers, weight, and dimensions; also called a packing slip.

Packing slip: see *Packing list*.

Per capita GDP: the value, per citizen, of the total goods and services produced within a country in a year.

Personal baggage entry: official customs entry designating import items arriving in a passenger's luggage.

Pro forma invoice: a price quotation in the form of an invoice.

QS 9000: international quality management certification for the automotive industry.

Republic of South Korea and U.S. Free Trade Agreement (U.S.–Korea Free Trade Agreement FTA): free trade agreement entered into effect in March 2012 between the U.S. and South Korea that has reduced tariffs on many products.

Retailer: the last conduit in the trade channel that sells the product to the consumer.

Revocable letter of credit: a letter of credit that can be rescinded by the buyer, or importer.

Sight draft: a draft payable when the merchandise arrives at the dock.

Sight letter of credit: letter of credit paid immediately upon fulfillment of the terms.

SME: small or medium enterprise.

Spot transaction: the sale of domestic dollars and the purchase of foreign currency, or the reverse, for immediate delivery, or on the spot.

SRCC: marine insurance term meaning strikes, riots, and civil commotion.

Standby letter of credit: an L/C that's set in motion if the buyer doesn't pay within a specified period of time.

State-controlled trading company: foreign government-sanctioned and controlled trade agency; often deals in raw materials, agricultural machinery, manufacturing equipment, and technical instruments.

Straight bill of lading: a nonnegotiable bill that prohibits release of the goods to anyone but the person specified on the shipping documents.

Strategic alliance: an agreement between domestic and foreign companies to work toward a common goal.

Tariff: trade barrier in the form of a tax.

Tariff-rate quota: a time period during which a specific product can be imported at a reduced tariff rate.

Temporary entry under bond (TIB): customs bond posted for goods, such as product samples, temporarily entering the country.

Terminal receiving charges (TRC): fees charged by the shipping line to load the goods.

Three-level channel of distribution: a trade channel that uses a middleman who resells to the consumer.

Through bill of lading: used when several carriers are involved.

TIB: see *Temporary entry under bond*.

Time draft: draft payable within a specified time period after the importer has received the merchandise.

To order of shipper: shipping term meaning the goods are consigned to the steamship line rather than the importer; also called a negotiable bill of lading.

TOP: Trade Opportunities Program; a trade leads program available from the U.S. Commercial Service.

Trade barrier: checks or hindrances on international trade set up by national governments to protect domestic industries from foreign competition.

Trade channel: the means by which merchandise travels from manufacturer to end user.

Trade preferences: privileges of being a trading partner or having normal trade relations with the U.S. and therefore paying standard duty rates.

Trading partner: favorable trading relationship with another country.

Tramp vessel: cargo ship that doesn't operate on a fixed schedule.

Transportation and exportation entry: official customs entry designating items arriving at a nondestination country's port and passing through to the destination country.

Transship: to ship a product into one trade region or country, offload it, and then reload and ship it on to another.

TRC: see *Terminal receiving charges.*

United States-Israel Free Trade Area (FTA): an agreement that provides duty-free entry for certain Israeli products.

USD: U.S. dollars.

US & FCS: the U.S. Foreign and Commercial Service, also called the Commercial Service, a division of the U.S. Department of Commerce.

Validated export license: license required to export U.S. goods on the Department of Commerce's Commodity Control List, such as articles of war, advanced technology, and products in short supply.

Value-added tax (VAT): a tax tacked onto domestic and imported products in European Union countries.

VAT: see *Value-added tax.*

Warehouse entry: customs entry for goods to be stored in a bonded warehouse, then withdrawn in portions.

Wholesale distributor: see *Distributor.*

Wire transfer: procedure in which funds from the importer's bank are wired to the exporter's bank account.

Index

CPSIA information can be obtained
at www.ICGtesting.com
Printed in the USA
LVHW060802240121
677243LV00004B/4